Founders and Builders
of
Greensboro

1808-1908

ILLUSTRATED

Fifty Sketches Compiled by
Bettie D. Caldwell

SOUTHERN HISTORICAL PRESS
INC

Book Publishers

This volume was reproduced from
An 1925 edition located in the
Publisher's private library,
Greenville, South Carolina

Please direct all correspondence and orders to:

www.southernhistoricalpress.com
or
SOUTHERN HISTORICAL PRESS, Inc.
PO BOX 1267
375 West Broad Street
Greenville, SC   29601
southernhistoricalpress@gmail.com

Originally published: Greensboro, NC 1925
ISBN #0-89308-753-X
All rights Reserved.
Printed in the United States of America

INTRODUCTION

The city of Greensboro is not one of those towns that just happened. It owes its existence and its location to none of the accidents of nature that have made the development of cities inevitable in certain localities—on the shores of land-locked harbors, at the confluence of great rivers, and at the junction of ancient high roads. The reason for the existence of Greensboro is not to be found in the geography and the topography of the region. In 1806 the citizens of Guilford County simply decided to build a town easier of access than Martinsville, and make it the county seat. Surveyors, therefore, were ordered to run their lines to determine the mathematical center of the county, and it was proposed to remove to that spot the county courthouse, which still stood in the hamlet near the field where the armies of Greene and Cornwallis had collided in 1781. That proposal was never carried out precisely, on account of a practical difficulty. It was. easy enough for the surveyors to locate the center of the county, but it happened that the spot was situated in the midst of a marshy valley, entirely unfitted for use as a town-site. The county authorities, therefore, compromised by going to a high plateau, half a mile south of the actual center of the county, and there they laid off their town. The actual center of Guilford County, therefore, must be in the neighborhood of Fisher Park, for the center of the original town is Jefferson Square, at the intersection of Elm and Market Streets, about half a mile south of Fisher Park.

The interesting point is that the city was created by the will and energy of the citizens of Guilford County, and not by any fortuitous combination of circumstances that favored the growth of a city on that particular spot. Greensboro owes its rise to the exercise of the same human will to create that produced the capital of the United States and the former capital of the Russian empire; but so far as the records show it was the collective will of the citizens, not the decree of some one outstanding personality, some local equivalent of Peter the Great or George Washington.

The genesis of the town is not in this respect unique. Raleigh, the capital of the State of North Carolina, was founded in similar fashion. In the western states scores and hundreds of town sites were surveyed, platted and staked out before a single house had been built. The western towns, however, were frequently the work of a transcontinental railroad company, and not the joint effort of the residents of the surrounding territory. Raleigh was built to serve mainly as the seat of government, as were the great capitals founded by the Emperor and the first President. Greensboro, on the other hand, seems to have been founded by the men of Guilford with the expectation that it would grow to be the principal town of their county, the place where they would attend to their daily business, as well as to legal matters that might bring them to the courthouse. It was to be in fact, as well as in name, the burgher's town, the borough, the marketplace of a democratic and vigorously independent people. Then, as if the more strongly to emphasize the fact that here was no overlordship, no baronial proprietary right, instead of giving the place the name of any of its founders they chose to call it after a man from Vermont, Nathanael the Blacksmith, whose mighty arm had done much to free the land where the new town stood from the dominion of a foreign king. So it became Greene's borough.

Surely, it is no dishonorable origin for a democratic town to have sprung from the people. By the will and energy of the people it was created, and by the same power it has been maintained, enlarged and beautified. Upon that sustaining force it must rely for whatever the future holds for it of advancement, materially or culturally. For a city does not consist of a certain number of parcels of land, with a certain number of houses thereon, nor of some thousands of people gathered within a restricted area. An army cantonment meets those specifications, but it is not a city. From Nineveh to Los Angeles cities have been recognized by every thoughtful observer as lands, houses and people, with something more—a common interest binding them together, a common aspiration toward advancement, a common pride in achievement. One of the most intensely human touches in all that is recorded of Saint Paul, is his remark when he thought back upon Tarsus, and to the astounded captain of the Roman guard explained with dignified pride, "I am a citizen of no mean city!"

This civic consciousness, operating in Greensboro, is this book's reason for being. Some years ago the Greensboro Public Library, already a treasure-house of irreplaceable records of the past, instituted the policy of collecting pictures of the men who had a conspicuous share in the work of making the town of Greensboro in the first century of its existence. The work was vigorously prosecuted by Miss Bettie D. Caldwell, then recently retired from active duty after many years' service as librarian. It was Miss Caldwell's intention to collect for each picture all available facts concerning the subject and to file them in the archives of the library. At this juncture the Greensboro Daily News offered to publish the sketches in its columns, believing that there would be sufficient local interest in them to justify publication, and realizing that the records would be more easily available to future students in the bound files of the newspaper than in loose typewritten sheets in the vault of the library. Several of the sketches were published under the general heading, "Founders of Greensboro", and the great and wide-spread interest that they aroused surprised even the originators of the venture. There followed immediately a demand that the sketches be put in book form, a demand which finally took the extremely practical form of pledges by a hundred different people of enough money to finance the work.

Therefore, the book, like the city whose history for a hundred years it outlines, is a creation of the people. Even its authorship has been a community affair, for its represents the joint labors of some twoscore writers whose reward has been merely such satisfaction as they have gotten out of the task.

Here, then, in every imaginable sense of the word, is a book of the people of Greensboro. If it is not a particularly brilliant, or spectacular, or startling book, the reason is not far to seek: Greensboro is not now, and never has been, populated exclusively by geniuses, any more than whatever other city you choose to name, and this is a record of people as they were, in so far as that record is traceable now that all the people who made it have been dead for many years.

But if it is an honest book, if the reader finds in these pages the traces of such old-fashioned virtues as honor, fidelity, piety, industry and kindliness, let him not forget that it is still the book of the people of Greensboro.

Perhaps it is permissible for one who was merely a sojourner there, wholly without either ancestral or commercial ties with the modern city, to add that while this is a book of the people who lived in Greensboro many years ago, it was produced by the people who lived in this city in the twentieth century. They produced it because they admire the virtues of their predecessors and wish to maintain them and to pass them on to the city that is to be. Therefore, while it is a book of the Greensboro that was, it is also in a sense not too subtle to be easily understood, a book of the Greensboro that is. The things that the writers of this volume have found worthy of transcribing out of the annals of the past are the things that the Greensboro of today would fain hand down to the future.

In the main, they seem to be simple and homely virtues. There is not much of earthly glory, and less of great wealth, in these narratives. They are, for the most part, stories of labor, first to reduce a wilderness to order, then to wring subsistence, comfort, and finally, some modest degree of luxury from a stubborn soil; afterward, to make good the losses of catastrophic war, and, toward the end, to build, on the wreckage of an old civilization, a greater and more splendid one. All these efforts succeeded but the last, and that one has been passed on to the generation that has written the story. Yet involved in this uneventful narrative are qualities that all men, everywhere, have found worshipful: courage that not only faced death on the battlefield, but that faced the severer test of life without wavering; faith that clung to a promise unfulfilled through years and generations; hope indestructible under the fiercest blows of misfortune as under the attrition of grinding and barren years; and charity, mantling the frailties and follies of God's children and striving incessantly to implant in this city that spirit of human brotherhood emanating from the Love that, dispensing with sun and moon and stars, itself is the sole light of the city not made with hands.

But these are not homely virtues. These are the metals from which is wrought all that humanity can know of the sublime. Yet they run like veins of precious ore through all our common clay. To smelt them out, not from the lives of heroes and saints and sages, but from the lives of what we call ordinary men and women, may be a tedious, but surely is no mean or unworthy task. Greensboro has valued them highly enough to strive to perform that task, using the men and women of her early history for the purpose; and that very effort is enough to give every townsman a right to assert with the great Apostle, "I am a citizen of no mean city."

Gerald W. Johnson.

CONTENTS

DANIEL GILLESPIE

DANIEL GILLESPIE

1743 - 1829

The pre-colonial history of Col. Daniel Gillespie's ancestors carries us across the sea to the liberty loving land of Scotland, with her rugged and massive hills emblematic of the strong and sturdy character of her noble and distinguished sons. In the Gaelic the name is spelled "Gillespuig", and means "servant of the bishop." As early as the fifteenth century, however, the spelling "Gillespie" was common and is the modern form of the name.

The ancestors of Col. Daniel Gillespie were of the MacPherson clan, whose ancestral home was Cluny castle. The MacPhersons were Celts, and the chief was called Cluny MacPherson, deriving his name from the ancestral home of Cluny castle, which dates back to the year 1438. The clan, as the name indicates, is of ecclesiastical origin, MacPherson meaning "son of the parson," and was common over the Highlands in the fifteenth and sixteenth centuries. The members of the MacPherson clan were among the best of Prince Charles' army.

An ancestor of Col. Daniel Gillespie was one of the one hundred and fifty-nine representative men composing the Westminster Assembly called by the English Parliament in 1643. Seven commissioners were from Scotland, and one of the seven was George Gillespie, the youngest and one of the ablest of the whole body.

Coming to America the Gillespies settled in Frederick County, Virginia, and there were born of "pious and worthy" parents two boys, John and Daniel Gillespie, in the years 1741 and 1743, respectively. Little is known of their father and mother except that they were godly and industrious, but judging from their distinguished sons, they must have been characters of sterling worth.

In 1783 a grant from the state was made to Daniel Gillespie of three hundred acres of land on South Buffalo "for fifty shillings for every one hundred acres." To this many other tracts were added from time to time. A part of the original grant is now in possession of his great grandson, the author of this paper, and on this section Col. Daniel Gillespie's son, Robert Gillespie, settled and his grandson, Daniel D. Gillespie, was born.

From the formation of Guilford County in 1770 to 1808, the county seat was Martinsville, now known as Guilford Battleground. An act of the legislature in 1808 granted its removal on certain conditions, namely, "that the location is geographically in the center of the county, and the net proceeds from sales be sufficient to pay all costs of removal from Martinsville of the courthouse, jail, stocks, and whipping post, and rebuild the same." A tract of forty-two acres was purchased at a cost of ninety-eight dollars and laid off into forty-four lots, which now constitute the center of Greensboro. One block of four of these lots, bounded by East Market, South Davie, East Sycamore and South Elm Streets, was sold at public auction for $306.85. Col. Daniel Gillespie purchased the corner lot on which the United States postoffice building now stands for the sum of one hundred and thirty-six dollars.

When the struggle for national independence came, there was no doubt as to the stand to be taken by the Gillespie brothers. They were Whigs of the deepest dye. The spirit of the Gillespies is aptly illustrated by the following excerpts from the "Life of David Caldwell" by Caruthers: "In a conflict between Tryon's men and a band of Regulators, among whom were two MacPherson brothers and John and Daniel Gillespie, the royalist party was forced to fall back and the cannons were seized by the MacPhersons, but having no ammunition and not knowing how to operate them, they were useless in their hands." In describing this battle, an old Regulator said to Dr. Caruthers: "O, if John and Daniel Gillespie had known as much about military discipline then as they knew a few years after that, the bloody Tryon would never have slept in his palace again."

"Both these brothers were in the battle of Alamance; but John distinguished himself so that he attracted the notice of the governor. He was about the last man to leave the ground —I mean of those who were under arms—and he would have been taken on the spot probably, like Captain Pugh, had not two of his acquaintances, who had no share in the engagement, taken him, one by each arm, and led him away. Tryon, having learned his name, offered a reward for his apprehension, and sent two or three men in pursuit of him, who overtook him at the distance of a mile or two from the scene of action, at the far side of a rye field which he had just passed; but not suspecting, from his dress and appearance, that he was the man of whom they were in pursuit, they asked him if he knew one John Gillespie. With perfect composure he replied that he did, very well, and that they could probably overtake him if they would hurry on, as he had seen him passing the rye field only a few minutes before. With that they put spurs to their horses, and went off at full speed; but he changed his course and hastened home, and then taking his wagon and servant boy he set off for the mountains. When Tryon came into the neighborhood, having learned where he had gone, he sent two men after him, and compelled one of Gillespie's neighbors, by the name of Reese Porter, to go along as a pilot. They overtook him in a place called the Hollows, in Surry County; and knowing their business as soon as they came in sight, his servant requested him to make his escape and let him take care of the horses in the best way he could; but he said that he never had run from man and he would not do it then. Being armed with a rifle, pistols, etc., he let them come within about a hundred yards, and told them not to advance another step, or he would kill one of them at all events. As neither of them felt willing to die just then, and knowing the determined spirit of the man, they remained there; and after talking for sometime at that distance, they left him. When he learned that Tryon had left this part of the country he returned home; and when independence was declared he embarked in the cause with irrepressible ardor. Several of his neighbors retired to the mountains as he did, and remained there until they could return with safety, but never surrendered, and never took the oath of allegiance.''

Another incident related by the same author shows very clearly what manner of men the Gillespies were: "He, John, was then captain; but was raised to the rank of colonel soon after the Declaration of Independence. He was too daring and impetuous perhaps to have the command of a large body of men; but with a small number of kindred spirits such as the Forbises, the Halls, the McAdoos, and others, he was

admirably calculated for the service in which he was engaged
as a partizan officer; and while the exploits which he performed were sufficient in number and importance to furnish
the material for a novel or romance, one will suffice to illustrate his character. Not long after the war commenced he
was out on an expedition against the Tories below Deep River,
within a few miles of the place where quite a large body of
them were encamped. Most of his men, having by some means
or other separated from him, were captured in the evening
and taken to the encampment. Early in the morning, having learned what had happened, he proposed to the few who
were with him to go and release the men, but they told him
that it was folly to think of it, for the Tories were ten or
twenty to one; and if they should get him in their power they
would be sure to take his life. This was true; for although
they had never seen him, they knew him well by character;
and would rather have had him put out of the way than a
dozen others. However, he determined on making an effort
to save his men, whether anybody went with him or not; and
set off alone. When he arrived at the camp he found a large
body of Tories collected around his men, and heard them telling John Hall, one of his best men, that he might be saying his prayers as fast as he could, for he had but a few
minutes to live. Gillespie rode a very fleet animal and,
throwing her bridle loosely over a bush, he walked up care-
lessly into the crowd. His men saw him, but were careful not
to betray him either by looks, words or actions. The Tories
felt a little disconcerted by the sudden appearance of a
stranger among them under such circumstances, and they
hardly knew how to proceed; but they soon asked Hall if he
knew John Gillespie. He replied that he did, very well, and
that he gloried in being one of his men. He was then asked
if he knew where he was. He said if he did he would not tell.
They offered him his life if he would give them such information that they could get him in their possession; but he nobly
refused to save his life on any such terms. The question was
then put, 'Is he in this place?' Keeping his back to Gillespie
and casting his eyes over the crowd, he replied, 'If he is I do
not see him.' He was then commanded to mount a stump
close by, and look all over. Keeping Gillespie again in his
rear, and looking over the company from this more elevated

position, he made the same reply. He was now ordered to turn around and tell them at once whether he was on the ground or not; for they would be trifled with no longer. He turned round, but looking entirely over Gillespie, he still gave the same answer: 'If he is here I do not see him.' With that they became angry, and told him with an oath that he had but three minutes to live.

When Gillespie saw that his men would not betray him, even to escape an ignominious death, and that there was no more time to lose, he walked off to the English filly, as he called her, and as he vaulted into the saddle, told them he was John Gillespie and they might make their best of it. That was enough; the shout was immediately raised; the men flew to their horses; and in their eagerness to get him, let the others escape; but he was as much at their defiance in flight as he was in battle, when the disparity of numbers was not too great.''

Daniel Gillespie was captain during the Revolutionary War and was promoted to the rank of colonel in the state militia after this mighty struggle. He fought at Alamance and Guilford Courthouse, being sent afterwards to join Washington's army in Virginia, where much of his war record was destroyed by fire. The North Carolina Colonial Records give us some glimpses of his war activities in the Old North State. In the Halifax Congress of 1776 committees from the several counties were appointed to raise arms for recruits and Daniel Gillespie was chosen to represent Guilford. In this capacity, he purchased all arms fit for use, except from the militia, and those that could be repaired, such repairs being deducted from the price paid. Quakers, Dunkards, and Moravians were expected to sell to the government, as they would have no use for arms, but no compulsion was to be used. The arms captured from Tories were all to be delivered, with those purchased, to the colonel in command, for use by the state. Repairs to arms were ordered made in local shops if possible, and if not, were to be sent to the national armory ''to be established by Congress.'' This committee to be paid a ''genteel and generous compensation for their services in proportion to the fidelity and dispatch with which they shall execute their trust.'' James Martin, who was made colonel commandant of Guilford regiment in 1774, raised troops to fight the Indians, and in 1776 to disarm the Tories. He speaks of "ordering out Daniel Gillespie, captain of the Light Horse company," for various expeditions to quiet Tory insurrections in Randolph and other points. The records show that Governor Martin wrote to Daniel Gillespie, as officer commanding state troops, to control Bladen riots and to suppress Tories, acting alone or jointly with local militia. He was instructed to manage with prudence and address in order to suppress riots promptly and told to use strict discipline with no cruelty.

After doing his full duty in the achievement of our national independence, Col. Daniel Gillespie played no small part in determining the policies and shaping the government of the new democracy. He sat with David Caldwell and other noted men as a member of the Halifax Congress called in April, 1776, for the purpose of forming a new system of government. He was a member of the House of Commons in North Carolina in 1779 and the Senate in 1790-1795. He was also a member of the Provincial Congress which adopted the state constitution, and of the convention of 1789 which adopted the federal constitution, and the North Carolina Colonial Records add that he "filled other offices of trust and responsibility."

Col. Daniel Gillespie was born in Frederick County, Virginia, October 13, 1743, and died in Greensboro, Guilford County, January 17, 1829. His remains were laid to rest in old Buffalo churchyard just north of Greensboro. There are numerous descendants of the third, fourth and fifth generations whose lives and labors owe much of their merit to the sterling worth of their honored and distinguished progenitor, Col. Daniel Gillespie. Upon a large slab of marble, in the peaceful cemetery of old Buffalo Church, marking the resting place of all that is mortal of this "Founder of Greensboro" are the words of a tribute paid him by those who knew him best and which fittingly close this sketch:

"Born October 13, 1743, in Frederick County, Virginia, a son of pious and worthy parents, endowed by nature with a mind above the ordinary grade, with a strong love of liberty and great decision of character, though without the advantages of a liberal education, he will nevertheless be ranked by a grateful posterity among that noble band of patriots whose skill and valor in the field of battle during our struggle for national independence and whose wisdom and integrity in the council chamber where the principles were discussed and the platform constructed of the happiest government on earth, were the pride, the ornament, and the security of their country. Having through a long life discharged the duties of husband, father and friend, of soldier, statesman, and citizen, with uncommon fidelity, he died in a good old age, January 17, 1829.''   E. E. GILLESPIE.

WILLIAM D. PAISLEY

WILLIAM D. PAISLEY

1770 - 1857

The name Paisley in Guilford County suggests patriotism, and the first Guilford officer to give his young life in the World War was Lieut. John C. Paisley, to whose name was awarded the distinguished service cross for heroism in Belleau Wood, France, June 21, 1918. Nearly a century and a half ago, Col. John Paisley, founder of this same Guilford family, was a brave soldier and prominent officer in the Revolutionary War. A native of Pennsylvania, he came in youth with neighbors and friends from Lancaster County to Guilford, North Carolina, and later married here Mary Ann Denny, long remembered as a woman of devoted piety and unbounded faith in a covenant-keeping God.

William D. Paisley, the subject of this sketch, was born of this union October 26, 1770, the eldest of nine children, the home of his parents being in the Alamance congregation, six miles southeast of Greensboro. His education, both classical and theological, was received from his pastor, Dr. David Caldwell, and he is said to have been the best Greek scholar of the Caldwell school in that day. Mr. Paisley was licensed to preach by the Presbytery of Orange, September 30, 1794, in his 24th year, and his first sermon was preached in the pulpit of his venerable pastor and teacher at Buffalo Church, two miles north of Greensboro. A short time after his licensure he went as a home missionary to the then wild and sparsely settled frontier state of Tennessee, where he spent three years in pioneer work.

Between 1797 and 1799 he came back to North Carolina and accepted the pastorate of Union and Lower Buffalo Churches, in Monroe County. Remaining there until 1800 he was called to Hawfields and Cross Roads Churches, in Orange County. Here Mr. Paisley's ministry of 20 years was signally blessed of God. Soon after his coming to this field the great revival of 1801 followed a communion service at Hawfields. A full account of this revival will be found in Foote's "Sketches of North Carolina." According to Foote, this seems to have been the beginning of camp meetings in this state, certainly in the Presbyterian church. In Hawfields and Cross Roads Churches Mr. Paisley spent the prime of his manhood, and his labors in this field were tireless. The new flame of holy love with which he and his people were baptized at the beginning of his ministry burned brightly and steadily during the whole time of his abode with them. A love for souls and for the honor of Christ fired him with great enthusiasm, and this same enthusiasm and zeal for the honor of Christ's Kingdom has followed these churches to the present day.

In 1799, the year before his removal to Orange County, Mr. Paisley married Frances, daughter of General Alexander Mebane, of Orange (a man of the same Scotch-Irish lineage and one who had filled many offices of honor and importance). For 48 years they lived together, a beautiful instance of youthful attachment, mellowed, but not diminished, by years.

In the month of January, 1820, he was led in the providence of God to return to the home of his youth and in that year had the privilege of establishing his church (Presbyterian) in Greensboro. Here, at fifty years of age, he did double duty as preacher and teacher, the village responding loyally to his leadership. He built up and fostered both a male academy on Sycamore Street, just west of the present Y. M. C. A. site, and a girls' school called "The Female Academy", beyond the western corporate limits of that day, but now 316 West Gaston Street. The girls' school was taught for a long time by Polly Paisley, his eldest daughter. Both schools had been chartered in 1816, but it was clearly Paisley who established their excellent service to the youth of the town. One was succeeded by Caldwell Institute for boys in 1833, the other by Edgeworth Seminary for girls in 1840.

Of his scholarship we have already spoken, so we are not surprised at his eminent success as a teacher. Of his force of character and personal courage there is abundant evidence. In his early missionary days a desperado once defied an officer of the law in his community and a tragedy seemed imminent when the young preacher, chancing upon the scene, unhesitatingly arrested the offender and so restored physical safety of the ones endangered.

In his dealings with Greensboro boys of one hundred years ago a story is told of some mischievous lads who thought it great sport to roll the teacher's carriage to Orrell's pond one night, thereby causing the owner some concern is regaining its use. Delighted with their success the prank was tried a second time, but with different results, for, just as the carriage was being left to its fate, Paisley's gentle voice spoke from the robes which had concealed him on the rear seat, thanking the boys for the pleasure of his ride and bidding them "now roll him back to town", which they did with alacrity.

From 1820 to 1824 he preached regularly in the male academy. In 1824 he organized the Presbyterian church, which was the first and only organized church in the village. He continued to conduct service in the academy until 1832, when a brick church was erected by his people at the present intersection of Davie and Church Streets, the ground for both church and adjoining graveyard being a gift from Jesse H. Lindsay, then a young man of twenty-four years.

This first Presbyterian church building of the village served the congregation until Mr. Gretter, the succeeding pastor, erected a larger structure upon the same site in 1846.

Mr. Paisley served the Presbyterians of Greensboro for twenty-four years in a most acceptable and helpful manner. Of his preaching a contemporary (Rev. J. J. Smythe, from whom this paper has already quoted) writes: "His sermons were thoroughly scriptural, their distinguished characteristic being an urgency of appeal and exhortation to the impenitent. The meek and gentle Christian in private life became the fearless ambassador of God in the pulpit. Few ministers have been more faithful in the denunciations of vice and every practice inconsistent with the high morality of the gospel. There is little doubt that Mr. Paisley's efficiency as a minister was due to this happy union of meekness and courage, of humility and a lofty sense of duty."

He was abundantly blessed in his work and in his family. Of his six daughters the eldest was the wife of Rev. Jesse Rankin, mother of the late Mrs. J. K. Hall, grandmother of Dr. W. P. Beall. His two youngest daughters were Mrs. John A. Gilmer, Sr., and Mrs. Robert M. Sloan, of Greensboro. In 1844 he retired as minister of the church because of infirmities of age, but lived until March 10, 1857, to exert a most wholesome and beneficent influence. Only a few days before his death, he whispered in the ears of his successor as pastor of the church, "I can still pray for the conversion of souls."

In the death of Mr. Paisley, Greensboro lost one of her most noble citizens and greatest benefactors. The whole town was greatly moved, a fact evidenced by the suspension of business and a general solemnity pervading the entire village. The writers who mentioned his name and influence always referred to him as "Father Paisley," also in the old Patriot he is so mentioned, and he was father as well as leader to the whole community, often rebuking with affectionate severity the worldly tendencies of his day.

It has recently been noted as a matter of curious interest in the early minutes of the village council that while usual penalties for small offenders ranged from one to five dollars, there was one exception in a drastic resolution of June 27, 1839, which ordered "a fifty dollar fine for each and every offense of playing cards within the corporation." This measure was passed in the days of Paisley's and Peter Doub's greatest influence and the men who framed the ordinance so typical of that time were John A. Mebane, Jesse Lindsay, John M. Logan and James Sloan.

Among old Greensboro homes that of Paisley alone remains the residence of a descendant, Mrs. J. E. Logan, a granddaughter occupying the house built in part by him in 1820 upon a block now found between Eugene Street and Library Place—but which was then just outside the corporation limits. Timbers used in its construction were purchased from the county commissioners and had been a part of the historic Martinsville courthouse moved to Greensboro in 1808. The purchase price of this block, which Paisley paid to his neighbor, Thomas Caldwell, was eighty dollars, doubtless a fair figure of one hundred years ago. Mrs. Logan's mother, Mrs. Robert Sloan, inherited the family dwelling, while her sister, Julia, wife of John A. Gilmer, Sr., lived for many years in an adjoining home built on that part of the Paisley block now occupied by West Market Methodist Episcopal Church and the city library.   R. MURPHY WILLIAMS.

THOMAS CALDWELL

THOMAS CALDWELL
1777 - 1859

From the viewpoint of 1924 it is strange that so grave and reverend an author as William Henry Foote, in his "Sketches of North Carolina," should give space to the appointment of young Thomas Caldwell as first clerk of Guilford Superior Court.

So far as the records available go, this term of court was held at Martinsville in 1807. The historian states that "Presiding Judge McKoy saw fit to keep both anxious candidates and impatient spectators waiting while, with a substitute clerk for the day, he took time to confer with his former teacher, Dr. David Caldwell, and inquire if one of his sons would be suited for the new office. The father thought not, as no one of them had been trained for such work, but upon the earnest request of his old pupil, agreed "to look them over at home and report next day." He returned in the morning with his son Thomas, and saluting the court, said, "Well, judge, I have done the best I could."

The appointment was made forthwith, and Dr. Foote, in 1846, adds kindly comment on fidelity in office, which justified Judge McKoy's decision. There is abundant evidence that no public servant of the county ever felt greater appreciation of a trust. His work, or the memory of that work, in old age, was ever his greatest pleasure and the portrait from which the accompanying photograph is taken shows a significant quill in the right hand.

The clerk's birthplace in 1777 had been the plantation home of his father, Dr. David Caldwell, three miles west of Greensboro, and his education, with that of his seven brothers and one sister, was received at the hands of that pioneer teacher and preacher. He was married in 1813 to Elizabeth Doak, also of Guilford, and their first home was on a farm purchased by the husband in 1812, and just half way between the father's plantation and his own post of duty in the village. Their double log house was on a high and beautiful hill, its homely entrance shaded by a large locust tree, and here their eldest child, the late D. F. Caldwell, was born November 5, 1814.

Only a few scattered stones are left on this western hill in 1924, but an old locust tree, with the story of a hundred years in its heart, looks down in friendly fashion on the asphalt of West Market Street Terrace and the three score young couples who also have chosen to begin life in its neighborhood.

The village home to which the Caldwells moved in 1815, had been bought with the first sale of town lots in 1808, just inside the western limit of the corporation, and was to be later known as the southeast corner of West Market and Ashe Streets. They built this house of brick, facing West Market, with an amply shaded yard on the east. The adjoining corner of Greene and West Market, now in part occupied by the Daily Record, was for many years the home of David Caldwell, Jr., village physician and twin brother of Thomas. Brick servants' quarters stood on the dividing property line, and it throws light upon the domestic conditions of that far off day to know that when these crumbling walls were to be removed for safety in 1905, a loving old ex-slave protested with tears. "You wouldn't tear it down," she said, "the house where we all was borned."

Three more children came to the clerk's new home, two sons and a daughter. Here the remaining years of the parents were spent and the long life of the eldest son. In time the three sons, who had been christened by their book-loving father Franklin, Newton and Addison, became busy men of affairs in the village. They ran a country store of general merchandise where the postoffice now stands, under the name "T. Caldwell & Sons," the father's connection being merely nominal. A flaming poster still in possession of the family, shows publicity methods almost startling in their modern trend.

In 1848 the wife, Elizabeth, died. In 1849 the clerk retired and his youngest son, Addison, for many years deputy, was elected in his place. The father's service, therefore, was given in the first three courthouses in the village, the log building to which the court was first moved from Martinsville in 1809 and which stood on East Market about seventy-five feet from South Elm corner, a second temporary building, never very clearly described, but in use for one decade after 1820, and the brick edifice of 1830 built in the center of old court square. He doubtless rejoiced in the stately structure of 1858, from which the courthouse of 1872 was rebuilt without change, but it could hardly have been finished the last year of his life.

In a sheltered old age the clerk's still active mind was occupied with much reading and not a little writing. He had, like many others, written for diversion in early manhood, and there was a queer little book of homely jingles, published by Gales, of Raleigh, in 1816. As poetry these verses having nothing to commend them, but because of local color one hundred years ago, some are of curious interest.

They depict the daily farm life: ''Light-Foot,'' the preacher's favorite horse; ''Stump and Golden,'' the patient oxen, with ''Tom and Joe,'' their cruel negro drivers. A highly satirical bit of verse on ''The crowd of election day,'' seems peculiar tactics for an office holder until we remember that until 1833 such clerkships were by appointment and not ballot. There is an ode of sympathy to his friends, the judges, who had been compelled by the law of 1806—most unjustly the poet avers—to visit every county in the state each year. Still another ode is to the ''Muses,'' imploring their presence in New America, and most of all on Guilford Battleground. He pleads their gift of fame for Greene and his heroic followers, adding the pathetic comment—''unsung before.''

No hint of longing is found for the world to which his older brothers had fared forth. Instead he says:

''Give me content on Guilford's hills,
My native vales and sounding rills,
This blessing every wish fulfils.''

Nearly all the writing of his last days was on religious subjects, and one quotation is given for its relation to the times. ''I think,'' he writes, ''that I have learned something of the meaning of sin from sitting as servant of the rulers of the country. Judge A. D. Murphy, Judge Cameron, Governor Morehead, Governor Graham, John A. Gilmer and other illustrious men came to the court where I sat—sat for thirty-five years—and if the law be the strength of sin, I have learned something of it workings.''

Thomas Caldwell has slept at old Buffalo since 1859, and today a beautiful new temple of the court he so greatly revered stands directly across the western border of old Greensboro—half in and half outside the village of 1808. By a strange chance its cornerstone rests upon the site of that humble brick home where an old clerk, resting from a long day's task, as men seldom rest in our day, found his greatest joy in memories of service for Guilford.

BETTIE D. CALDWELL.

HENRY HUMPHREYS

HENRY HUMPHREYS
1790 - 1840

"The first trace of the Humphreys family, from which Henry Humphreys sprang, was in the person of Biron De Humphreys, who came into England with William the Conqueror. From Biron De Humphreys are descended the Humphreys of Pennsylvania, Virginia, Mississippi and the North Carolina branch of the family."

"That John Humphreys came to Virginia from England in 1635 is upon record. He was probably well to do and of sufficient consequence to have been extradited for his religious opinions. From this branch of the family the southern Humphreys undoubtedly came." Quoting further from Dr. F. Humphreys, of New York City, who compiled the history of the family: "The Humphreys never go together, anywhere or to any place, except under compulsion, according to my observation. This self-reliance and impatience of restraint render them quite too independent to do the common sense thing."

Unfortunately our people are not careful in keeping family records and only vague traditions enable us in any way to trace our forbears; but from the foregoing the characteristics of the Humphreys rang true in the personality of Henry Humphreys, as he was markedly "self-reliant and impatient of restraint," and further to bear out their traits "that the Humphreys never go together" is the fact that the only brother of Henry Humphreys, "Jack" or John Humphreys, settled in Vancouver Island after a life partially spent on the sea. Jack accumulated a large fortune and having no family of his own the Henry Humphreys children were his heirs, their father having died first. The matter was taken up by my grandfather, Thomas R. Tate, son-in-law and executor of Henry Humphreys, through his attorney, and papers prepared to substantiate the claim. Owing, however, to the outbreak of the Civil War the matter was dropped and the estate after several years reverted to the English crown.

Henry Humphreys came from Virginia to Caswell County, North Carolina, moving afterwards to old Jamestown, in Guilford, and finally to Greensboro, where he established his home and became a leading spirit in the upbuilding of the town. The date of his last move was probably about 1820. The first census of the village in 1829, giving a population of 269 and the value of all real estate as $53,485, shows Humphreys' lands valued at $12,000 of this total. The minutes of the town council tell that he was chosen by the people as a member of that body and was made chairman by the council in 1832 and 1834.

In 1837 the corporation was extended, making Greensboro one mile square. All citizens were drafted in four squads to work the streets of the enlarged municipality and Humphreys was one of four overseers chosen to direct the service. This seems clear testimony from his neighbors that he knew how to make friends as well as make money in Greensboro.

In that early day the number and variety of his business activities seem remarkable. Under date of April 25, 1831, I find an inventory of the stock of goods of Humphreys and Stockton, who ran a store at Statesville, N. C.; this inventory shows assets of same to be $13,093.53¼. An agreement, dated 23rd of January, 1831, with Thomas R. Tate, my grandfather, shows they were opening a store at Wilkesborough, N. C., in addition to the one operated in the old Tate corner in Greensboro. Other of his papers show that he was a stockholder in various local mines and one where he paid an account with 890 pennyweight, 15 grains of gold ($730.31). In addition to this he was a large dealer in real estate both in Guilford and other counties. I have a memorandum given by him to Michael Hoke, his agent at Lincolnton, N. C., showing deeds for various tracts in Lincoln County aggregating 750 acres, value $4,000. So he must have been a very busy man, yet his active, self-reliant Humphreys brain was long before 1828 planning the erection of the first successful cotton mill in the south, which was completed in 1833. I have before me an agreement between Henry Humphreys and Leonard Allen, of Lincoln County, N. C., under date of June 25th, agreeing to pay said Allen $1,000.00 per annum for setting up machinery in the mill and operating engines after the work has been done, which is to be on December 1, 1832.

As I go over these papers and see the remarkable grasp of detail the man had and the systematic manner in which widely different business was reduced to concise statements the thought comes that he must have been a wonderful personality.

The Mount Hecla Steam Cotton Mill, begun in 1828 and completed in 1833, the crowning enterprise of Humphreys' busy life, was long the pride of old Greensboro. Stockard's history of Guilford says: "To build a cotton factory then was a great undertaking. The machinery had to be hauled in wagons either from Petersburg, Virginia, or from Wilmington, North Carolina. Postage on letters was twenty-five cents. Mr. James Danforth came down from Paterson, New Jersey, to set up the machinery, and spent a year or so teaching the people how to run it. The hands were white people from the neighborhood."

A bill of lading for Mr. Humphreys' machinery says that "seventeen boxes had been shipped on the Schooner Planet whereof Capt. I. Cole is master for this present voyage now lying in the port of New York harbor and bound for Petersburg, Va. Goods to be delivered in good order and well conditioned at the port of Petersburg, Va., (the danger of the seas only is excepted). Freight for said machinery is eight cents per cubic foot. These goods were insured, marine insurance, policy costing $1.25."

Another letter bears date of August 5, 1835, Paterson, N. J.:

To Mr. Henry Humphreys:

"Wages with mechanics have advanced in a much greater ratio and there is a scarcity of workmen. Besides the Trades Unions have created throughout all the whole Northern and Eastern sections of the country much insubordination. Workmen have struck in many places for a reduction of the hours of labor. The cotton mill hands have been standing out for eleven hours per day for more than four weeks.

"We trust the reasons stated are sufficient to justify the increased price of the 120 spindle frames.

"ROGERS, KETCHEN AND GROWNOR."

The mill was built of brick and contained five stories, with a basement. It was one hundred and fifty feet long by fifty feet broad. Three thousand spindles and seventy-five looms were run. Sheeting, shirting and osnaburgs were woven, and also cotton yarn, which was put up in five pound packages and sold throughout the country round to be woven on old-fashioned looms. When the mill was first established the yarns were so popular that people from the country camped all round the factory, waiting for the yarns to come off the machinery. Other products of the factory were hauled in large wagons to Virginia, Tennessee, Kentucky and western North Carolina.

This, the first cotton mill in this state, stood on the corner of Bellemeade and Greene Streets, in Greensboro, N. C. Edwin M. Holt, who became the leading cotton mill owner in the state and in the south, learned the cotton manufacturing business from Henry Humphreys. (See letter of Governor Thos. M. Holt in the "History of Alamance.")

Currency was issued by Mr. Humphreys. This bore a picture of Mount Hecla Steam Cotton Mill. Fifty-cent bills, dollar bills and three dollar bills were issued in 1837. Many of these were made payable to Thomas R. Tate, his son-in-law. These steel plates are still in possession of the family.

The Patriot of May 13, 1833, edited by William Swaim, O. Henry's grandfather, printed enthusiastic comment for this new factory and the progressive spirit of the pioneer manufacturer. A later edition of the paper gives the editor's indignant protest upon legislative action which proposed to cripple the infant industry by taxation.

Henry Humphreys was twice married, his first wife being Mary Baldwin, of Caswell, who died in 1820, leaving a daughter, Annie, who married Thomas R. Tate and became the mother of the Tate family known in Guilford and Mecklenburg Counties. Her sons were Henry, George, Charles, John, Thomas, Turner, Ferd and Ernest, and there were two daughters, Louisa and Katherine. The second wife was Letitia Harper Lindsay, daughter of Col. Jeduthun Harper and widow of Col. Robert Lindsay. She died in 1835, leaving two Humphreys children who grew to maturity, a son Absolum, and a daugher, Sarah Watson.

The home of Henry Humphreys was located on the southwest corner of West Market and South Elm Streets where the Greensboro Drug Store and Cline's Drug Store now stand. Cline's Drug Store is a part of the old residence and the store of Henry Humphreys was on the present site of the

Greensboro Drug Store. The building was three stories, all but the corner room being the residence. It was the first building of its kind in Greensboro and people came for miles to see it and by some it was called "Humphreys' Folly".

Known in his own day and ours only as a man of affairs with every energy concentrated on business, we find his one recreation to have been a great love of music and that he was accustomed to play his violin for the frequent dances of his employees. Two heirlooms once prized in the Humphreys home serve to illustrate life interests of its master. One is the iron-bound safe with an intricate lock, which held his orderly accounts, the other an old hand organ in a mahogany case, with its repertoire of eighty old Scotch tunes.

Buffalo Church was the church which he attended until his death in 1840 and beneath the sombre cedars and thickly intertwined periwinkles of its graveyard he sleeps, a plain marble gravestone marking his resting place. As you stand here in the gathering shadows the faint hum of thousands of spindles comes borne on the soft evening breeze from Proximity, Revolution and White Oak, past the tomb of Ceasar Cone and a few yards on passes to the clinging vines of Buffalo, singing its restful requiem to these two master workmen. There could be no more fitting threnody to two valiant souls bidding them rest in peace than the twinkling lights in factories and houses and the work going on—and on—and on.

THOMAS H. TATE.

JOHN McCLINTOCK DICK

JOHN McCLINTOCK DICK
1791 - 1861

William Dick, the first of the family to settle in North Carolina, was of Scotch-Irish Presbyterian stock and came south in the migration which from about 1760 to 1770 gave us a number of names since prominent in local history.

An iron worker by trade, he settled on a grant of land adjoining the courthouse square at Guilford Courthouse, and shared with Robert Lindsay the commercial honors of the settlement, Lindsay conducting a general store and copper-smith shop, while Dick made the wagons and agricultural implements for the early settlers.

James Dick, the son of William, as a young man, fought with the North Carolina militia at the battle of Guilford Courthouse, and shortly thereafter obtained a grant of land in what is now Rock Creek Township, in the eastern part of Guilford County, and became a large landowner and successful farmer.

On this farm in eastern Guilford, John McClintock Dick, the son of James Dick, was born in 1791.

When John reached manhood his father offered him his choice, either a good farm or a college education. The choice was made, the farm was sold, and John went to the University of North Carolina. College life was succeeded by "reading law" in the office of an active practitioner, the while serving as the lawyer's clerk, as was then the custom of applicants for admission to the bar. His law license obtained, he began the practice in Greensboro and made it his home until his death.

All records of his early life at the bar have faded out, and he first came into local prominence in 1819, being in that year elected from Guilford County to the State Senate, an unusual honor for a man of his age. After serving one term he returned to the bar. He was re-elected to the State Senate in 1829 and served for three consecutive terms.

In those days the judges of the Superior Court were elected by the legislature for life.

In 1835 there was a vacancy on the Superior Court bench, and two of the most brilliant lawyers of the central part of the state were candidates before the legislature for election. Both men were of the type which makes strong friends and bitter enemies and feeling ran high. At the same session of the legislature Mr. Dick went to Raleigh as a candidate for solicitor, but the result was that the deadlock over the judgeship was broken by the election of Dick, who seems to have been an acceptable second choice to both factions, and in this office he served until his death on the circuit in 1861.

His record on the bench is almost entirely a matter of tradition, but tradition has it that the same qualities which elevated him to the bench by making him acceptable to all factions were the outstanding characteristics of his judicial career. He was a sound, though not a brilliant lawyer, patient, painstaking, level-headed and industrious, though perhaps a bit slow; and a man of spotless character and even temper, universally liked and trusted. The late Levi M. Scott, a distinguished member of the Guilford bar, expressed the general opinion, when writing of Judge Dick, he said: "There have been greater but few more irreproachable public men in all our history."

Outside of his professional and official duties, his chief interest was in the University. While in the legislature, he was its devoted, though not always successful, champion in its struggles for financial assistance, and later served as an unusually active member of its board of trustees from 1842 to 1860.

His methodical habits and simple life, coupled with a successful legal practice and later an official income, large for those days, enabled him to accumulate considerable property. His home on North Elm Street, directly opposite the present site of the O. Henry Hotel, was one of the show places of the village, while his principal recreation was in superintending a farm of several hundred acres, worked by his slaves, in the northern part of the county.

Being on the bench, he took no active part in the public discussions preceding the Civil War. His privately expressed opinion was that he was opposed to secession, but that his first duty was to be loyal to his state whatever course the state might take.

He was married to Parthenia Paine Williamson, of Person County, a women of unusual force of character, and reared a large family, the most noted of whom was his son, Robert P. Dick, afterward for many years a judge of the Supreme Court of the state and of the District Court of the United States.

The death of Judge Dick was peculiarly in keeping with his life. The sense of methodical devotion to duty, so characteristic of the man, prompted him, though in failing health, to undertake the riding of an eastern circuit in the summer of 1861. In the latter part of September he held his last court in Bertie County, and then in the words of an early account ''the faithful and upright old man cleared off his court docket and went as a visitor with Mr. Abraham Riddick, the clerk of the court, to his beautiful country seat, Manneys Neck, hoping thereby to recover from his illness. There on the 16th of October, 1861, far from home and family, his long and conscientious discharge of public duty found its conclusion, and he sank to his rest.''   ROBERT DICK DOUGLAS.

JOHN MOTLEY MOREHEAD

JOHN MOTLEY MOREHEAD
1796 - 1866

In the second quarter of the nineteenth century North Carolina received the impetus of a group of men distinguished from their fellows in ability and disposition to think far forward beyond their environment, and in terms of the common welfare. Poverty held the state in thrall, and many, abandoning a hopeless struggle with adverse conditions, fled westward, anywhere, that seemed to offer hope of a more tolerable existence to be won by their labor. The greatest need of those who remained was the means of profitable exchange of the product of their fields and their strength. But they lacked not only facilities of commerce; government was inert, remote from the people; of public education there was none worthy of the name; the deaf and dumb, the blind, were unregarded by the state, the insane were confined in the county jails. Culture and comfort were for the privileged few, ignorance and a bleak existence, which those disposed to grinding toil could little alleviate, the portion of the many.

There were not lacking those of vision keen enough to penetrate the drab mist of the times. Some of them could see even to this day. We of the present have not completed translating into actuality all of the dream-fabrics of their creation. John Morehead, a young lawyer practicing in Greensboro, had been the law pupil of the man whose brilliant mind was, perhaps, most prescient of all in projecting the North Carolina that was to be. Morehead became the leader of that group.

The history of the steam railroad may be said to have begun with the opening of the Liverpool and Manchester in 1830. Our North Carolina progressives were prompt to realize its possibilities, but years before that they had begun to dream and to plan, and so their first ideas for transportation other than by water were limited to highways. They talked and wrote of a network of roads covering the state, with a central highway from ocean to mountain top; of the deepening and widening of the channels of the rivers; an inland waterway connecting Beaufort harbor with Pamlico Sound, and the opening of Roanoke inlet; of great ports for the world's commerce at Beaufort and Wilmington; of mills and factories, utilizing the energy of the streams; the drainage of swamps, a geological survey, and later on of great railroad lines traversing the state and linking it up with the commerce of the continent. Their vision was not confined to the material. It included education made accessible to the mass, a government brought nearer to the people, asylums for the insane, schools for the deaf and dumb and for the blind. To all these things Morehead subscribed with the vigor and tenacity which characterized his career. In the general assembly he opposed a bill to prevent the education of negroes, moved the appointment of a select committee on the colonization of slaves, introduced a bill for their emancipation under certain conditions. In his first legislative term, 1821, he voted with the minority for a resolution providing for a constitutional convention; he was member of the convention of 14 years later and supported the amendments which placed representation in the house of commons on a basis of federal population, and made the office of governor elective by the people instead of by the legislature. At this period John Motley Morehead was becoming the commanding figure of the state.

He was the son of John and Obedience Motley Morehead and was born on Independence day, 1796, in Pittsylvania County, Va. The family removed in 1798 to Rockingham County. In 1810-'11 John was tutored by his father's neighbor and friend, Thomas Settle—we have no record of his earlier education. He next attended the academy of Rev. Dr. David Caldwell, near Greensboro, where his preparation for college was completed. Doctor Caldwell was then nearly ninety. "Governor Morehead never wearied of praising his skill as a teacher and his range and acumen as a scholar," C. Alphonso Smith tells us (Biographical History of North Carolina, Ashe). He entered the University of North Carolina as a junior half advanced, having been appointed a tutor in his junior year. After graduation he studied law under the instruction of Archibald D. Murphy, settled at Wentworth in 1819, after receiving his license, and represented Rockingham County in the House of Commons in 1821. The same year he was married to Miss Ann Eliza Lindsay, daughter of Col. Robert Lindsay, of Guilford, and removed to Greensboro. In 1826-'27 he represented Guilford in the house, and he was a delegate from his adopted county in the constitutional convention of 1835. He was elected governor in 1840 and re-elected in 1842. He was the permanent presiding officer of the national Whig convention at Philadelphia in 1848; in 1858 again represented Guilford in the House, two years later served a term in the Senate, and was one of the North Carolina delegates to the peace conference in Washington the following year. In 1861-'63 he was a member of the provisional congress of the Confederacy.

Governor Morehead, from the completion of his law course until his middle fifties, devoted himself mainly to the practice of his profession. He had engaged in business ventures of increasing scope, had long since reached a position of outstanding prominence in public affairs and of leadership in his party, but when he began his first campaign he was not the equal of his opponent in knowledge of the history of politics and political parties. During these years he had accumulated a substantial fortune based on his practice, and had established his place in the state's legal history. Following his retirement from the chief magistracy he was mainly absorbed in business, public and private; he spent "five years of the best portion of my life in the service of the North Carolina Railroad," in development of what then appeared the most stupendous of the many plans that had been projected for the betterment of North Carolina.

Morehead was the sixth alumnus of the University to be made governor of North Carolina—from 1828 to 1866 he served on the board of trustees, and in 1849 was president of the alumni association. The five-months campaign between Morehead and Romulus M. Saunders was the first in which candidates for public office ever made a canvass of the state; and he was the first governor to sit in the present capitol. He won by a majority of more than 8,000 votes. The Greensboro Patriot recorded that his inaugural was delivered without the use of notes, and without the slightest appearance of faltering. Commerce, agriculture, methods of internal improvements, the needs of the University and the common schools, were his theme; he said "it is to our common schools, in which every child can receive the rudiments of an education, that our attention should be mainly directed."

Dr. C. A. Smith describes his appearance at this time as he stood at the threshold of his larger career, as "singularly winning and impressive. His shoulders were broad, his forehead was massive, his face clean shaven, his hair touched with gray, his carriage erect but not stiff, and his expression a blending of kindliness, sagacity and unalterable determination." Two years later, confusion having arisen in Whig ranks, he was re-elected by a majority of about 5,000 over Louis D. Henry. When the legislature next met the governor presented a program which he had matured during his first term. It embraced insistence upon the Roanoke inlet and Pamlico-Beaufort canal plans as federal projects; recommendation for a charter for a turnpike road from Raleigh to some point westward, selected with a view to its ultimate continuance to the extreme west and perhaps its eastward extension to Goldsboro (then Waynesboro); a charter for a turnpike from Fayetteville to some point above the narrows of the Yadkin, and thence ultimately westward. The policy of the Democratic party, in control of the legislature of 1842, was hostile to public improvements. But the governor hoped to do no more than to lay definite plans for the future, realizing the heavy burden their cost would entail. In his final message to the legislature before retiring to private life the governor urged the establishment of a state asylum for the insane and better treatment of the deaf and dumb and the blind. By the act establishing the North Carolina asylum for the insane he was made chairman of the board to locate and build it.

The legislature of 1849 passed the act to charter the North Carolina Railroad Company, the foremost enterprise of the state in that era of its history terminating in the War of the Sections, in which enterprise Morehead was to lead. In June of that year he presided over an internal improvement convention at Salisbury, at which measures were taken for securing stock subscriptions. At a meeting held at the same place the following July the company was organized and Morehead was unanimously chosen president, in which office he continued until 1855, when he declined to accept another election, and was succeeded by Charles F. Fisher. The charter act had been passed when a tie vote was broken by the speaker,

Calvin Graves, of Caswell, in the Senate. Governor Morehead said, in his first report as president to the legislature:
"The passage of the act under which this company is organ-
nized was the dawning of hope to North Carolina; the securing
of its charter was the rising sun of that hope; the completion
of the road will be the meridian glory of that hope, pregnant
with results that none living can divine." In his final report
to the stockholders shortly before his death, he gives this
terse chronology of an achievement which he regarded as the
crowning event of his life:

"On January 29, 1856, trains could run from Charlotte to
Goldsboro, a distance of 238 miles. June 7, 1858, found the
roadbed of the Atlantic and North Carolina Railroad ready
for trains from Goldsboro to Beaufort harbor, and a few
months thereafter found trains running to within a few miles
of Morganton on the western extension." "In seven years,"
said he, "we have built of this great line 352 miles in one
continuous line." It was in 1858 that charters were granted
incorporating the Atlantic and North Carolina Railroad Company, and the North Carolina and Western Railroad Company, referred to by Governor Morehead as "the contemplated extensions of the North Carolina Railroad," and
immediately Governor Reid ordered President Morehead and
the directors of the North Carolina Road to make surveys.
Work on both these roads was inaugurated under Morehead's
supervision.

Governor Morehead went to the "peace congress" or convention of 1861, at Washington, a strong union man who, says
John Kerr (the Kerr Memorial) had "always denied the
right of a state to secede." He was among those who "went
to that congress opposed to a secession of the Southern States
from the union, returned in favor of it, as a measure of
unavoidable necessity." "With his whole soul he espoused the
cause of his native land, and devoted all his resources of mind
and estate to its defense." He did not long survive the Confederacy, his death occurring August 27, 1866.

Governor Morehead was by far the greatest man that North
Carolina had ever produced, was the declaration of Thomas
Settle, the son of John Morehead's first preceptor in Latin.
Settle had often heard the opinion expressed; he first realized
the truth of it at the session of the legislature of 1858-'59.

John Kerr, of Caswell (quoted above), was then a colleague of the ex-governor in the House. Upon him, also—although there then existed between the two a friendship of long standing—the dramatic event of the session, Morehead's reply to attacks upon him and the plans for permanent improvements then in process of development, made an impression which figured largely in his appraisal of Governor Morehead's abilities. Citizens of the piedmont had sought (a decade before) to have the legislature charter a company to build a railroad from Charlotte to Danville. This was opposed by the east and the Charlotte to Goldsboro charter was adopted as a compromise. At this legislature of 1858 the scheme was revived in application for a charter to build a railroad, without state aid, to connect the North Carolina Railroad at Greensboro with the Richmond and Danville at Danville. Governor Morehead was the principal champion of the measure. It was opposed by eastern members and Raleigh newspapers as prejudicial to the interest of the North Carolina Railroad, and Governor Morehead's administration of that company was assailed with intense bitterness; he was charged with breach of faith in that while soliciting subscriptions to the North Carolina Railroad stock he had promised to abandon forever all advocacy of the Danville connection. For five days he sat in silence under these attacks. C. S. Wooten had said that "there has never been another instance in the history of the state of such moral courage, such heroic firmness, and such a grand exhibition of iron nerve," as Morehead displayed in his reply. Chroniclers of the period agree that, to the amazement of friends and opponents, he achieved a great personal victory, although the Danville connection charter was defeated by a strictly partisan vote. This incident appears to have marked the supreme forensic triumph of Morehead's life and to have determined, to no small extent, in the opinion of distinguished members of his own profession, his rank in ability. Said Judge Kerr: "In such times as he lived, with such knowledge and influence surrounding him, and with such rivals as he had—to have won such eminence and fame as he did win, proves John M. Morehead clearly entitled to be ranked in his profession among the great." "Once in every age," writes Prof. R. D. W. Connor ("Ante-Bellum Builders of North Carolina") "appears that rare individual, both architect and contractor, both poet and man of action, to whom is given both the power to dream and the power to execute. Such men write themselves deep in their country's annals and make the epochs of history. In the history of North Carolina such a man was John M. Morehead."

Morehead was not rated by scholars as of eminent scholarship, by lawyers as one notable for wide learning in the law. He spoke in the broadest vernacular, as did most popular orators, when addressing the populace; his state papers and other formal utterances come down to us in the careful English of the student of the classics. He had a practical knowledge of engineering and architecture, and a discriminating taste in art and music. As lawyer, statesman, farmer, pioneer manufacturer, railroad builder, business administrator, he is to be judged by a combination of qualities. His power with the people, which increased throughout his active years—in that lay much of his strength for accomplishment, his talent for leadership of great minds; and this alone would go far to prove to posterity that steadfastness of soul and sterling integrity to which his contemporaries testified.

Eulogists who had been Morehead's contemporaries thought it worth while to take notice of an impression that he was cold and selfish, but the earnestness with which this is denied leaves no doubt of the sincerity of the denial. There was a general belief that he had the Midas touch; a girls' school that he built in Greensboro, even, was supposed to be a profitable enterprise. This was Edgeworth "Female Seminary," and was founded the year he was nominated for governor: the only girl's school of the period founded and owned by an individual. Mrs. Mary Bayard Clarke said he erected the school in order that he might keep his daughters at home, having been always opposed to sending southern girls to be educated in northern schools. "He spared no expense on it: the buildings and all appointments were in the best and most appropriate style; the grounds cultivated and adorned, and a corps of the best teachers always employed. It was a benefit to the state. . . . He never received even a fair interest on the money he invested in the buildings," ("Social Reminiscences," the Kerr Memorial volume.) She also tells us: "Those who cried against the terminus of the Atlantic road being at Morehead City, and asserted that it was carried there because of the large bodies of land owned by Governor Morehead at that point, did not look far enough back, or they would have seen that he owned the land because he was convinced that the railroad should, and eventually would, be run to that point, and did not run it there because he had first purchased the lands. An old sea captain who lived at Beaufort, and whose property would have been greatly enhanced in value had the road run to that point, remarked, when someone regretted that it did not do so: 'Governor Morehead was striking for the best anchorage, and he hit it as true as if he had been bringing a vessel into this harbor for 20 years. Morehead City is the point for the terminus; vessels of any draught can lie right up to the wharf there, and they can't anywhere in Beaufort.'"

"Blandwood" is referred to by Judge Kerr as the governor's "delightful suburban seat." At the close of the War of the Sections the Moreheads, although impoverished, were in better condition than many of their erstwhile wealthy neighbors. Dr. Smith says this was because he owned comparatively few slaves. Mrs. Morehead had been reared in the abolitionist community of New Garden Church, and had always opposed her husband's investing largely in negroes. He is frequently referred to as the pioneer manufacturer of this section. He had a big cotton mill at Leaksville, among other manufacturing enterprises, and "even while he was expiring in the mountains of his native state, his spindles and his looms were still running." He was a prophet never without his full meed of honor and respect amongst his neighbors of Greensboro and the surrounding country. The Greensboro Patriot files of some 75 years ago bear many a story testifying to the pride and affection of the town, the county and this entire section. From all Guilford and neighboring counties they flocked to hear him, for instance, at the time of his second campaign, when the governor spoke four hours—and neither speaker nor audience showed fatigue. Crossing a county or so to attend a political speaking was in those days rather an enterprise, and he who undertook it expected to hear a considerable speech.

Of the dreams that they dreamed, Murphy, Morehead, Gilmer and all that company of far-visioned seers, little remains of dream-fabric only, save a great river commerce and two ports attracting the shipping of the world.

EARLE GODBEY.

PETER DOUB

PETER DOUB
1796 - 1869

Facing the eastern aisle of West Market Street Methodist Church a familiar memorial window in dark rich colors bears the name of Peter Doub. This is Guilford's claim to a pioneer Methodist preacher who built the first church of his faith in Greensboro (318 South Elm) in 1830, forty-seven years after Guilford circuit was established in 1783, and sixty years after Methodism entered this section in 1770.

John Wesley, defining the church he established, said in part: "A Methodist is one who rejoices evermore and prays without ceasing. He keeps God's commandments from the least unto the greatest. He follows not the customs of the world and fares not sumptuously every day. He cannot lay up treasure on earth, nor can he adorn himself with gold or costly apparel. He cannot join in any diversion that has the slightest tendency to evil. His heart is full of love to all mankind."

Wesley went to his reward in 1791, and five years later Peter Doub, who was to carry his banner in far off America, was born in Stokes County, North Carolina, March 12, 1796, a life destined to exemplify in a marked degree the ideal Methodism of Wesley. These two apostles of the early church had many characteristics in common. Both were men of power, rugged and sturdy, yet exceeding kind; both had all the courage of strong convictions, with a burning zeal for the betterment of humanity, and both would gladly sacrifice all other aims to spread the kingdom of their Lord.

Of all the folk, Scotch, English, Irish, Dutch and German, who furnished bone and sinew for North Carolina, none were superior to the patient plodding Germans and thrifty Dutch. Persecuted for their religious views they had emigrated from Switzerland and the Palatine to America a few years prior to the Revolutionary War, casting their lot first with Pennsylvania in the counties of York and Lancaster, but soon moving south where they settled permanently in the fertile valley of the Yadkin.

Of such lineage were Johan Doub, father, and Mary Eve Spainhauer, mother, of Peter Doub. These young people met in the backwoods of North Carolina and were married about 1780. The husband, Johan, was born in Germany, and it is recorded that "he was well instructed in mechanics and the tanning business as was customary in that country, and in all the arts of skin dressing." Fluent in his own tongue, he became a good English scholar after he was fifty years of age.

The great event of the father's life was being brought to a knowledge of truth under the influence of Rev. William Otterbein, founder of the United Brethren, who had been received into the Doub home as a circuit preacher. From that good hour this home was not only thrown open for the entertainment of the itinerant Methodist, but became one of the regular preaching places in the circuit and was the beginning of Doub's Chapel in Forsyth County.

Johan Doub became a licensed preacher, a local deacon, and a man of great piety. He possessed a fine knowledge of the Bible and of Methodist theology. Mary Eve, Peter Doub's mother, a member of the Dutch Reformed Church from her fifteenth year, joined the Methodist Church with her husband and became a mother of all Methodists in that section. Her strong mind, deep piety, Bible knowledge, cheerful disposition and great firmness of character made her a fitting help-meet for her husband. Into this home Peter Doub was born, the youngest of nine children, among a simple-mannered, God-fearing people. His brothers bore such names as John, Joseph, Henry, William, Jacob, Michael, and his sisters were called Mary and Eve. Is there something a little prophetic in the fact that he was called "Peter?"

The earliest fact he could recall after entering the ministry was a camp meeting held on his father's land in 1808, when as a lad of twelve, he and a brother four years his senior were deeply impressed by the claim of an atoning Savior and both resolved to consecrate their childish lives to His service.

Schools and good teachers were few in that day, but the Doub parents were tireless in their home training and Peter, youngest of the nine, was required to recite a scripture catechism daily so as to be letter perfect for examination by the itinerant preacher on his next round. More than that we are told that he was required to tell in his own words the spiritual truths of these lessons.

In time this youngest son was also sent away to school. Under the spell of new associations the early religious impressions were chilled and we are told that "he was led into a course of carelessness rather than outbreaking wickedness," but 1817 brought another great camp meeting, when he obtained the pardon of his sins and proclaimed his full deliverance to the people. He shouted for two hours, exhorting the congregation and encouraging the penitents.

He immediately joined the Methodist Episcopal Church, and now at twenty-one the call of the gospel ministry, never entirely absent since childhood, filled his mind with great perplexity; feeling it his duty to preach he was for a long time deterred by great natural timidity and limited education. It was in this period of indecision that he and a brother "commenced the concern of a farm," but, "seeing that his eternal salvation depended on his own compliance, he fully resolved to offer himself to the church."

He was received as a "probationer in the traveling connection," at the Annual Conference held in Norfolk, Va., February, 1818, and after two years in the regular work his doubts all left him and he secured the entire surrender of himself, body, mind and soul, to the work of the ministry.

"His first appointment was to the Haw River circuit, as a colleague of the venerable Christopher S. Moring. In the course of the year, Mr. Moring told him that the people objected to his preaching—not as to the matter nor as to the manner, but because his sermons were too short. He answered that he could not make them longer without repeating what he had said. Mr. Moring replied: "You must read more, think more, and pray more, and then you can preach more." This circumstance so discouraged him that he almost concluded to quit his work and go home; but he survived the struggle, and took the good old man's advice, and "his profiting soon began to appear to all, and the rich results in his later years are known in all the churches." (Minutes of North Carolina Conference, 1869.)

His life work thus begun covered fifty-one years, twenty-one spent on circuits, twenty-one on districts, four on stations, two as a temperance lecturer, and in regaining his health, and the last three as professor of Biblical Literature at Trinity College. Seven times he was sent to the General Conference, and when the Southern Methodist Church was organized in the Louisville Conference of 1845 the name "Methodist Episcopal Church, South" was his suggestion. The degree of doctor of divinity was conferred upon him by Trinity College in 1855.

In Greensboro his work for education alone is an interesting record. Almost as soon as the first Methodist church of the village was built under his guidance in 1830 a school for Methodist children was opened directly across the street and served the town for at least ten years.

In 1837 he was one of a committee of three appointed to petition the Virginia Conference for a charter to establish Greensboro Female College, and among many valiant workers in the campaign which followed he was said to have been the most active and influential.

When success crowned their efforts he was chosen as one of nine trustees to open and control the early college. His own home (405 S. Mendenhall) stood just beyond the western boundary of its beautiful campus.

In October, 1856, Doub's Chapel was dedicated, a comfortable brick structure built to continue the gospel work begun long ago in the Doub home. In "The Annals of Southern Methodism" Dr. C. F. Deems writes in cordial praise of the day's services, especially the dedicatory sermon preached by Rev. Peter Doub—son of the chapel founder—from the text "The Lord hath done great things for us whereof we are glad." Lorenzo Dow, traveling through the south at this period, and preaching often to an audience of thousands, found time for a night service at Doub's Chapel and later commended it in his records. It is cheering testimony to work accomplished here that from one class taught first in the Doub home, fourteen men went out to preach the gospel.

Minutes of the North Carolina Conference for 1869 tell us that "Peter Doub's labors for his church were enormous, that he studied and traveled and prayed and preached incessantly. It is estimated that over 40,000 people were brought into the church directly or indirectly through his ministry. In the first year of his district work 1,000 names were added on profession of faith in that district and in meetings conducted by him in the Yadkin circuit in 1826 there were 2,738 conversions.'' This writer of 1869 further says, ''To those who do not know the people and preachers of the North Carolina Conference it is difficult to convey the veneration and tenderness with which Dr. Doub was regarded. He was a great man physically, mentally and spiritually.''

He was more than six feet tall and his face, like his life, held always something distinctly characteristic of his Fatherland. It has been said that ''German blood, American environment and the Methodist itinerancy combined to make him what he was.''

His marriage in 1822 to Miss Elizabeth Brantley, of Chatham County, North Carolina, was a happy union to which seven children were given and the cheer of their fireside was a powerful factor in all those loyal years of service to his church—service gladly given with one end ever in view, the saving of souls for the kingdom of his Lord. The seventy-three years allotted him were in a time which knew little of modern industry and transportation as familiar today, yet it was a period of momentous changes when great questions of state and national importance were constantly dividing the people and with his old age came the shadows of a great Civil War.

It was in Greensboro at the home of his daughter, Mrs. Charles G. Yates, that his life went out August 24, 1869, but the light of that life will shine to the end of all Methodism. His farewell message to his church is characteristic of the man: ''Tell my brethren of the Conference,'' he said, ''that if I am alive I am fighting my way to the skies; if I am dead I am alive.''   LAURA GREY DOUB.

JOHN McCLINTOCK LOGAN

JOHN McCLINTOCK LOGAN
1797 - 1853

On October 18, 1821, the stage from the north came into the little village of Greensborough, carrying as a passenger, a young Scotch-Irishman, lately lánded, who was seeking to better his fortunes in the New World. Though no one knew him, he received a kindly welcome—such as the people of the town have ever given the stranger—and he soon decided to remain, and make his home among them. There for more than thirty years he lived, taking an active part in the affairs of the community, and at his death, holding the respect and confidence of all.

John McClintock Logan was born October 15, 1797, at Raphoe, County Donegal, Ireland.

He was the son of Alexander and Isabella McClintock Logan, and the grandson of James Logan, all of whom lived in the province of Ulster. His ancestors were originally from the highlands of Scotland.

Alexander Logan was an army officer; his sword and pistols are still kept in the Masonic Hall in Raphoe.

In early childhood John M. Logan lost his father, and before he reached maturity, went to live in the city of Londonderry, where he was connected with a mercantile house.

Like so many thousands of his countrymen, he was dissatisfied with conditions in Ireland, and his thoughts turned more and more to the Irishman's Land of Promise—America.

An elder brother had emigrated already, and settled in Pennsylvania. In the summer of 1821 he also bade farewell to kindred and friends; looked for the last time on the familiar scenes of his boyhood, the quaint old town with its ancient castle; then embarked at Londonderry on the British ship, "Hannah," for America, and landed at Philadelphia the first of September.

Six weeks later he came to Greensboro. According to tradition, when he reached Petersburg, Virginia, coming south, a new acquaintance told him of the thriving little place in North Carolina, whose merchants bought goods at Petersburg, and he concluded to go on and see it for himself.   Soon after his arrival he became engaged in merchandising, and according to a chronicler of those days, was for many years a leading merchant.

Incidentally, there were five stores in the town in 1829.

In 1825 he made application for citizenship and in 1830 received his naturalization papers.   These papers, containing facts of his early life, are still in the possession of the family.

Perhaps no act of his life gave him a deeper feeling of satisfaction than this, the renouncing forever of all allegiance to any foreign power, "especially to the king of Great Britain," and becoming a citizen of a republic.

That it was his earnest desire to have an intelligent understanding of what it means to be an American citizen is evidenced by the number of books which he possessed, relating to the history and institutions of his adopted country.

At the organization of a town government in 1829 he was made tax collector and public officer; and with T. Early Strange, was appointed to assess each man's real estate and take the census.   The population inside the corporate limits was three hundred and sixty-nine.

Between 1830 and 1842 he served six times as town commissioner, and in 1837 was elected clerk of the county court, which office he held until his death in 1853.

Always an ardent advocate of Masonry, in 1823 his name appears as Secretary of the Greensboro Lodge No. 76; and in after years he was raised to the degree of Master Mason.

In 1849 the Greensboro Lodge No. 76 established a Masonic Lodge at Jamestown, and dedicated it three years later, giving it the name "Logan Lodge."

John M. Logan was keenly interested in military affairs, and assisted to the best of his ability in the training of the state militia.

It is probable that he joined the militia soon after coming to Greensboro, for in 1829 he was captain of a company, and in 1834 was colonel of the First Regiment.

He received his commission as Brigadier-General of infantry over the Eighth Brigade in 1841.

The annual military review, or "general muster," seems to have been held, usually in October, and was an exciting event in the quiet little town.

In a newspaper report of the review of October, 1842, mention is made of General Logan's knowledge of military tactics, and a description given of his appearance in the field with "his aids, Majors Gilmer and Lindsay, in their rich suits of regimentals." The aids were John A. Gilmer and A. C. Lindsay. The colors of the said regimentals were the beautiful blue and buff of an earlier day, which had been revived in 1835, and worn by the militia almost to the time of the Civil War.

Since the military held a somewhat prominent part in the life of the town, it would be interesting to know where the parade ground was situated. The orderly sergeant's announcement in the "Patriot" that the Greensboro Guards would drill on "tin shop hill" is not very definite at the present day.

In 1847 a volunteer company was formed in General Logan's Brigade for service in Mexico, and the name "The Logan Guards" was adopted in his honor. It was made up of young men from the counties of Guilford, Rockingham and Stokes, and led by Captain Patrick M. Henry, who was instrumental in raising the company. Captain Henry, it is recorded, was a grandson of the Revolutionary patriot whose name he bore.

In 1848 General Logan was raised to the rank of major-general, "having been elected thereunto by the officers of the Brigades of the Ninth Division".

He was twice married, the first time in 1825 to Mrs. Nancy Dick Patrick, of Greensboro, daughter of Thomas Dick, of Guilford County. They had two children, a daughter Isabella (Mrs. Lyndon Swaim) and a son who died in infancy.

Miss Elizabeth Ambler Strange, of Bedford County, Virginia, was his second wife. Of their four children only one lived to maturity. This was a son, Dr. John E. Logan.

A Scotch-Irishman from Ulster, it hardly needs to be told that he was a Presbyterian. He lies buried in the old First Presbyterian churchyard, his death occurring April 3, 1853.

The following is copied from the Greensboro Patriot: "General Logan filled various offices of public trust in the county, with strict honor and punctuality. For the last sixteen years clerk of the county court, chosen at each recurring term by the voters and filling the office to the satisfaction of the public.''

In its resolutions on his death the Greensboro Lodge No. 76 expressed itself as ''deprived of one whose counsels gave Wisdom, whose character gave Strength, and whose amiable nature imparted Beauty to the ancient institution of Freemasonry, of which he has so long been a devoted member.''

The Logan home was at the intersection of North Elm and Gaston Streets, on the southwest corner.

There was the usual garden in the rear, where the owner, as a recreation after his duties in office and store, liked to spend his leisure time cultivating new varieties of shrubs and flowers; often friends at a distance sent him rare specimens. By this means, it is said, various ornamental plants were first introduced to lend their touch of beauty to the town.

His wife, who shared his enthusiasm, was the proud possessor of the first red rose in Greensboro.

All nature appealed to him; he loved a good horse and the wide out-o'-doors, and a daily pleasure was his early morning horseback ride, with his children, over the hills of Guilford.

ISABELLA L. SWAIM.

ELI CARUTHERS

ELI CARUTHERS
1799 - 1865

Old Alamance Church, five miles southeast of Greensboro, is rich in its traditions and established facts of Guilford County's ancient lore—and let us hope that someone who has the time and abilities may soon write a history of Guilford County, that its history, which is fast slipping away from us, may not become forever a "forgotten lore" for failure to record it.

This sketch is of one who, in his time, preserved in history what was then current and common knowledge among the older inhabitants—but had such a record not been written, later historians would have sought in vain for a dependable account of many of the events he recorded. And so the historians who will write of the past century will seek in vain for reliable data pertaining to Guilford's history if someone does not soon record the events of this period.

Alamance Church, so rich in Christian endeavor and accomplishments for more than a century and a half, would be worthy of real interest if only on account of the two remarkable men who served it as pastors: David Caldwell, for a period of sixty years, and his successor, Eli Caruthers, for a period of forty years. Dr. David Caldwell, eminent as preacher, as physician, as teacher and as patriot—a man fulfilling in its widest and truest sense the ideal of a "cultured" man—was the pastor of Alamance from 1764 to 1824.

Eli Caruthers was graduated at Nassau Hall, Princeton, in 1817. A few years later he came to visit Dr. Caldwell, and so impressed was Dr. Caldwell with this young man that Caruthers was asked to remain over the coming Sabbath and preach to the Alamance congregation. Appreciating the true worth of Caruthers, Dr. Caldwell recommended to his congregation that they call him to serve as assistant pastor for Buffalo and Alamance Churches, and this recommendation, meeting with approval, was promptly acted upon by the congregation.

In 1821 Dr. Caldwell retired from active duty, though he still preached, and Caruthers succeeded to the pastorate of these two churches until the union of the two churches was dissolved in 1846, and he then served Alamance as pastor until the time of his resignation in 1861.

Unfortunately there is no written record, or diary, of the life of Dr. Eli Caruthers, and it is impossible to write a complete sketch regarding a man whose life, though zealous and influential in his time, was almost all given to his one great calling in so far as "massive deeds and great" are concerned; though rich and no doubt eventful enough in its daily routine of work faithfully done among the people of his congregation and neighborhood.

It is known that Caruthers was born in Rowan County, North Carolina, on October 26th, 1799; that he was unquestionably of Scotch or Scotch-Irish descent, and possessed the unflinching integrity and patriotism of those people. An old picture of him, long lost, was located some twenty years ago. It shows him in his old age to have been a man rugged in appearance, with the sandy, distinctively Scotch hair, and with strong intellectual features. This picture shows him with a high "stove-pipe," or "beaver," hat. He looks the typical Scotch divine, and you might well imagine him lifted bodily out of Barrie's "Little Minister."

Although he perhaps little dreamed it, Caruthers will be remembered longer, not as a minister, but as a historian. When his life work in the ministry is forgotten, he will live in the ages to come as the author of his "Sketches of the Old North State," in two volumes, known as "Series First and Second."

When he became pastor of Alamance his life became linked and interwoven with the life and history of Guilford, and caused him to search for the truth of Guilford's history. In 1842 he published "The Life of David Caldwell," in which the plant and early growth of Presbyterianism in Central Carolina under the fostering care of Dr. Caldwell, is written in pleasing and interesting style, and many incidents of Revolutionary history in Guilford heretofore unrelated are published by him in this book. This book was cordially received and encouraged him to write his "Sketches of North Carolina." Most notable of his Sketches is his second series, which contains his refutation of the slander of the North Carolina militia at the battle of Guilford Courthouse, which slander has been effectually disproven by the further research and defense of a later historian.

Caruthers died November 14, 1865, and from men who remembered him some facts were collected and recorded about twenty years ago.

He was an uncompromising foe to the making and use of alcoholic liquors—and in a time when its use was much more customary and respectable than it is in these latter days, when John Barleycorn totters with "one foot in the grave."

He was opposed to another "established order of things" of his time—slavery—and remained so to his death. He refused to take a slave even to save a debt due him, notwithstanding the fact that he was a man "poor in this world's goods"; for it is recorded in the early census of the village of Greensboro in 1829 that Caruthers had no property for taxation; and in another old record that his "poll tax for two years being excused."

In 1861 he offered a prayer that: "The young men at the front might be blessed of the Lord and returned in safety, though engaged in a bad cause." As a result of this prayer he was caused to resign his pastorate of the church and he devoted the remaining four years of his life to writing in a clear and legible hand the manuscript for a book against slavery, entitled, "American Slavery and the Immediate Duty of Southern Slaveholders," in which every passage in the Bible relative to slavery is cited. This book, however, was never published.

Although he was a gentleman of broad culture and refined literary taste, yet he was unquestionably a man of rugged type —rugged in his manner and his integrity.

It is recorded of him that he was somewhat negligent of his personal appearance, lacking in grace and refined manners, and in an old sketch this is attributed to the fact "that he deprived himself of that which is the best corrective of these evils—a refined and intelligent wife"; but he never made any effort and never manifested any disposition to change his condition in this respect.

He seems to have loved to wear his characteristic "stovepipe" hat, for it is said that some of his flock resented his not removing it when he visited them, and when the dictates of politeness would have made him do so.

With just what significance I cannot say (unless it be another indication of his ruggedness) it is recorded that he was an inveterate consumer of molasses, and that at the wedding of Governor Morehead's eldest daughter to Mr. Waightstill Avery, that Caruthers left before the wedding supper, and one of the wags of the time said that he had "nosed about" the dining room, and finding no molasses, had left in disappointment and disgust.

In his own life those who remembered him state the dominant guiding principles were: "Is it right?" "Is it God's will?" and he drove home these stern and solemn inquiries to the ears and consciences of his congregation, and it appears that he had the old-fashioned solemn conception of religion, because an old citizen who remembered him stated, "I have no recollection of ever having heard him indulge in a hearty laugh."

His life was linked with the lives of the early builders of Greensboro and of Guilford—with Gorrell, Dick, Morehead, Swaim, Humphrey, Porter, Sloan, Caldwell, Lindsay, Logan and other forebears of the present day families.

Nowadays when the fame of General Nathanael Greene, the hero of Guilford Courthouse and Greensboro's namesake, is commemorated by an equestrian statue at the scene of his greatest battle, it is interesting to know that the citizens of Greensboro in 1857, 1858 and 1859 started a movement to erect a monument to Greene and raised what was then a very considerable sum ($600) for this purpose. The approaching War Between the States prevented the consummation of this laudable purpose at that time. Even then the citizens of Greensboro believed that the national government should erect this monument, for they passed resolutions, which were in effect as follows:

"Resolved, that the National Government should erect a monument to General Greene; but

"Resolved, that if the National Government does not erect it, that the State of North Carolina should erect it; but

"Resolved, that if the State of North Carolina will not erect it, that the citizens of Greensboro will erect it."

Caruthers was one of the committee appointed to carry on the work of collecting the funds and erecting this monument. One of the methods of raising funds for this purpose was a series of lectures, and we find that in October, 1859, at a large meeting at the Methodist Church in Greensboro, Caruthers delivered a lecture on "The Life and Character of General Greene," which was warmly praised by the contemporary "press" of the day.

He lies buried in Alamance churchyard in the midst of his own people, and they have erected over his grave a neat marble shaft to commemorate his life, and there is something both pathetic and touching in the inscription which reads:

"Erected by his Congregation and Friends," as he had no family to mourn his parting. The further inscription, which is both true and prophetic, reads:

"A sound theologian, instructive preacher, painstaking historian of his native state, a friend and promoter of education, and a public-spirited citizen; the influence of his life and labor was widely felt and the fruits will be lasting."

In this age of hurry and commercialism, if you should visit this old churchyard, a certain reverence and tendency to meditation would no doubt steal over you, and you could but feel that it is a fitting resting place for Eli Caruthers, for even today this is a country churchyard where:

"The lowing herd winds slowly o'er the lea.
The ploughman homeward plods his weary way."

PAUL W. SCHENCK.

JAMES TURNER MOREHEAD

JAMES TURNER MOREHEAD
1799 - 1875

Among the sturdy pioneers who came in early days from Scotland to wrest a home and living from the wilds of the new world, was Charles Morehead, who located, about 1630, in the northern neck of Virginia. A son, John, and wife, Mary, lived in the section afterwards known as Fauquier County, and judging from his will probated August 8th, 1768, John was a prosperous planter surrounded by a large family. Two of their sons, Charles and James, married Mary and Elizabeth Turner, daughters of James Turner and Keren-happuch Norman, of Spottsylvania County, Va., whose monument now stands on the famous battlefield of Guilford Courthouse, erected there in honor of her courage and help in the cause of freedom.

John, youngest son of the two children of James and Elizabeth, married Obedience Motley, a daughter of Captain Joseph Motley, of Amelia County, Virginia, and descendant of Forrest and Ellington families of Amelia and Gloucester Counties, Virginia. They moved into Rockingham County, N. C., and there reared a large family. One of their sons, John Motley Morehead, became governor of North Carolina and another, James Turner Morehead, is the subject of this sketch. Family records speak of young John as a soldier of the Revolution who would without doubt have taken part in the battle of Guilford Courthouse under General Greene, in whose command he served, but for the fact that he had been sent away the day before that of the great battle with prisoners taken to Cowpens. His elder brother, Captain James Morehead, on March 23, 1779, was appointed officer in the 10th North Carolina Regulars under General Sumner. In the records of Mrs. Annie Morehead Whitfield, a daughter of James T. Morehead, she speaks of the many stories her grandmother, Obedience Motley, who lived in her home, told of the beloved husband John Morehead—his benevolent spirit and kindly heart, of the little church, Mount Carmel, he built in Rockingham, and the love of the community which he served as squire, as dancing master or preacher, as friend or creditor. Obedience herself seems to have been a stern business woman, managing the plantation and a large family of children with austerity tempered by kindliness.

Their son, James Turner Morehead, inherited from them traits which made him a greatly beloved and honored citizen. A true standard bearer of a line of forefathers of rugged character, courage and kindliness, for "the bravest are the tenderest." He was born in Rockingham County, North Carolina, January 11th, 1799, married Mary Teas Lindsay May 13th, 1830, and died in Greensboro May 5th, 1875. Mary Teas Lindsay was a daughter of Captain Robert Lindsay and granddaughter of Col. Jeduthan Harper, of Randolph. They lived in Greensboro, and to them were born four sons, Robert Lindsay, John Henry, James Turner, Jr., Joseph Motley, and two daughters, Annie Eliza (Mrs. Theodore Whitfield) and Mary Harper.

In a sketch of her father, James T. Morehead, Mrs. Whitfield speaks of him as a favorite with all who knew him. Even the boys and girls rejoiced when "Uncle Jimmy", as they called him, came in sight, for there was always some fun or music or "goodies" for the young folks.

"He was tall, large and 'erect as an Indian', as he loved to say, handsome, with dark hair, blue eyes and ruddy complexion. He was fond of music, poetry and literature, of which he seemed to know everything ancient and modern."

"Widowed, his 'heart poured out like water' over his six motherless children, making him not only their protector but companion and recipient of their confidences. This same tenderness toward his own filled his heart for all children. He petted them and his servants, and especially his dogs, which were companions of his earlier sports (he was very fond of hunting) and also beguiled him of the loneliness and sadness of later days." To his servants he was always the kind helpful master and friend, their physician, carrying medicines in his pockets for the sick ones and nicknacks for the pickaninnies.

"The nephews who loved to throng his office in winter evenings and hear wonderful stories of the chase, used to call the office the arsenal because of the guns stacked there. One of these guns, an old-fashioned flintlock shotgun, 'Lady

Callagran' had 'brought down' scores of deer and turkeys and was greatly prized.'' His office was a square brick one-room building at the home place on Sycamore Street and faced the present new courthouse square.

"Grandfather's earliest teacher was Rev. David Caldwell, D. D., and his preceptor in law, Chancellor Taylor, of Virginia. He graduated at the University of North Carolina in the class of 1819, and settled in Greensboro, where he practiced law until his death."

In the "History of the University of North Carolina," Hon. K. P. Battle quotes from a letter written by Mr. Slade about the students a few years after graduation, in which the writer says: "J. T. Morehead is the same blunt, plain old fellow, respected by all, and loves to hunt and fish as well as ever." "At commencement exercises of 1849 an oration was delivered by Hon. James T. Morehead, who was a successful lawyer and a member of the General Assembly of the Congress. It was said to exhibit much of a practical nature and allusions to great minds. He was a favorite with the members of the bar in his circuit who affectionately called him 'Uncle Jimmy.' He was naturally a lauditor temporis acti. The last time I saw him he was denouncing the code of civil procedure, then recently imported from New York, and declaring that he would spend the rest of his life procuring its abolition and return to the good old practice. The code, modified, outlived him and has come to stay." He served the university as a trustee from 1836 to 1868 and was a leader in his profession and patriotic service to his state.

In the story of the early days of Greensboro James T. Morehead is found serving the town with true public spirit. In the "Minutes of the town of Greensboro from 1829-1848" he appears as commissioner in 1832, '34, '35, and at the meeting of the commissioners February 24, 1832, "agreeable to a resolution of the last meeting James T. Morehead, Esq., submitted rules of regulations for government of the town for the next year, which were adopted," etc. There are three chapters of these "regulations", interesting indeed because of their quaintness and practical character. "Teams could not be watered at the public pumps nor could produce be sold nearer than one block to the Central Square at public times." "Litter of straw, leather, shavings and ashes, could not be thrown in the streets, wood could not be piled there nor lumber (except for building)." "Horses (and by a later edict hogs also) might not be fed in the streets."

James T. Morehead served the state as a member of the Assembly in the Senate in 1835, '36, '38, '40, '42, and in the House of Representatives of the United States Congress. He took his seat in 1851 at the time Daniel Webster was rising to prominence. He did not care for this phase of life, and his simplicity of character leading him to prefer home and his home town, he resigned after two years and returned to Greensboro and practiced there. He loved the law as a true statesman and was a busy successful practitioner. Among his associates and friends were "the brilliant galaxy of legal wisdom, Ruffin, Badger, Iredell, Graham," and others.

His daughter, Mrs. Whitfield, again speaks of her father as "grieving over secession, feeling it better to demand right under the flag which he almost worshipped. He honored and loved his country with true patriotism and wept and grieved as he walked the floor all night during the winter of '61 when secession was going on, predicting failure—no great country has been disrupted without bloodshed. He foresaw prophetically "our young men slain upon the hills." When, however, it did come he gave to the Confederate Army his four sons. These kept his name untarnished and served their country with the dauntless courage of father and grandfathers.

They were Robert Lindsay Morehead, captain, 45th Regulars, North Carolina; John Henry Morehead, colonel, 45th Regulars, North Carolina; James Turner Morehead, Jr., colonel, 53rd Regulars, North Carolina; Joseph Motley Morehead, lieutenant, 2nd Regulars, North Carolina.

Robert L. became a planter and died a few years after the war. Col. J. Henry Morehead contracted malaria while stationed at Drewry's Bluff, and though too sick to be moved, insisted on accompanying his regiment to Gettysburg, but being too ill to remain, he was carried back to Martinsburg where he died the night before the battle.

Col. James T. Morehead, Jr., served through the war. He was wounded several times, captured within the enemy's line at Petersburg, imprisoned at Washington and Fort Delaware, and finally released after the surrender. He became a successful lawyer and a man honored in the state for his public spirit and legal sagacity.

Joseph M. Morehead became president of the Guilford Battleground Company, devoting many years of his life to the development of that historic place. Its many monuments and adoption as a national park speak his vision successfully wrought out.

Unable to recover from the shock and distress of the war or to adjust himself to changed conditions, the father soon retired to private life. For many years in leisure weeks his plantations and mills were recreation to him—never profit. "Hamburg" mill and "Troublesome" iron works, where were also mills, gave him frequent occupation. While return-ing from one of these trips a chill came on and illness from which there was no rallying. In a few hours murmuring, "Lord Jesus, have mercy upon my soul," he passed away.

With pleasure and satisfaction I add the following sketch by Lyndon Swaim, written at the time of the death of James T. Morehead, which voices the sentiment of the people among whom he lived:

"Mr. Morehead belonged to the past age. For one so long and so honorably distinguished in professional and public life, it is fitting that we recall some of the prominent points in his character and career. In mental and moral culture, in his sense of humor, and in his manners, he was a gentlemen of the old school. In his profession, he was laborious and faith-ful to his clients; well learned in the law; observant of those amenities of the bar which made the practice agreeable to his brethren; as an advocate, original, interesting, and as occasion required, rising into those higher flights of eloquence which stirred men's souls. Occasionally called into the legisla-tures of the state and the nation, his course was marked by sound judgment, independence of thought and act, and honor above reproach or suspicion.

"Mr. Morehead was less clannish or partisan in his dis-position than most public men. While in Congress, he voted with only some half dozen others against paying national hon-ors to Kossuth. And he often voted with very lean minorities in the state legislature. But perhaps in every instance time has vindicated his sagacity and illustrated his independence."

We recall two distinguishing traits in the character of our

departed friend: his love of his profession and his love of nature. A ramble in the woods with his gun and dogs, among the free wild scenery of the hills of Dan, he enjoyed with keenest relish and next to that the discussion with his legal brethren of the "beautiful points" arising in their cases at law. His literary attainments were of a description that afforded to himself and the social circle high enjoyment. We hardly knew a man better acquainted with the old classic literature of England or more ready in illustration from its exhaustless stores.

On religious matters he was reticent. Evidently governed in his business intercourse and public life by the stern commands of the Decalogue—yet he talked little of these things, except, perhaps, in the inner circle of his friends. An expression which fell from his lips forty years ago has nevertheless come frequently up in the memory of the writer, like the sound of a far-off bell: "I would not exchange my hope of the resurrection for all the world!"

His later years, during and since the Civil War, have been more and more marked by bodily and mental failure, caused by age, and the public troubles, but his declining days were soothed by the unfailing duty and affection of his children, the kindly and hearty sympathy of his neighbors, and the affectionate respect of his former servants. His dead face, impressed with all the manliness and more than the benignity of his earlier and better days, was bedewed with no heartier tears than those which fell from the eyes of these old servants who had lost in him the faithful friend of a lifetime.

After a solemn and impressive funeral service conducted by Dr. Smith and attended by a large concourse of citizens his remains were laid to rest beside the grave of his wife in the Presbyterian churchyard.

EMMA MOREHEAD WHITFIELD.

PETER ADAMS

PETER ADAMS

1802 - 1883

Much water has passed under the bridge since the writer was a citizen of Greensboro, though it has been his proud boast wherever his sacred wanderings have led him that he was a Greensboro boy. That he is still at heart a loyal son of Greensboro the writing of this article proves, for it is a well known test of a loyal Greensboro man that he will not refuse to do anything his home town commands him to do, and this authority has penetrated even to the city by the side of the Pasquotank where the children used to say, ''the bull frogs jump from bank to bank.''

Under other circumstances the privilege of paying a tribute to ''my father's friend and mine'' would be pure joy, but as far removed from Greensboro as it is possible to be without going out of the Old North State and therefore wanting the opportunity to search its records, or as perhaps in this case would be far more important, to talk with the gray-haired few who knew the eccentricities, yet admired the worth of Uncle Peter Adams, the writer is reluctant to offer a paper which must be, of necessity, in large part simply recollections of his early childhood. But the command has been received and must be obeyed.

''Recollections of early childhood!'' How the name of Peter Adams brings back the memory of years that busy manhood had well nigh obliterated! Care free years, years of the two-piece garment, of one-hole cat and two-hole cat, of shinny, of the old swimmin' hole, of gazing at the distant line of blue from the top of the college, of crawling through the darkness and spider webs under the college, of wading in Tommy Owen's branch and catching minnows in the beach. My, what years they were! and wherever the writer went Will Hughes went, and Will Hughes was ''Uncle Peter's'' grandson and the apple of his eye.

Oftentimes the writer would make a day of it. The two families were almost as one. Joys and sorrows borne in common had made them one. Leaving his own home before breakfast, he would join Will Hughes and Uncle Peter in eating "buckwheat cakes swimming in maple syrup." Then for the old barn with its many unused stalls eloquent of activity past, but just the place for playing boys, and its great loft where you could roll in the hay or toss it or burrow in it, or to the carriage house where side by side stood the handsome modern carriage, seldom used, and the ancient coach with its letdown step which had made its last trip years before. Or to the tool house, or to the garden, or to the orchard. Or best of all on rainy days, through the old house with its many treasures, its spinning wheel, its candle moulds, its bullet moulds, its relics of the war, its "Boys in Gray" and "Gray Jackets," in which the southern lad, then at least thoroughly unreconstructed, could lose himself. Then couldn't "Aunt Adams" and old Hannah cook? Ginger bread, sugar cakes, fried apple turnovers—well might that humorous writer offer a reward of a thousand dollars for any one who would cook a ginger cake which would taste like those he ate when a boy. Then remember the delicacy nowhere else seen, "persimmon leather," with persimmon pudding and persimmon beer, honey and buttermilk biscuits and milk out of the cool water of the dark dairy.

"Recollections of childhood," and all of them when interrogated telling something about "Uncle Peter" himself. The children stood in awe of him. He was too positive a character for it to be otherwise. But his kindness to us all and especially to his motherless grandson, tell of his kind heart. A sneaking notion arises out of the recollection of the years that certain things have not changed so much after all. "Uncle Peter" was the head of the family, oh, yes, but then "Aunt Adams," his "dear Sarah," was a power to be reckoned with, even by "Uncle Peter." How many tales she had to tell of the times when they kept the Inn and the travelers stopped to eat with her, of the Indian chief who would eat only cake, saying that the "sweet bread was good enough for him." To the writer those were joyous years, but he fears they were not such to the subject of his sketch.

There were still evidences of large business activity and success, but the increasing infirmities of age and one unfortunate business venture had greatly curtailed both activity and success. The old man always seemed full of jollity and humor, but looking back with eyes opened by the experience of years one can suspect that the old home was lonely to those dear old people. How they must have missed those two daughters, Sarah Jane, whom all the village called "Queen", and Mary, who had passed away in the strength and beauty of young womanhood. How often they must have thought of the brave, handsome, dashing young officer, Captain William Adams (second captain of the Guilford Grays), who had fallen leading his men at Sharpsburg! And Peter, their last and only son, away from them and they alone in the big house where there had been so much of gayety! But all this was hidden to us then. When we would enquire of Uncle Peter, "How are you today?" back would come the answer bright and cheerful, "Jam up, jam up. Darling, give me buckwheat cakes swimming in maple syrup this morning. Jam up, jam up." Or if the infirmities of age were too insistent, "Just a few growing pains today. Just a few growing pains." He might be seen any day riding to and from town in a cart, on a load of wood, or in a dray, anyway so that it was riding, but always careful to deny that he would rather ride than walk, "for", said he, "walking is my usual gait."

The block of brick stores down in the heart of the city, the wide sweeping acres of the home place, the capacious outhouses, the orchard, garden and fields, the stone posts to the fences and the granite curb to the well, all bore mute testimony to the kind of business man he had been. His affectionate title, "Uncle Peter," and the greeting of high and low, told of the place he had won in the hearts of his townsmen. Such is the light which the recollections of the writer's early childhood cast on the subject of his sketch and this must be his contribution to the memory of Peter Adams. A more detailed history of his life and labors follows in the mature estimate of a contemporary published in the Greensboro Patriot at the time of his passing:

"Mr. Adams was born in the southern part of Guilford County, February, 1802. He died in Greensboro at the residence of S. C. Dodson, December 4th, 1883, in the 82nd year of his age.

"Born nearly coeval with the century he lived through eight decades thereof, 'with their fluctuations and their vast concerns.' He was the oldest man in town; and for about 60 years had been a citizen of Greensboro. His familiar form and cheery face, and genial salutations, so long daily encountered upon the streets, have passed away forever, leaving a blank no one living can fill.

"With little school education, but with fine natural ability and energy, Mr. Adams was successful in business life. He commenced as a hatter; afterwards engaged for some time in merchandise; became a partner in stage and mail contracts on the old Piedmont line and on the line between Raleigh and Charlotte; was secretary and manager of the Greensboro Mutual Fire and Life Insurance Company; besides engaging at times in mining and other enterprises. With his knowledge of men, and his marked shrewdness as a trader, he made most of his enterprises pay, until the war. And after that his business habits stood him in good stead for the preservation of considerable remnants of his effects.

"Mr. Adams' native ability and aptitude for business were recognized by his fellow-citizens of the county and various representative trusts committed to his hands. He represented his county in the Legislature, where he made an active and useful member of the House of Representatives during 1836-1846 and 1850, and in the State Senate, where he was sent in the troubled days of 1862. He had served as town councilman frequently while a young man and for a long time held a commission as justice of the peace, in the old days when the justices were selected from among the ablest and most substantial citizens; when the office was one of honor, held pro bono publico; profitless as to pay or perquisites; its duties discharged 'without fear, favor or affection, reward or hope of reward.' For a series of years he was chairman of the county court of Guilford, under the old regime—a place of efficiency which required intuitive knowledge of human nature, soundness of judgment, and promptness of decision —all of which qualities he possessed in a remarkable degree. In those days a finance committee annually investigated the money affairs of the county. Peter Adams and Harper Lindsay were standing members of that committee; and when, after a crucial interview with the sheriff and the county trustee, they made their report to the body of justices, in open court assembled, everybody went away satisfied that there had been no crookedness and no mistakes.

"Amid the trials of his chequered life, he was remarkably free from the personal dissipations which frequently overtake men of the world. As husband, father, master, he was true, affectionate, indulgent. The writer (Editor Lyndon Swaim) after an acquaintance of fifty years, can say that he never heard him swear a profane oath, nor ever saw him take a drink of liquor. When invited to drink, he had the habit of saying in his short dry manner, 'I never drink before dinner.' If similarly invited afterwards, his reply was, 'I never drink after dinner.' This habit amid the associations and temptations of his time, shows a power of will which all who live after him might profitably imitate.' "

The location of the various Greensboro enterprises cited in Peter Adams' busy career are added below from the dictation of Mrs. S. C. Dodson in whose home, 327 East Market Street, stands an old chair used by her uncle during his service in the State Legislature at least sixty years ago.

Garrett's store on the northeast corner of Greene and West Market, now Beall Hardware Company, was the scene of young Peter Adams' work as a hatter, sometime from 1820 to 1829, his specialty being high silk hats worn by the more prosperous citizens of that day.

In 1830 he had so far prospered that he was one of three leading Methodists able to contribute most toward the first church of his faith built in Greensboro that year under the leadership of Rev. Peter Doub.

It was in the early forties that "The Inn" was under his management on the present site of the Southern Life and Trust building. To this inn came the stage coaches of the Piedmont line, largely under his management, each stage drawn by four horses. Mrs. Dodson recalls the pleasure of a journey by this service in early girlhood from Greensboro to Hot Springs, N. C., via Charlotte and Asheville.

The Peter Adams "business houses" are to be found between the Greensboro Drug Company's store, once Humphreys' corner, and the Weatherly building, which was the long ago McConnell's store, 109 West Market.

With the fifties Mr. Adams again changed his business. A Greensboro Insurance Company was organized with every well known man of the village among its promoters. David

Wier was its first secretary, but Adams was soon afterward called to this arduous office.

As chairman of the county building commission he advertised in 1857 for contractors' bids on the new courthouse from the home office of this company (now Lindley's store, 115 South Elm). It is doubtless to him that Greensboro history owes two pamphlets clearly stating the work and aims of his company which were placed in the historic corner stone of June, 1858, and brought to light by the steam shovel of June, 1922.

After the hatter's shop, the church, the inn, business block and insurance company, there remains but the location of his beautiful home built in 1854, the hospitable abode depicted above. This we find in 834 West Market, opposite Greensboro Female College which, with other schools, its owner had befriended. Magnolias and firs still living were part of a large shrubbery collection, once the pride of the neighborhood. In a recently remodeled residence this is still a beautiful home.   N. H. D. WILSON.

RALPH GORRELL

RALPH GORRELL

1803 - 1875

In the late fifties there could be seen a tall, straight figure of a man, with a gold-headed cane, emerging from a large red brick house in a grove of great oak trees, and walking down the curved walkway of his stately home in South Greensboro to his law office which was located in his yard. This was the Honorable Ralph Gorrell, southern aristocrat. Of distinguished parentage, of cultivated and well trained mentality, of spotless character and of substantial estate, he might well be taken as the type of ante bellum North Carolina gentleman. Born in 1803, in Guilford County, five years prior to the founding of Greensboro, he was for more than half a century an influential factor in the social, political and economic life of our city and section.

Ralph Gorrell was the grandson of Ralph Gorrell who landed in Boston, from the north of Ireland, in 1750, in company with Robert Lindsay. This first Ralph Gorrell came immediately to Guilford County and settled near Alamance Church, where he purchased a large boundary of land and lived in affluence and with open hospitality. In addition to his successful financial ventures and social activities, he took an active political interest in the founding and development of the new commonwealth.

He was a member of the House of Commons and a member of the North Carolina Constitutional Convention held in Halifax. During the Revolutionary War he was authorized and commissioned to raise forces and supplies wherewith to keep the Indians in check. He was a consistent member of Alamance Church. All in all, he ran true to form to the best traditions of the Scotch-Irish race, who came to the wilderness of this country with a Bible in one hand and a rifle in the other. It is a tradition in Guilford County that he furnished large supplies to General Greene's army just before the battle of Guilford Courthouse. Uncle Bob Sloan had talked with men who had seen Ralph Gorrell, but their description was very vague. "He rolled into Greensboro in a big coach, and wore shining knee buckles."

The peculiar connection, however, of Ralph Gorrell with Greensboro is that he gave, for the munificent sum of $98, the land on which the new city was founded. This occurred in 1808 when the seat of Guilford County was moved from Martinsville to Greensboro. In a real sense, therefore, he was one of the founders of Greensboro.

Ralph Gorrell had several children, and his descendants are scattered over the United States. The late Col. Albert B. Gorrell, of Winston-Salem, was a descendant, and also Rufus Weaver, president of Mercer university. Ralph Gorrell died in 1816 and is buried at Alamance Church.

From such ancestry did Ralph Gorrell, the subject of this sketch, descend. Born in 1803, he was a graduate of the State University in 1825, being the first native of Guilford County to complete the course in that institution. He studied law and was admitted to the bar. In 1834 and 1835 and 1854 he was a member of the House of Commons from Guilford. He represented Guilford County in the State Senate in 1856 and again in 1858, when the Whigs cast their vote in favor of him as presiding officer. He delivered several notable speeches in the Legislature. One speech in the Senate particularly arrested the attention of the state, when he advocated an ad valorem tax which would include negro slaves.

However, he was not an aspirant for political honors, and never accepted public office except for the purpose of effect-ing some particular legislation. But throughout his long career his advice and counsel was sought by his political brethren. He was invariably put forward by unanimous con-sent to preside over the political meetings of the Whigs in this county, and being a public speaker of force and ability, he was called upon many varied occasions to address his fel-low citizens. Some of his most noted efforts were his Fourth of July address in Greensboro in 1839; his speech receiving the Tippecannoe Club banner in 1840; his speech in 1842 receiving Governor Morehead in Greensboro; his speech before the Agriculture Society of Guilford in 1858; his commence-ment address at Davidson College. The subject matter of these addresses reveals the broad scope of his mind, and the treatment of them exhibits him as an orator of no mean ability.

The newspaper accounts of these speeches throw some interesting side lights upon Greensboro's method of doing things in those days. For example, in describing the speech receiving the Tippecanoe Club banner, it seems that the Whig ladies of Edgeworth Seminary decided to bestow a flag upon the Tippecanoe Club of Guilford County. Great preparations were made properly to receive this banner. The club members and citizens generally assembled at the Presbyterian Church at 6 o'clock a. m. (if the ancient chronicler can be believed) and formed a line of march. The Log Cabin was in front, followed by the Tippecanoe Club, next the Greensborough Guards, and then all the citizens who happened to be awake, the total assemblage being about 1,500 people. The procession moved through town and halted in front of the Edgeworth School. Here the ladies of the school presented the club with a large white banner appropriately embellished and inscribed. One of the young ladies made a presentation speech. And young Ralph Gorrell was put forward to receive it, which he did in a manner befitting one of the Knights of the Round Table.

Another interesting event was the occasion of Governor Morehead's return to Greensboro during the campaign of 1842. It seems that the Whigs of Guilford determined to give him an ovation. Accordingly on the morning of his expected arrival the Whigs in front and the rest of the citizens in the rear (for it appears that everybody attended all political demonstrations of either party) formed in double lines in front of Caldwell Institute, a famous seat of learning in those days. A committee on horseback met his Excellency on the Fayetteville road at South Buffalo bridge, one and a half miles from town, and escorted him to the border of the village. The Greensborough Guards, with General Logan and his staff in their gorgeous regimentals, and a large number of people on horseback and on foot, attended by Meller's brass band, went out to meet him at the border of the corporation. When the governor arrived in sight he was saluted by a round from the guards. He was received by Ralph Gorrell, and followed by the band, the general and the staff, the guards, and a long procession of citizens, he was escorted into town amid the enlivening airs of campaign music. His open carriage halted between the waiting lines of people and Honorable Ralph Gorrell arose and delivered a rousing political speech of welcome.

On the political side of Ralph Gorrell's life, one of his most striking and valuable public contributions was his action in regard to the doctrine of nullification asserted by Calhoun and South Carolina. A meeting of Whigs of Guilford County was called with Ralph Gorrell presiding as was customary. The doctrine of nullification was denounced, and although opposed to the political party of President Andrew Jackson, the unanimous opinion of the meeting was that the Federal Union must be preserved. A set of resolutions embodying this idea was prepared and indorsed and broadcasted over the country. For elevation of sentiment, for clarity of diction, for cogency of reasoning and for a deep spirit of patriotism, these resolutions deserve to take rank with the great state papers of our nation.

Political life was distasteful to Ralph Gorrell. It took him away from his dearest interests—the companionship of his family, the exchange of social amenities with his friends and the practice of the law. For these reasons he refused the offer of a committee of his friends to run him for Congress. He devoted his working hours to his profession and the management of his large plantation. His leisure hours were spent in the company of his family and the companionship of his friends. His large and hospitable home was a meeting place for lawyers, statesman, preachers and elders of the Presbyterian Church.

In his profession of the law Ralph Gorrell furnishes an example to every young member of the bar who would achieve an honorable reputation and a lucrative practice. In the practice he was a man of tremendous energy and industry. His judgment was good, his insight keen, his legal knowledge extensive, and above all his integrity above question. No man was ever betrayed by Ralph Gorrell. He was engaged in active practice for about fifty years, and unquestionably occupies a position as one of the leading lawyers of the State of North Carolina at that time. One of the old court calendars is said to reveal the fact that his name appeared as plaintiff's or defendant's attorney in every case set for trial at that term. He was clerk and master in equity for many years and held that office until it was abolished in 1868. He was also a director of the North Carolina Railroad.

In 1858 when the Greensboro Mutual Life Insurance and Trust Company issued its two dollar bill the picture of Ralph Gorrell was put upon it as typifying those qualities of solidity and reliability which this paper currency was desired to represent.

His professional advice was sought not only by laymen, but by lawyers as well. He was frequently requested by other lawyers to become associated with them in the trial of their cases. He was also consulted by the law makers in regard to rules of practice and procedure. For example, Governor Worth wrote him: "Why should not the county courts have concurrent jurisdiction with the Superior Courts in actions of debt and indebitatus assumsit?" and asked his advice upon the matter. This is but one illustration from among many.

In his religious life Ralph Gorrell joined the Presbyterian Church in Greensboro in 1843. He was made a ruling elder in 1849 and held that position continuously until his death. Faithful as he was in his professional life, he was equally so in his church relations. The solid qualities of his mind were used for the benefit of the church organization. He was often a delegate of his church in Presbytery and in the Synod of North Carolina, and was once a delegate to the General Assembly of the Presbyterian Church at Philadelphia.

Ralph Gorrell married Mary Chisholm, who was a first cousin of William Stainback, of Richmond County. This union was blessed with ten children. But only two descendants now survive, Miss Charlotte Gorrell, a daughter, and J. Henry Fariss, a grandson.

Ralph Gorrell's last days must have been sad ones. With Robert P. Dick and John A. Gilmer he represented Guilford County in the Constitutional Convention of 1861 and strongly opposed secession because he thought it wrong in principle, unjustified by events and because he clearly foresaw the inevitable calamities that would result to the entire country and especially to the South from an armed conflict. One of his latest public speeches was delivered in Winston in April, 1861, with Messrs. Settle and Gilmer, appealing to his fellow citizens to remain in the Union. But the force of circumstances carried North Carolina along with the torrent; and like Robert E. Lee and others Gorrell felt his highest allegiance was to his state. His son, Captain Henry Gorrell, was killed leading his troops in the Confederate Army; and Mr. Gorrell lost a large portion of his money which he gave to help finance the "Lost Cause." The Treasury Department of the Confederate States selected him as its depositary at Greensboro. And in connection with this office, Ralph Gorrell rendered valuable service in establishing in this section the financial credit of the Confederacy.

After a lingering illness, he died in Greensboro August 14, 1875, beloved of all citizens of Greensboro as one of its founders. For in every station he was distinguished by fidelity and the wisdom and sound judgment of his counsels. He was a gentleman of charming social graces, a lawyer of distinction, a counsellor and advisor in affairs of state, a Christian in practice without ostentation, in short, a southern aristocrat. May he rest in peace.

MARTIN F. DOUGLAS.

JOHN ADAMS GILMER

JOHN ADAMS GILMER
1805 - 1868

John Adams Gilmer is one of the half-lights of history. He belongs in the category of the Saracen Army leader—his very name now unknown to all save a few specialists in history—who all but broke Charles Martel's line at Tours, that is, all but made Europe Islamic instead of Christian; of Grouchy, marshal of France, whose failure to hold the Prussians from Waterloo extinguished the Napoleonic Empire, and saved England from sinking to the level of such powers as Denmark and the Netherlands; and that Russian minister of foreign affairs who saw the catastrophe impending in 1914, but could not persuade Sir Edward Grey to speak out in time to stop it. Gilmer was the man selected by Abraham Lincoln to save a union already disrupted.

All the experience of the ages teaches that speculating on what might have been, had certain men at certain crises been able to accomplish what they wished to accomplish, or what was demanded of them, is the most fruitless activity of the human mind; but all the experience of the ages teaches likewise that it is one of the most fascinating. We all know that a thousand things might have intervened after the battle of Tours to turn history back into the channel through which it has flowed, even had Charles the Hammer been defeated; yet we constantly say that had the Saracen been but a little stronger, or a little cleverer, a Mohammedan civilization might control the world today; and that lends to the defeated general's memory an interest that will never fade. Similarly with Grouchy; had the Napoleonic bubble not been pricked then, had the mighty Corsican been able to found the dynasty of his dreams, all subsequent history would have been radically modified; so Grouchy we cannot forget. And Savanov—he implored Sir Edward to declare flatly that England would fight if the threatened assault on civilization were made; but during those hectic seven days the Englishman could not believe that Germany had gone stark mad, and instead of smiting the kaiser between the eyes with the announcement that the most formidable power in the world would be hurled against Germany as soon as the first shot was fired, he made a pacificatory speech. Savanov almost persuaded him, but not quite. Had his eloquence been a trifle stronger, Germany might have been cowed, and Europe left smiling and prosperous, instead of the red ruin that she actually became in the first quarter of the twentieth century.

And had John A. Gilmer, of Greensboro, North Carolina, been able to accomplish what Mr. Lincoln hoped of him; had he, the stout Whig, the slave-holding southerner, but the strong friend of the union, entered the Lincoln cabinet and drawn with him the vast host of conservative, union-loving men in the south, the war of the sixties would have been rendered impossible. Some means of abolishing slavery by peaceful means would have been devised, but the south might have continued its development uninterruptedly, instead of having a great chasm, 50 years broad, torn out of the path of its progress.

But it was not to be. Even if Mr. Gilmer had become Lincoln's secretary of the interior (if that was indeed the post offered him) he probably could not have carried many even of his own class with him. For they felt as he did; and he declined the cabinet appointment because he felt that his first duty was to his state. Nevertheless, the world will always speculate on what might have been, and therefore Gilmer's name will always be remembered for his brief appearance in the spotlight of history in those stormy days.

However, it is irrefutable proof of a man's reputation with his contemporaries when the dominant personage at a time of world crisis selects him for a tremendously important task. The Saracen must have been an officer of outstanding ability to be selected to encounter Charles Martel. Napoleon certainly considered Grouchy the best man available for the job of holding Blucher. The Russian was a diplomatist of the first rank, even if he failed at the most terrific crisis of his life. And John A. Gilmer certainly was a man who loomed prodigiously upon the political horizon of his time, since Lincoln picked him as the one man who was perhaps capable of saving the union.

Furthermore, in the city of his nativity there is convincing proof of the hold that he had upon the imaginations of the men of his day. Greensboro bestrides two townships of Guilford County; one of them is named "Morehead", the other "Gilmer". Those were still names to conjure with in the new city, long after the town that their bearers knew had passed completely away. Gilmer has been in his grave for many years, yet still there cluster around his name traditions of rugged honesty, of physical and moral courage, of candor, truthfulness, and kindliness that make it eminently fitting, in the eyes of the citizenship, that half the city should rest upon ground that is honored by that name. Few, indeed are the men who can so impress themselves upon their own generation that half a century after they are dead they will still be remembered for sheer character.

It is related of John Adams Gilmer that once he swept the national house of representatives from its feet—that members wept under the spell of his eloquence as he pleaded for the already destroyed union, and that followers of every party standard crowded around him when the great effort of his life was ended. But such dramatic moments in his life were few. For the most part, there is nothing for the chronicler to relate, save a story of quiet days, the ordinary life of a gentleman of North Carolina; yet for him who looks closely the story is unusual in its recital—in the very monotony of its recital—of duties cheerfully accepted and competently discharged, of a heart inclined to love the ways and institutions hallowed by ancient custom, yet unswerving and unfaltering in its loyalty, even when loyalty seemed to call for the shattering of those institutions.

"Sir, I must confess, whatever be the consequences of such a confession, that the word 'union' has had some charms for me," he said in an address to the North Carolina State Senate —an address that riddled the claims of those who asserted that secession was not revolution. How sadly many there were like him in those fearful days—men who looked back with heartache to the union that had charms indeed for them, but who nevertheless walked steadily and unhesitatingly into the roaring pit of war when it came to a choice between the union and the state to which they felt that they owed first allegiance. We can see the pathos of it now. We can understand better the pain that the decision cost many thousands of them. And with that in mind we can better appreciate the heroism that enabled them to make their decision and adhere to it resolutely through the hellish years that followed.

But in Greensboro courage and resolution were rather to be expected of one who bore the name of Gilmer. The first of the family, William Gilmer, a Scotch-Irishman who had come to the Alamance neighborhood by way of Pennsylvania, was a member of Captain Arthur Forbis' Company at the battle of Guilford Courthouse—the one militia company that did honor to the name of the state by standing its ground in the face of the British charge. The presence of his grandfather in that heroic company John A. Gilmer never forgot. Time and again he referred to it as motivating his love of the government that his ancestor had faced death to establish; and the memory of the old soldier of the Revolution unquestionably nerved him to follow the path of duty to the bitter end. His maternal grandfather, Major John Forbis, also bore arms in that struggle; so Gilmer was eminently justified in claiming to be an American of the Americans.

He was born on his father's farm in the Alamance section, November 4, 1805, and lived the life of a country boy of that date until he was 17. Incidentally, it is tradition that he never wore anything but homespun until he was in his 20th year. At the age of 19, he entered the "Grammar School" in Greensboro taught by the Rev. Eli W. Caruthers and Abner Gay. But the establishment of Caruthers and Gay was a very different thing from the grammar school of today. The "grammar" taught there was taken from crabbed texts in Latin, Greek and Hebrew, and the man who finished their school had not merely the ability to read and write and a little arithmetic, but an excellent grounding in the classics. The mind that could struggle with and overcome the difficulties in the lessons they assigned had necessarily acquired toughness, suppleness and endurance.

So had Gilmer's; and after teaching in South Carolina long enough to pay off the debts with which his education had loaded him, he returned to Greensboro in 1829 to enter the law office of Archibald Debow Murphy. To anyone familiar with the history of North Carolina judicature, that simple statement will go far to explain Gilmer's subsequent career, and especially his outstanding quality—moral and intellectual probity. To have had at 24 the privilege of intimate association with the venerable jurist, whose reputation for nobility and personal integrity lasts to this day, must have shaped the mental habits of the young man to a material degree. But of all the eminent men whose minds Murphy assisted in training, none reflected more credit upon the preceptor.

In 1832 Gilmer was admitted to the bar, and in the same year he married. His wife was the daughter of the first Presbyterian minister in Greensboro, the Rev. William Paisley, a clergyman of the Jonathan Edwards type, less the shepherd of a flock than the fearsome and awe-inspiring prophet of wrath to come.

Mr. Paisley at that time possessed a home on the outskirts of the straggling village of Greensboro, and he settled the young couple in a house which he built for them on a corner of his own place. That house occupied the spot where West Market Street Methodist Church now stands, opposite the new county courthouse—almost in the heart of the city.

It is evident that it was not all smooth sailing in the beginning, for tradition has it that his wife helped out in the first few years by taking boarders; but presently the young attorney was elected county solicitor, evidence of the truth of the statement made by writer on old Greensboro sixty years later: "I have heard it said of Gilmer that he had a better knowledge of mankind and greater influence over a jury than any of his contemporaries."

In 1846 he went to the legislature as member from Guilford County in the State Senate, where he remained for eight years. He first acquired state-wide fame by a speech in that body in which he favored the establishment of an asylum for the insane, who were then treated in North Carolina with a barbarism that today makes the blood run cold. He also participated in the memorable session of 1848 that started a program of internal improvements not duplicated since until the legislature of 1920 undertook the task of building a state-wide system of roads.

For this generation the assumption by the state of the task of building first-class highways everywhere was the first instance within their memory of a really great effort by the State of North Carolina at internal improvements. It has long been forgotten that the men of 1848 were as public spirited and as progressive as any of our day. A list of the public improvements initiated by that body is astounding—it includes navigation works, railroads, plank and turnpike roads in every section, the inauguration of a progressive public school system, the establishment of schools for the deaf, the dumb and the blind, hospitals for the insane, the geological survey and the State Agricultural Society. By comparison with that, the program even of 1921 looks pitifully small.

Nor was it an isolated outburst, followed by backsliding into civic stagnation. It continued right to the outbreak of the war. In 1854, indeed, we find the senator from Guilford leading the fight for a state appropriation of $1,000,000 to finish the North Carolina Railroad. Had catastrophe not overwhelmed the state six years later it is easy to believe that North Carolina would today be among the leading states of the union in material development.

In 1857 Gilmer went to the National House of Representatives as member for the fifth North Carolina district. He served until the outbreak of the war. After the crash came, he was transferred to the Congress of the Confederate States, of which he was member in 1865. He did not long survive the Confederacy, dying in Greensboro, May 14, 1868.

Compared to the long records of other men, it was only a brief term of service that Gilmer had in the National House, and yet in those four years so deeply had he impressed himself upon the minds of thinking men that Abraham Lincoln selected him as the ideal man to fulfill Lincoln's hopes of reconciliation. ''I hope,'' Mr. Lincoln wrote to Seward as late as January 12, 1861, ''Mr. Gilmer will, on a fair understanding with us, consent to take a place in the cabinet.'' Miss Stockard, in her History of Guilford County, asserts that the post Lincoln had in mind to offer Gilmer was that of secretary of the interior.

But Gilmer was unable to accept. Up to the last he hoped against hope; and on January 26, 1861, he rose to make that appeal to his northern brethren upon which his fame as an orator principally rests. ''Long before the close Mr. Gilmer's emotions were so powerful that his voice failed,'' said a Washington dispatch published in the Baltimore Clipper the next day, ''and when he sat down there was scarcely an eye in the house not filled with tears.   Dozens of Republicans and southern union men rushed forward to congratulate him, and it was conceded by every Republican last night that some compromise must be made to save John A. Gilmer from being carried down by the secession tide.''   Yet on April 18 of the same year the same man stood in the courthouse at Greensboro, along with other prominent men of the village, and urged the Guilford Grays, who had volunteered in a body in answer to the call of Governor Ellis, to defend their state against any invader, no matter whence he came.

He was fulfilling his own prohecy to the House of Representatives, when he had said in January: ''Whenever that struggle comes, you will find, north and south, that the men who have sought most to preserve the union, who have been the last to give it up, will be the first men to be found in the rank and file on both sides of the bloody contest, their means most liberally and freely be devoted to helping and maintaining the great, terrific, and bloody struggle, and they will enter it on either side for victory or death; and if they fail in their efforts for the first, they will be found with their back to the field and their feet to the foe.''

So, indeed, it proved, not of individuals alone, but of states as well.   North Carolina, for whom like Gilmer the very word ''union'' had charms, who left it so slowly and reluctantly as to incur the criticism of her more impetuous sisters, and of her hot-headed sons, nevertheless left more men ''with their back to the field and their feet to the foe'' than any other southern state, and than Virginia, Georgia, and Mississippi combined.   Gilmer's personal tragedy was the tragedy of the state.   It was with her voice that he spake when he declared, in that impassioned address in the house: ''When these things come, when this bloody strife ensues, as it certainly will unless this spirit of disunion can be checked; when, mark you, this country shall be laid waste; when all our channels and communications of trade shall be broken up; when the shipping in our ports shall be destroyed; when our institutions of learning and religion shall wither away or be torn down; when your cities shall be given up for plunder and for slaughter; when your sons and my sons, your neighbors and my neighbors, shall be carried from this bloody field of strife; and our mothers, our sisters, our wives and our daughters shall assemble around us, and with weeping eyes and aching hearts, say: 'Could not you have done something, could not you have said something, that would have averted this dreadful calamity?' I want to feel in my conscience and in my soul that I have done my duty.''

In making that speech John A. Gilmer filed North Carolina's protest against the madness that overwhelmed the country. The state that had spoken so strongly against disunion could go to the field feeling in her conscience and in her soul that she had done her duty.

With that speech Gilmer passed from the stage of national affairs. He had done his best, and it was not enough; so he belongs forever among the half-lights of history, a figure glimpsed but dimly in the storm—glimpsed for a moment, then lost in the night. Yet he is among the most tragic and most appealing of such figures; for the beam that picked him out of the gloom for his moment of illumination, was not such a red and menacing glare as lights up the figures of the Saracen and Grouchy, but the peculiar splendor that always touches the last vain effort of a gallant and a loyal heart.

GERALD W. JOHNSON.

JEDUTHUN HARPER LINDSAY

JEDUTHUN HARPER LINDSAY
1806 - 1881

The poverty of Scotland, the wars waged upon her by England, religious persecution, and her internal dissensions, sent many of her sons and daughters throughout the world. Almost every country has been enriched by an infusion of blood from the sturdy people of this little land. Although only a little more than half as large as North Carolina she has helped to populate and rule England, Ireland, Canada, Australia, Africa and other sections of the globe. No country, however, is more indebted to her than the United States. The Scotch were a thrifty, hard working and God-fearing people. They were used to danger and privation. They believed in education and carried the Bible with them as their best beloved book. They were ideal colonists for a new and wild country.

They trooped to America, and every section of the United States was helped and influenced by them. Many of them first went to the north of Ireland and afterwards came to this country and were known as Scotch-Irish. To this last element Guilford County is especially indebted. Their first settlements, in what was then an almost uninhabited country, were around Buffalo and Alamance Presbyterian Churches. Dr. David Caldwell was their preacher, their physician and leader. With their Quaker neighbors on the west and their German neighbors on the east, they have builded the great County of Guilford.

Until 1808 the county courthouse was at Martinsville, near the Guilford Battleground, but in those days roads were not hard surfaced and there were no motor cars, and if there had been probably not a dozen men in the county would have felt able to buy and maintain a Ford; so it was unpardonable for a courthouse to be six miles from the center of the county, and accordingly it was moved to what is now the site of Greensboro. Martinsville lingered for a while and died and Greensboro was the proud possessor of the gaol, the stocks, the whipping post and the log courthouse.

The Lindsays of Scotland were a powerful family. Many of them went to Ireland and then emigrated to Pennsylvania and the lower part of Maryland. Later a number of them decided to find homes further south, and came to North Carolina. Most of these settled in Mecklenburg County.

Robert Lindsay, the grandfather of Jeduthun Harper Lindsay, pitched his camp in Guilford on the waters of Deep River, about twelve miles from the present site of Greensboro. He was a man of influence and represented Guilford County in the first House of Commons in 1776. He raised a large family, consisting of six boys and two girls. The oldest son, John, moved to Davidson County and had a large number of descendants; Samuel settled in southern Guilford; William lived near his father's place; Andrew afterwards maintained the old homestead; David located at Jamestown; and Robert, the father of the subject of this sketch, lived in Martinsville. This Robert was born on September 26, 1776, and was about four years old when the battle of Guilford Courthouse was fought in and around his native village. On June 9, 1803, he was married to Miss Letitia Harper, born February 27, 1785, and the daughter of Lieutenant-Colonel Jeduthun Harper.

Robert was a man of wealth and influence, but died at the early age of 42 years, on the 26th day of October, 1818. His wife survived him 17 years and died on July 25, 1835. Shortly after the founding of Greensboro, Robert built a store where the American Exchange National Bank now stands. This store was for many years known as the Lindsay corner, even after it was purchased by Captain Fisher.

Of this union between Robert and Letitia Harper, there were three sons and two daughters as follows: Jeduthun Harper, Jesse Harper and Robert Goodloe, and Ann Eliza, the wife of Gov. John M. Morehead, and Mary, who married Governor Morehead's brother, James T. Morehead, both brothers being able lawyers and distinguished men. At the time of Robert Lindsay's death North Elm Street stopped at Church Street and nearly all of the northern part of the present city of Greensboro, including the Fisher Park section, belonged to him and was known as Lindsay's woods until sold to Capt. B. J. Fisher. The family tradition is that the three sons built the large brick house which stopped North Elm at Church Street with the understanding that the first one that married should have the house. Jeduthun Harper married Miss

Strange, of Kentucky, and became the owner of this house, afterwards known as the home of Judge John A. Gilmer. Jesse built for himself the house on North Elm Street afterwards owned by his grandson, Clem G. Wright, and but recently removed; and Robert Goodloe had a handsome home on Sycamore Street where the Elk's Club now stands.

Jeduthun Harper Lindsay was born on the 8th day of October, 1806, two years before the founding of Greensboro, and he moved to Greensboro from Martinsville in 1821 when but fifteen years of age. He was a man of affairs and of great public spirit. Among his business interests was a saw mill located where Lindsay Street crosses the Southern Railway. He advanced the public weal in many ways, sometimes even in the humblest capacities, for we learn from the minutes of the city that in 1837 all the men of the town were divided into four teams and required to work the streets, and Jed. H. Lindsay was assigned along with his brother Jesse to division third with Henry Humphreys as overseer. History does not tell us whether or not he was as efficient as our present street mender. In 1837, 1839, 1840 and in 1861 we find that he was one of the commissioners of the town, which office he seems to have held for several years longer, and he was town clerk in 1837 and 1838. Lyndon Swaim, in writing of Mr. Lindsay, said:

"For some twenty years before and during the war he took a prominent part in the management of county affairs. In his position as chairman of the county court, member of the finance committee, or whatever other duty devolved upon him by his fellow justices, he brought to bear the well trained business habits and honesty of purpose which illustrated his private life. Most of his contemporaries in active duty have passed away, but a few remain. Theirs was a station of labor and responsibility, without much of pay or of honors. The performance of duty was its own reward. The deceased was an admirable representative of that class of unpretending citizens on whom depended more than any other the peace, order, prosperity and healthy social progress of the country."

He was for a while also the county auditor. In 1872 the courthouse built in 1858 was destroyed by fire, and Jed. H. Lindsay was appointed by the county court to have charge of rebuilding, which was accomplished at a cost of $21,000. Lyndon Swaim tells us that the names of Peter Adams and Harper

Lindsay were left on the county finance committee for years after their service ended.

Greensboro was early noted for its schools, and Harper Lindsay was also active in their promotion. The first free school was the Lindsay Street School, and Mr. Lindsay sold in 1854 to "James Sloan, Andrew Weatherly and Jed H. Lindsay, school committee for the common school district No. 38" for the sum of $37.50 the present site of the Lindsay Street School, the description "beginning at the N. E. corner of the graveyard of the Presbyterian Church."

Harper had eight children, seven of whom grew to maturity. Mary died in young womanhood, Jesse died unmarried, James, who married in Baltimore and lived there, Henry died during the Civil War of fever, and was unmarried, Harper was in the Civil War and was never married, Ernest, who married in St. Joseph and left one son, Edward, who is still living in Missouri, and Dr. Edward Lindsay, who married Lizzie Kirkland and left four children, Letty, Edward, Harper and Ernest.

Mr. Lindsay was always a reverent attendant upon public worship, and during the latter years of his life was a member of the Presbyterian Church. His was a religion of principles, consisting of the fear of God and keeping His commandments and dealing justly with his fellowmen.

He died in the year 1881 at the age of seventy-five. Swaim says:

"He had always enjoyed fine health and until weakened by age had taken an active part in county affairs and the transaction of public business. He was a man to be trusted—and he was trusted—in every situation of his life, public and private. His business transactions, for himself or others, were illustrated by the strictest integrity and by sound judgment. Prompt decision was a marked trait of his character. On questions of public concern, where intelligent and inquiring minds were expected to have opinions, you always knew just where to find him. He was quick to make up his mind, and as quick to express it. Like all impulsive men he doubtless committed errors, but no one ever doubted for a moment the absolute honesty of his professions."

ALFRED MOORE SCALES.

JESSE HARPER LINDSAY

JESSE HARPER LINDSAY
1808 - 1886

The United States of America will never fully realize and can never repay its obligation to Scotland. The descendants of the Scotch have played a great part in the conquest and settlement of every state of the union. They put iron in the blood of America. They helped greatly to make this a God-fearing nation. In no state and in no county is this better illustrated than in North Carolina and in Guilford County. They came by way of the north of Ireland, and thus became known as the Scotch-Irish. Among these people were the Lindsays, who went first to Pennsylvania and Maryland, and then came to North Carolina. Most of them settled in Mecklenburg, but Robert Lindsay, the grandfather of Jesse Harper Lindsay, settled in Guilford on the water of Deep River west of the present city of Greensboro. The county was at that time almost an unbroken forest. The deer, the bear and the buffalo roamed unmolested in the woods and in the cane-brakes of Buffalo, Horsepen and Reedy Fork Creeks, and of Deep River. Years later in 1781, when the battle of Guilford Courthouse was fought, both General Greene and Lord Cornwallis commented in their reports upon the dense forests of the county. A similar comment was made afterwards by George Washington, who passed through the county in making a tour of the south. At this time the county seat was called Guilford Courthouse, though its name was after the Revolution, changed to Martinsville in honor of Governor Alexander Martin. A courthouse, a jail, a large coppersmith shop, and a few other straggling buildings made up the village.

Robert Lindsay represented North Carolina in the first House of Commons and was a man of distinction. He had a family of six boys and two girls. His son, Robert, was also a man of prominence and acquired considerable wealth, although he died at the age of forty-two. He married Miss Letitia Harper, daughter of Lieutenant-Colonel Jeduthun Harper. This Robert moved to Greensboro shortly after it was founded in 1808. He had five children, three sons and

111

two daughters, as follows: Jeduthun Harper, Jesse Harper, Robert Goodloe, Anne Eliza, the wife of Governor Morehead, and Mary, the wife of James T. Morehead the first.

Jesse Harper Lindsay, the subject of this sketch, was born in Martinsville, on December 17, 1808, a few months after the founding of the city of Greensboro, and was, therefore, a baby when brought to Greensboro by his parents. He was educated at the University of North Carolina, where he was graduated with the class of 1827. He delivered one of the orations at commencement. Well equipped for life's work, he returned to the village of Greensboro at the age of nineteen, which village was also nineteen years old. The town had, in 1829, three hundred inhabitants, there being one hundred and twenty-four taxable polls, and gave little promise of the splendid city into which it has developed. There were five stores and three saloons—one for every forty-two citizens of poll tax age. Surely Mr. Volstead was little dreamed of in those good old days. The real estate of the town was valued at $53,495.00 and the total income of the town, including license taxes, was $160.00. Young Lindsay was at first engaged in the mercantile business with his brother Jeduthun, but retired from this after a few years trial.

When twenty-four years of age he was elected a member of the board of commissioners of Greensboro with Henry Humphreys, David Scott, George Albright and James T. Morehead. In 1840, together with James Sloan and Dr. John A. Mebane, he was authorized to set out trees on Elm and Market Streets, and this committee paid $34.00 to a colored man named Gill for setting them out. These trees grew into the splendid elms which were for years the joy and pride of the town. Although these trees were cut down recently when the town took on city airs, yet seldom has so small an expenditure resulted in so much beauty and comfort. Should not we learn a lesson from this, and pay more attention to the beauty and adornment of our city? Some day we will buy lands for parks and squares at enormous price which would now be secured at small cost.

In 1835, 1836 and 1838 he represented Guilford County in the House of Representatives and in the Senate in 1844.

Before the war Greensboro had three banks, all of which were prosperous, and Jesse H. Lindsay became cashier of one of these, the Bank of Cape Fear. All of these banks collapsed at the surrender except the one of which Lindsay was cashier. After the war the Bank of Cape Fear was succeeded by the Bank of Greensboro, and afterwards the name was changed to the National Bank of Greensboro, and then to the Greensboro National Bank, which is now the Greensboro National Branch of the American Exchange National Bank. For practically a lifetime Mr. Lindsay was in this bank and for seven years was its president. For many years it was the only bank in the city. He guided its destinies with rare prudence and consummate skill. "As punctual and particular as Jesse Lindsay" became a proverb of the town. "Probity, punctuality and exactness were the marked characteristics of his practical life." He merited to have such implicit confidence and esteem of the people not only in Greensboro, but throughout the state.

J. R. Wharton, now general manager of the Butte Electric Railway Company, was associated with Mr. Lindsay in the bank for seven years, and in referring to Mr. Lindsay, writes: "To me he looms up bigger and bigger as I grow older and more fully realize what a magnificent character his was. The thing about him which first made the greatest impression was the fact that from all over the state our best men and women seemed to have such implicit confidence in him. Politicians, statesmen, theologians, all seemed to want to know his opinions and be guided by them. Business men from Wilmington, Raleigh, Fayetteville, Charlotte, etc., were daily calling to see him or writing for advice, and as my desk was next to his I saw and heard many things which I shall always remember and many which I think helped shape my life for good.

"Zeb Vance was a great friend and admirer of Mr. Lindsay. On one occasion he called at the bank and said, 'Jesse, I am to stump the state with Tom Settle. Now, Tommy is not only a big, fine looking fellow, but he wears good clothes. Look at this shabby suit; it is the best I have got and I haven't got money to buy even a pair of pants.' Mr. Lindsay loaned him the money with which to buy two suits.

"On another occasion Vance came into the bank and said, 'Jesse, the boys are beginning to ask me my views on certain financial questions. I want half an hour's talk with you so that I can find out what they are.'"

Mr. Wharton also says: "He was just as courteous and kindly with the lowliest as with the powerful and rich. Alston was an old club-footed African Methodist preacher out in Warnersville. He frequently called on Mr. Lindsay both for financial assistance and advice, and was always treated with the same courtesy as Vance. Mr. Lindsay recognized the fine work done by Alston and regarded him as one of the really big men of his race."

Those who were closely associated with him say that they never heard him say an unkind or harsh word. He was a dignified, courteous, Christian gentleman.

He was a devoted Christian and was throughout his life one of the chief supports of the First Presbyterian Church. He gave the church its present site, and was always one of its staunchest supporters. He was elected a ruling elder in 1849. He was largely instrumental in the calling to the church in 1859 of Dr. Jacob Henry Smith, who continued as its pastor for thirty-eight years. Only God can estimate the blessing to Greensboro and the state that grew out of this pastorate. Mr. Lindsay was always his loyal friend and counsellor.

Mr. Lindsay was for many years the treasurer of Orange Presbytery, and later also treasurer of the Synod of North Carolina, and finally the treasurer of the General Assembly of the church.

He married his cousin Amelia Gozeal Ellison and had four children, only two of whom lived to maturity. Annette married Clement Gillespie Wright, a distinguished lawyer and a brave officer in the Confederate Army. Of this union there were two sons, Jesse Lindsay Wright, who died unmarried, and Clement G. Wright, who has just been elected to a fourth term in the House of Representatives of North Carolina. There was also one daughter, Annette Lindsay Wright, who died in early childhood. The other daughter, Sallie, married John A. Gilmer, an able jurist and a colonel in the Confederate Army, who was also for many years an elder in the First Presbyterian Church. There was born of this union two

sons and one daughter: Julia, the wife of Samuel W. Dick,
who had two daughters, Sadie Lindsay, the wife of Cummins
A. Mebane, and Mary Eloise, deceased, wife of James T.
Morehead; Colonel Ellison L. Gilmer of the United States
Army, and John A. Gilmer, in the service of the United States,
with headquarters in Washington.

Mr. Lindsay died in December, 1886, at the age of seventy-
eight, well beloved and full of honors.

ALFRED MOORE SCALES.

JOHN A. GRETTER

JOHN A. GRETTER
1810 - 1853

For the historic sources of Greensboro's moral and religious life and of all that is best in her domestic, civil, social, and commercial character, we must trace the stream back and up to the springs. Among those early fountains of worthy influence grateful mention is due the life and labors of John A. Gretter. For the following sketch of this gifted man the materials are drawn from Sprague's "Annals of the American Pulpit," personal reminiscences by Mr. John C. Wharton and Rev. James H. McNeill, secretary of the American Bible Society, a half column editorial and a two-column obituary published in the Greensboro Patriot of January 29, 1853, and certain other more private sources.

The Gretter family were of German origin, the immigrant ancestors first settling in Pennsylvania and later moving to Virginia. One member of the family living at Alexandria was an officer of the historic Masonic Lodge No. 22, of Alexandria, at the time George Washington was Master. The family tradition is that the first John Gretter owned an estate in Germany and sent his lawyer over to look after his interests, this person assuming the Gretter name and laying claims to all the Gretter holdings.

Through his mother, Joanna Hewlett, he was descended from the distinguished Clopton family, George Clopton III, of Virginia, being her maternal grandfather. The Cloptons were among the nobility, tracing back to 1212, and the owners of Stratford Manor since that date, Sir Hugh Clopton, being Lord Mayor of London and benefactor of Stratford on Avon.

John Augustus Gretter, the son of Michael and Joanna Gretter, was born in Richmond, Virginia, September 28, 1810. In 1824 when Lafayette visited America, young Gretter was captain of a boy's military company in Richmond which marched out to meet the distinguished visitor, the saber he carried being now a cherished possession of his grandchildren.

After going to school in Richmond he entered the University of Virginia in January, 1827, and graduated in July,

1829, at the age of 19. From February till July of 1831 he taught mathematics in Mr. Crawford's school in Huntsville, Alabama, whence he returned to Richmond to visit his friends with the intention of going back to Huntsville and becoming principal of the school. But a new influence now entered his life, changing its course and complexion. He became a devoted servant of Christ, living thenceforth under the guidance of His Spirit and for the advancement of His Kingdom.

In August, 1831, he was married to Mary Wynn, of Charlottesville, Va., and in October of that year they both united with the Second Presbyterian Church of Richmond, then under the pastoral care of Rev. Stephen Taylor. Deeply convinced of his call to the gospel ministry he entered the Theological Seminary at Princeton, but the northern climate proving unfavorable to his health, he returned to Virginia, and as a member of East Hanover Presbytery studied theology under his pastor, Mr. Taylor. He was licensed to preach in the fall of 1833, ordained in September, 1834, and soon after sent as a missionary to Genito, Powhatan County, Virginia, where he labored with great acceptance.

In the spring of 1836 he moved to Greensboro, North Carolina, and became a professor of mathematics in Caldwell Institute, a Presbyterial school opened in the fall of 1835 or the very beginning of 1836 and conducted under the control of Orange Presbytery. In 1837 the school building was erected upon a lot purchased from William H. Cumming. This building was completed and occupied January 1, 1838. Under the Rev. Alexander Wilson, D. D., as president and professor of Greek; Silas C. Lindsley, professor of Latin; and Mr. Gretter, professor of mathematics, the school was eminently prosperous and useful. Its popularity drew students from several surrounding states and one from Missouri, who in 1837, at the age of 15, came on horseback from his home in the extreme western part of that state, and on his arrival sold his horse and used the money thus obtained as part of his expenses.

Mr. Gretter's connection with the school did much to elevate its character and extend its influence, since he was a thorough mathematician, an excellent teacher, a man of wide culture and much personal attractiveness and an earnest Christian. But preaching was his favorite work, so he accepted a call from the congregations of Bethel and Gum

Grove, nine and twelve miles distant, to preach to them on alternate Sabbaths. This he did to their entire satisfaction for several years.

In 1844 he resigned his professorship and the care of these churches to become pastor of the Greensboro Presbyterian Church. Rev. William D. Paisley, the chief founder and first minister of this church, after serving it many years, in accordance with a resolution formed long before, announced to his people on reaching the age of 70 his purpose to retire from the active ministry and his desire that they should choose a successor. Mr. Gretter was with great unanimity called to the pastorate. In April, 1844, he was installed pastor of the Greensboro church and entered upon his labors with such zeal as to excite in the minds of many of his people the fear that he was overtaxing his strength.

A new and commodious house of worship was erected by his congregation in 1846, replacing on the same site the old church which had been built by Mr. Paisley in 1832. This second building served the Presbyterians of Greensboro until the church of 1890 was built, also on the old site, under the pastorate of Dr. J. Henry Smith.

In personal appearance and address Mr. Gretter was attractive and engaging. He was of slender figure and rather below the medium height. His face was pale, his complexion somewhat dark, his hair black and flowing, his eyes of the same color, large and piercing, his mouth broad and firm yet flexible, and his features generally, though not classically regular, possessed the greater charm of animated and varied expression. His manners were easy, his disposition social and friendly, while his buoyancy of spirit and ardor of temperament made him a pleasant companion, a warm friend, and an active leader in all enterprises.

Naturally quick and impulsive, he was transparently frank and honest. Dissimulation was impossible to him. Though the expression of his likes and dislikes was often outspoken, it was tempered with a Christian kindness that prevented offense. Strong, independent, self-reliant, he pursued what he believed to be the line of duty without any calculation of consequences. On his convictions of right he stood with all boldness, even though he stood alone, and he rebuked what seemed to him wrong with a fearlessness that gave his words authority and compelled respect.

As a scholar and thinker his inclinations lay rather in the line of mathematics, metaphysics, and theology than in that of belles-lettres. He was a man, however, of marked literary taste and culture with a particular fondness for classical studies. One of the last books he ever read was Morell's "History of Philosophy," and his love of such studies may be inferred from the fact that its perusal occupied but a day or two and was completed almost without interruption. But all his literary and intellectual pursuits converged upon theology, which was to him the highest, the all-embracing science. The Bible was his chief textbook and its methodical study occupied much of his time. The Old Testament and the New Testament he studied in the original and warmly advocated the advantage of such a course. The writings of standard theological authors he was familiar with and was ever on the alert to secure new and valuable works. In an age of doctrinal controversy he was an able and trusted champion of evangelical truth.

But it was in the pulpit that his varied powers found their fullest and noblest expression. His rich and musical voice, his pale intelligent face, his countenance uplifted, grave, earnest, animated, his very attitude, his whole person combined to fix the eye and ear of his audience and send home his message. While he used manuscript yet he did not confine himself to it, and in his later years dispensed with it altogether. His sermons, whether written or unwritten, were most carefully studied and methodically arranged. While from his very superior mental gifts and the severe studies which were his delight one would infer the intellectual quality of his discourses, yet he excelled also in pungent, faithful appeal. The substance of his preaching, as of all good preaching, was doctrine, clearly stated and proved. But he knew how to make doctrine practical. He knew how to grip with it the mind, the conscience, the heart. Though often called to preach before Presbytery, to the delight and edification of his brethren, yet to country and village congregations he preached with equal eloquence and power, drawing his inspiration not from the appreciation of his hearers, but from the grandeur of his theme and the spiritual and eternal needs of his audience. Almost from the beginning of his Greensboro ministry the quarterly communions were marked by the addition of members on profession of faith.

As a pastor he was untiringly energetic and faithful. Not content with preaching twice every Sunday, on two Sunday afternoons in the month he taught a Bible class which he formed in his congregation and which he instructed with great care. One Sabbath afternoon he preached to the colored people in the lecture room. The remaining Sabbath afternoons he catechised the children. On Wednesday night for many years he delivered written lectures on the prominent characters of the Old and New Testaments which were greatly enjoyed by his people. On Friday night of each week he held prayer meetings from family to family in the congregation. During his pastorate the communion was changed from a semi-annual to a quarterly ordinance. The first Sabbath night of each month a collection for foreign missions was taken. He gave great prominence to the sacrament of baptism, appropriating to it the whole afternoon of every communion Sabbath, and using it to urge upon the children of the church the Saviour's claims upon their hearts and lives. He would then turn to the parents and in the presence of their children would remind them of their duty and exhort them to its performance. These exercises, conducted with his affectionate earnestness and solemnity of manner, produced the happiest results. Under his charge family religion flourished, the membership increased, and the church greatly prospered. His people were devoted to him and rejoiced when he refused the frequent calls that came to him from other fields.

In the judicatories of the church he wielded great influence. To his thorough understanding of Presbyterian principles he added a quickness of apprehension, a faculty for business, and a remarkable power in debate that made his presence felt in any church court of which he was a member. Important commissions were entrusted to him. As chairman of the Synodical Committee on Colportage he directed that important interest throughout the state. As a member of the Committee on Domestic Missions of Orange Presbytery, he promoted the cause of church extension. He was a steady supporter of all the benevolent plans of the church. He was often called on by his brethren to conduct the devotional exercises at Presbytery and Synod and many were the signs of tenderness when all united with him in prayer or received from him the word of fraternal exhortation. Though comparatively young in the ministry at the time of his death, he was already looked upon as a leader and the profound grief which that event occasioned throughout the whole Synod gave evidence of the high appreciation in which he was held. His influence was rapidly extending, and had his life been spared his great abilities would have been recognized and acknowledged throughout the whole church.

It is a fact more noteworthy at that early date than it would be now, that he lived on terms of kindness and brotherly love with the ministers of other denominations, Presidents Shipp and Deems of the Greensboro Methodist College and the local pastors of the Methodist Church often filling his pulpit in his absence.

The genuineness of his personal piety, so manifest in his life, was triumphant in the approach and presence of death. One Sunday morning in March, 1852, he had risen in the pulpit to announce his text, when to his surprise he found that he could not speak. After a vain effort he sat down, while his devoted session crowded around him in the pulpit, and his people arose in a body filled with anxiety and alarm. This was his last attempt to preach. It was pathetic that this occurred when his people were still joyful over his refusal to accept a call from the Presbyterian Church in Wilmington. But that dread malady, consumption, had laid its hand upon him. He appeared, at church only twice more. The first time was when John M. Sherwood, then a licentiate just from Union Seminary, preached his first sermon in the church, having been invited to supply the pulpit during the pastor's sickness. In a few touching words he commended the young brother to his people. The second time was for the purpose of administering infant baptism, which duty he performed in a very solemn and tender manner. When the congregation was dismissed, he himself pronouncing the benediction, tears were in many eyes, as it was realized that his voice would never again be heard in the church. His decline was marked by the utmost Christian composure and a cheerful resignation to the Divine will. He passed to his reward on the night of the 21st of January, 1853, in the 43rd year of his age, leaving a wife and eight children. "Blessed are the dead who die in the Lord; yea, saith the Spirit, that they may rest from their labors, and their works do follow them."

EGBERT W. SMITH.

LYNDON SWAIM

LYNDON SWAIM
1812 - 1893

Anthony Swaim emigrated from his Holland home about the year 1700, and settled on Staten Island in the State of New York. Of his four sons, three remained in the north, while William came to North Carolina and settled on the upper waters of the Yadkin River. There his son, John, was born in 1748, reared in the pioneer surroundings of the times and became a friend and hunting companion of Daniel Boone. His wife was Elizabeth Vickery, a daughter of one of the Regulators who became the vanguard of American freedom on the field of Alamance. John Swaim settled in Randolph County, carved a farm and home out of the wilderness and became a successful farmer and raised a large family. One of the younger children, Moses Swaim, stayed in the family homestead, married Ada Swindell, of Hyde County, cultivated his farm in the summer and in the winter taught the neighborhood school.

Here Lyndon Swaim, one of Moses Swaim's eleven children, was born December 15, 1812. His early life on the farm was without special incident. Such education as he could get from the local schools was supplemented to good purpose by the intellectual guidance of his father and by extensive reading.

In 1834, at the age of 22, he came to Grenesboro and went to work in the printing office of William Swaim, a distant cousin, who was then the proprietor and editor of the Greensboro Patriot. However, William Swaim died in 1835, the Patriot passed into other hands and Lyndon Swaim returned to Randolph County. There he became connected with another printing office and printed for Benjamin S. Swaim, a cousin, "Swaim's Justice," a well known law book of that period.

But his absence from Greensboro was not of long duration. In 1839 a number of the leading citizens of Greensboro, with Jesse H. Lindsay as their spokesman, wrote Mr. Swaim a letter, which is still extant, complaining of the low estate into which the Patriot had fallen, saying that "we need a paper amongst us that will be regularly issued, that will be fixed in its Whig principles and that will advocate with spirit and fearlessness the Whig cause,'' and urging Mr. Swaim for the good of the community to come to Greensboro, purchase the paper and take charge. Heeding this call Mr. Swaim returned to Greensboro and in conjunction with Michael S. Sherwood bought the Patriot and became its editor, it being understood between the partners that Swaim was to handle the editorials and news while Sherwood attended to the mechanical and business side of the venture. He seems to have satisfied the aspirations of Mr. Lindsay and his friends for a stalwart Whig newspaper, but had far higher aims than to make the well known weekly simply a political organ. In his opening editorial he says, ''We shall advance all well-judged plans for the improvement of the internal commerce of the state and that system of school education which may reach every child in the land.''

During the succeeding fifteen years he remained the editor and followed his determination to make the paper a genuine upbuilder of the community. In this he was eminently successful, and the paper wielded a power hard to estimate and doubtless to a great extent planted the seeds which though apparently dormant for many years, have at last borne fruit in the scholastic and commercial prominence of Guilford County at the present day.

Having been elected clerk of the county court in 1853, Mr. Swaim in 1854 sold out his interest in the Patriot to Mr. Sherwood and devoted all of his time to his official duties. This office he held continuously until it was abolished by the new state constitution of 1868, and rendered such satisfactory service to the community that from time to time his re-election was practically taken as a matter of course.

But even during his busiest years he was steadily working for his town. He served as one of the commissioners of Greensboro in 1846-'50-'51-'52-'59-'60-'61 and '62; and in 1865 was appointed one of the town commissioners under the provisional government of Governor Holden.

Legislated out of office in 1868, he again entered the editorial field in 1869 as editor of the Patriot. This connection lasted only a few months, but during these trying times his voice was raised in no uncertain tones for the general good. He strongly opposed the ''radical'' party, but never hesitated to demand moderation of his own party associates and to counsel that their duty was to face actual conditions rather than live in the animosities of the past. Particularly was he outspoken—not a usual thing in those days—in preaching the doctrine that no man who sincerely tried to be a useful citizen should be proscribed on account of his political affiliations.

Severing his connection with the Patriot in the latter part of 1869, though then 56 years old, he boldly entered into a new field of endeavor and began the study of architecture and its practice as a profession. Success came promptly, and for the next twenty years, until ill health compelled a practical retirement, he was the town's leading architect, designed many of the better class of homes and public buildings of this and surrounding communities and helped in no small degree to educate the public taste.

During his years as an architect the only time he turned aside temporarily from his profession was to serve as a member of the State Legislature from this county in 1876-77.

Following several years of declining health, he died March 26th, 1893, at the age of eighty. He was a devoted member of the First Presbyterian Church, and one of its ruling elders from 1872 until his death.

In 1842 Mr. Swaim was married to Mrs. Abiah Shirley Swaim, the widow of William Swaim, mentioned above as former editor of the Patriot. By this marriage he left no surviving children.

In 1859 Mr. Swaim was married to Isabella Logan, daughter of General John M. Logan, one of the leading men of Greensboro. She died in 1900, leaving surviving her one son and three daughters, of whom the son and two daughters still live in our city.

So much for historical outlines. But what of the man himself? He might perhaps best be described as "A dreamer who worked." Tall, spare-built, studious, quiet and somewhat reserved, he had many of the qualities of a Puritan in his fearlessness, his directness of purpose and his hatred of shams; but had withal a gentleness of both thought and manner that made him as universally loved as he was respected.

First as the editor of its leading newspaper, then as a leading public official, and lastly as its leading architect, Lyndon Swaim may truly be said to be a founder and builder of intellectual, civic and material Greensboro.

ROBERT DICK DOUGLAS.

ROBERT MODERWELL SLOAN

ROBERT MODERWELL SLOAN
1812 - 1905

In 1827 Greensboro was a hamlet, barefooted, thinly clad, poorly fed, without a luxury and without an asset save the untouched wealth which nature spread before it in varied and bounteous measure. For nineteen years it had been cutting its way through an unbroken forest. A shabby court house and less than one hundred rude dwellings with a couple of stores and a log hut for a hotel were its star attractions. Two merchants and one lawyer were accused of gathering all the coin of the realm. One-half of one wing of the big office building of the Jefferson Standard Life Insurance Company, now soaring skyward, could have held every human soul within its unmarked boundary. The screech owl with its shrill outburst in the adjoining forest and the whippoorwill with its doleful cry were the Ku Klux of that day. The superstitious of the evil-doers trembled at the sound of these nocturnal birds. Hill and plain around were crowned with the stately oak. The rich valleys slept sweetly under their robe of unspoiled beauty. The running streams swept idly and peacefully by and down their homeward course, and the juicy trout had not a foe. Wild game reveled undisturbed over forest and fields and mocked the sport of those who dared attack. The pioneer found it a paradise.

It was during this year that a bright and handsome boy, born at Lexington, Virginia, on the 22nd of March, 1812, ventured from the parental roof and struck his tent in this lonely and lowly hamlet amid these scenes. His name was Robert Moderwell Sloan. He was the son of John Sloan, a native of the County of Donegal, Ireland, who was reared there, and when a young man came to America and later married Mary Shields, a native of Rockbridge County, Virginia. The issue of said marriage was seven children, named Alexander, James, Robert, Mary, Rachel, John and Martha.

Robert, our subject, was the third son, and after coming to Greensboro, became a salesman in the store of his uncle, Robert Moderwell, who at that time was the most successful merchant in said hamlet. His store was located on the site now 108-110 South Elm Street, and his residence adjoined it, so that the Moderwell property covered an entire half block extending to West Sycamore Street on the south and Greene Street on the west. Here Robert began a successful career and here by diligence and industry he and his brother James, after a few years, succeeded to the business and became successful merchants. Under this firm the business was continued until the Civil War.

In 1836 Robert married Sarah Paisley, a daughter of Rev. William Paisley and granddaughter of Col. John Paisley, who was also a native of Ireland. The Paisley family was later one of the most prominent in church and state. The issue of said marriage was seven children, namely: Col. John Sloan, a gallant Confederate officer, Mrs. W. C. Porter, Mrs. J. E. Logan, Mrs. C. Mebane, Mrs. Jeff Scales, Mrs. J. A. Barringer and Mrs. Neil Ellington.

The mere mention of these names attests the high place of this charming family and the prominent part its members have played in the social and civic life of Greensboro. They were the flowers that grew and bloomed from the beautiful garden of the home life of our subject, where he bestowed the wealth of his love and the beauty of his devotion. But his fine spirit reached beyond the sphere of his beautiful home. He loved his neighbors. His fellowman was his brother. His church was his idol. His business was his trust. His town was a constant object of his care and pride. He sought no honor outside of service to his own church and his town. When a commission as lieutenant in the state's militia was presented to him from Governor Dudley he wore the blush of a school boy. In spite of his modesty and his aversion to public office he was chosen mayor of Greensboro four times. in 1870-'71-'72 and '73. It was during his administration that the town charter was amended and the name of "City of Greensboro" was adopted. He was therefore the first mayor of the city of Greensboro. The beauty of its trees and the fragrance of its flowers enchanted him. The ruthless stroke of the woodman's axe grated on his fine nerve. He preached civic pride always and practiced civic righteousness. He had displayed during his long life all the fine qualities that make a model citizen.

After his retirement from the mercantile business during the War Between the States he was appointed the first agent of the Southern Express Company at Greensboro and held this position until his death. So faithful had he been that this company held him on its roll of honor long after the infirmities of age had stolen his strength and paid to his memory its finest tribute. For more than eighty years he was a leading spirit in all the forces at work for the betterment and upbuilding of his adopted town. Not less active was he in the affairs of his church—the old First Presbyterian. In 1867 he was elected to the highest office within the gift of his church, that of ruling elder. "But," says his pastor, "his modesty was even greater than his worth, and it was not until he was re-elected in 1882 that he could be prevailed upon to accept it. Till his death he was faithful and diligent in the discharge of this sacred trust."

It was in 1870 that he was induced to accept for the first time the highest honor within the gift of his town. No towering monument of marble or brass was needed to preserve his name and keep green his memory. His simple life was so useful, so full of service and so filled with kindly words and good deeds it has left a name and influence that will live when monuments are dust. His name may not shine on the historic page because it is not linked to any public policy of church or state, or any great act of legislation, but in his humble sphere, among his neighbors and his fellows, his name was linked for more than four-score years to "whatsoever things were true, whatsover things were honest, whatsover things were just, whatsoever things were pure, whatsoever things were lovely and whatsoever things were of good report."

In 1903, two years prior to his death, a unique and loving tribute was paid to him. One hundred of his friends and fellow-citizens, led by the late Dr. Charles Duncan McIver, united in procuring and presenting a Randall portrait of "Uncle Bob", as he was affectionately called, to the public library of this city where it still hangs and where friend after friend with moistened eye, and stranger with softened face, pause to study the benignant face of a man who for more than four score years lived and wrought in the fear of God and in the love of his neighbor. There was no exaggeration in the eloquent tribute of his pastor, Rev. Egbert W. Smith, who said, "He was the best loved member of his church and the best loved citizen of his town, and that to meet him on the dreariest winter's day was to enjoy a touch of summer's warmth and fragrance and melody." He died on the 27th of July, 1905, his long life having spanned the century lacking only seven years.

There are those yet living who cherish sweet memories of his kindliness. He believed that kindliness was the greatest thing in this life, and it is. There was a warmth in his hand shake and kindliness in his genial, sunny, jolly, every-day salutation, which always touched and cheered and made glad those who felt the one or heard the other. No life touched his that was not made the better and happier for it. In his sunny presence old age grew young and youth was led captive. His young life covered wars and peace and the wondrous transformation of the hills and valleys and running streams, over whose primeval face the feet of his boyhood strayed and played. It covers the most momentous and stupendous events of his country's history. He witnessed the birth and growth and the daring strides of his own queenly city. No gentler spirit, nor kindlier soul ever passed through this world.

                                        G. S. BRADSHAW.

CALVIN HENDERSON WILEY

CALVIN HENDERSON WILEY

1819 - 1887

The year 1819 is a memorable one in American literature. It saw the publication of Irving's "Sketch-Book" and witnessed the births of James Russell Lowell, Herman Melville, Walt Whitman, Julia Ward Howe, and J. G. Holland. It is no wonder that Calvin Henderson Wiley, whose infant cry was first heard on the morning of February 3 of this year, should have felt the promptings of a literary career. He was born in Guilford County, and neither his county nor his state had ever sent a representative to the high court of literature.

His training for a literary career was as thorough as North Carolina could then afford. He was prepared for college at the famous Caldwell Institute in Greensboro; he absorbed the best English classics available; he read widely in the theological literature of his day; and in 1840 he graduated with honor from the University of North Carolina. During this formative decade from 1830 to 1840 the two prose writers who dominated the English-speaking world were Walter Scott and James Fenimore Cooper. They were the respective founders in the Old World and the New of what we now call the historical novel. Both had shown that history is not a dead thing but capable of being recalled, re-enacted and re-vivified. They had proved not only that past events could be made entertaining to the present, but that the virtues and heroisms of the past could be re-invested in new lines and thus re-vitalized for new service.

With the high motive of continuing the tradition of Scott and Cooper, Wiley turned from a brief legal career in Oxford, North Carolina, to the serious pursuit of historical fiction. The early history of North Carolina was to be his theme, and no author ever entered upon his task with a purer patriotism or a more devoted determination to make the past of his state a living and exemplary present. That part of Guilford County that he knew and loved best was to be his chosen *locale*. This was the region around Alamance Church, the church that Dr. David Caldwell had made famous. Three miles west of this church, in a house built by his father, David Wiley, in 1815, Dr. Wiley was born. The house is still standing, though additions have been made to it, and is occupied by a nephew of Dr. Wiley, William C. Rankin, who bought it to keep it in the family. Let me suggest that a memorial tablet be immediately erected by the State Literary and Historical Association dedicating the building to the love and care of all patriotic citizens of North Carolina.

With the manuscript of a novel called "Alamance, or the Great and Final Experiment" in his pocket, Dr. Wiley, at the age of twenty-eight, starts for New York City. The following letter from Philadelphia, dated August 31, 1847, is peculiarly interesting and informing. He is writing to the Greensboro editors of "The Patriot," Swaim and Sherwood. The Harper Brothers had already curtly refused even to consider the publication of the new book, but Wiley was not a man to be easily daunted. The Graham that he meets in Philadelphia, by the way, was the famous George R. Graham, firm friend and loyal defender of Edgar Allan Poe. Graham was at this time proprietor of "Graham's Magazine," which under Poe's previous editorship had become the leading magazine in the country:

"Well, I came on to Yankeeland and went in New York to the most eminent literary gentleman there and one who had the confidence of all the publishers. He kindly examined my book and then gave me, in writing, a very favorable opinion; one more favorable than I care to say. In fact, he became so much interested that he went at once to the Harpers, and after a conference with them the Messrs. H. were glad to take my book without pay and at their own risk.

"My letters brought me acquainted with nearly all the publishers and many of the editors and literati of New York and this place, and all, without an exception, express astonishment at my bargain.

"I stopped here to see Graham, the great and noble patron of American authors; told him of my bargain with the Harpers and showed him the opinions of the critics on my book. He at once offered me $500 for a new tale of 100 pages to be published in his magazine, and I to retain the copyright. He says my novel is to be the great feature in the magazine for

1848, and you will see a flourishing announcement of it in the numbers for November and December.

"Having always cherished a desire to immortalize my old mother state, I have laid the scene of my book there and much of it in old Guilford. 'Alamance' is the name of the book and the critics, especially Johnson, the literary editor of the Nat. Intel., tell me that the finest scenes in all the book are laid in that old church. There, thank God, will that dear old edifice (now no more) be handed down to fame just as it was when, a white-haired boy, I worshiped there. Our debt of gratitude is now paid; there are others on my list which, if God spares my life, shall be discharged with compound interest. Where I am not remembered, I remember everything, and, unlike many, I have made my native place shine in the glories of my attempts at fame."

The book appeared late in 1847. Chaper 47 describes the Battle of Guilford Courthouse. Dr. David Caldwell and Captain Forbis are leading characters. The highest tribute ever paid the book is in a mention of it by William Dean Howells, late primate of American letters. In Mr. Howells' volume of youthful reminiscences called "A Boy's Town", he names the books and authors that he and his brothers used to read with most delight. Among these were the histories of Greece and Rome, by Goldsmith; "Don Quixote," "Handy Andy," by Samuel Lover; "Harry Lorrequer," by C. J. Lever; and "The Bride of Lammermoor," by Scott. But the book that they preferred above all the rest, the book that "bewitched" them, was "Alamance, or the Great and Final Experiment." Mr. Howells had forgotten the name of the author and every character and event in the story. He remembered, however, that "it was about the life of some sort of community in North Carolina." Two other novels complete Dr. Wiley's contribution to historical fiction. "Roanoke, or Where is Utopia?" appeared in 1849 and was republished in London as "Old Dan Tucker and His Son Walter, a Tale of North Carolina." In 1852, when the country was in turmoil over "Uncle Tom's Cabin," Dr. Wiley issued "Life in the South," adding as an alternative title, "A Companion to Uncle Tom's Cabin," though the story takes place in the eighteenth century and culminates in the Battle of Moore's Creek Bridge.

I hope that some one will yet make a thorough study of these laudatory attempts of Dr. Wiley to clothe with romance the Revolutionary history of North Carolina. No one can withhold his admiration of the spirit that dictated these ventures. The man had a feeling for big things and was the first North Carolinian that labored to do for his state what other writers had done and were yet to do in lifting definite localities into literature. But he was ahead of his time. Had he written after 1870, when regional literature scored its most conspicuous triumphs in the American short story, the result might have been different; but Dr. Wiley would have had to change with the times. He had knowledge and a measure of fancy; but he lacked an interpretative and constructive imagination. He could not reproduce the local in terms of the universal. The defect was not in his subject; it was in the man himself. His love scenes are stilted; his humor is bizarre; his plots are loose-jointed; his English, though uniformly correct, is lacking in charm and flexibility; while his conversations are, let us say, as ceremonial as Cooper's.

But the year 1852, that saw the publication of his poorest novel, saw also the beginning of a career that was to inaugurate a new epoch in his own life and a new era in the history of his beloved state. In that year he was elected our first Superintendent of Education. Now began a period of terrible toil, but a period of fruitful and cumulative achievement. The reason why Wiley is almost forgotten today as our pioneer in historical fiction is because his greater fame as the father of the public school system in North Carolina has absorbed his lesser fame. The public schools were in a deplorable condition and, worse still, there was no organized public opinion back of them.

Freedom was the catchword of the time, but it was still used in the narrow political sense. It meant freedom from outside oppression. It was passive, not active. It meant "free from", not "free to." It was an inert laissez-faire doctrine that bragged loudly of its past but stood powerless before the opportunities of the present or the challenge of the future. It was not destructive, but it was not constructive. It was Wiley's mission to inaugurate a campaign for freedom in the larger and more dynamic sense, freedom through education, freedom from narrowness, selfishness, provincialism, and inefficiency. The word to him meant equality of opportunity, but he realized with all the passion of his nature that there could be no equality of opportunity in actual life without equality of opportunity in preparing for life.

With this vision before him, Dr. Wiley visited in his old-fashioned buggy every secton and corner of the state; he prepared a series of North Carolina Readers that stirred a new pride in our past and a new realization of our agricultural possibilities; he made a simplified digest of our conflicting school laws; he mobilized teachers, preachers, farmers, and politicians in a crusade for public education at public expense; he established the "North Carolina Journal of Education"; he denounced the idea that the public schools were a charity and proclaimed instead that democracy was impossible without them; he requisitioned every newspaper and printing press in the state for the cause of educational propaganda; and from every platform and pulpit to which he had access he preached the doctrine of a new and greater North Carolina.

His success may be measured in part by these victorious figures: In 1853 there were 800 teachers in the public schools of North Carolina; in 1860 there were 2,286. In 1853 there were 83,373 pupils; in 1860 there were 116,567. In 1853 the receipts were $192,250; in 1860 they were $408,566. In 1858 North Carolina had a larger school fund than Georgia, Virginia, Maryland, New Jersey, Massachusetts, or Maine. But his greatest work was done between 1861 and 1865. During these years, though our soldiers were suffering for the bare necessities in the field, Dr. Wiley persuaded the legislature to preserve the school funds intact and thus keep the schools continuously in session. In his last report made to Governor Worth on January 16, 1866, he writes: "To the lasting honor of North Carolina her public schools survived the terrible shock of cruel war, and the state of the south which furnished most material and the greatest number and the bravest troops to the war did more than all the others for the cause of popular education."

In 1862 Dr. Wiley married Miss Mittie Towles, of Raleigh; in 1866 he fulfilled the lifelong prayer of his mother and became a Presbyterian minister; in 1869 he moved to Jonesboro, Tennessee, as agent for the American Bible Society; in 1874 he settled permanently in Winston; in 1876 the position of Superintendent of Public Instruction was again tendered him but he declined it, believing that, as the office had become the football of partisan politics, he could not as a minister take part in its personal polemics; in 1881 he received the degree of doctor of divinity from the University of North Carolina; in 1883 he organized the public school system of Winston and remained chairman of its board of trustees till his death in 1887. In 1904 the school children of Winston erected a monument to him bearing the inscription: ''Erected by the pupils of the graded schools of Winston to the memory of the Rev. Calvin H. Wiley, D. D., as one of the founders of the schools of this city and as the father of the public school system of North Carolina.''

Dr. Wiley was more than a ''founder of Greensboro.'' Among North Carolinians he was the first to reveal the storied possibilities that lie latent in the history of Guilford County; he was the first to recognize that, though it is well to memorialize the past, it is better to emancipate the present; he was the first to actualize in a state-wide crusade the conviction that education is not a luxury but a life-preserver. In the latter sense he was one of the founders not only of Greensboro, but of every city and hamlet in the state that sets a little child in the midst as the central concern of constructive statesmanship.

C. ALPHONSO SMITH.

TURNER MYRICK JONES

TURNER MYRICK JONES
1819 - 1892

A man who was president of a college for more than a quarter of a century consecutively and for nearly fifty years was closely identified with the educational development of the state necessarily possessed outstanding characteristics that marked him as an executive and a leader.

Such a man was Dr. Turner M. Jones, who for thirty-six years was president of Greensboro College save the interim that elapsed between the burning of the old building and the completion of the new when the school was carried on at Louisburg and Warrenton.

Turner Myrick Jones was born in Franklin County, near Louisburg, in 1819. His father was Rev. Amos Jones, a Methodist preacher, and his mother, Mary Ann Myrick, a devout and cultured woman of Puritan stock.

He was the sixth son in a family of eleven children and one of two brothers who became presidents of colleges for women.

His education began in "an old field school" where, besides the regular studies, he spent much time reading and studying the Bible, classical poems and, for lack of adequate instruction and brain stimulus he memorized Murray's English Grammar.

At the age of sixteen he was sent to a boys' boarding school not far from his home where he was prepared for college and in 1841 he entered Randolph-Macon, which at that time was the Methodist Episcopal College for young men of both the Virginia and North Carolina Conferences.

In the first month of his senior year ill-health forced him to leave college, but later he recovered sufficiently to take charge of a boys' school and at the close of the spring term he went to Randolph-Macon, where he stood his examinations, receiving his diploma and A. M. and A. B. Later in life he received the degree of D. D. from Trinity College.

Soon after leaving college Dr. Jones was married to Miss Frances Stone, of Franklin County. Ten years later Mrs. Jones died, leaving four children.

For ten years Dr. Jones was at the head of boys' schools and in 1852 he was licensed to preach by the North Carolina Conference, but never entered the pastoral field.

In 1853 he was elected as head of the departments of literature and mathematics at Greensboro College, and the following year, after the resignation of the president, Dr. Charles F. Deems—who for many years following was pastor of The Church of the Strangers in New York City—he accepted the presidency of the college and from that time dedicated his life to the higher education of young women.

It was in 1857 that Miss Lucy McGee, of Raleigh, became the wife of Dr. Jones and proved a helpmeet in every sense of the word.

During the twenty-seven years of her married life Mrs. Jones was a wonderful mother, friend and teacher to the hundreds of young women under her care. She was the busy mother of eight children, yet could always be relied upon to give of her best in the interest of the college family of girls and teachers. A woman of remarkable gifts, highly cultured, deeply religious, exceedingly diligent in administering the onerous duties of her high calling, she was a "tower of strength" to her husband and her wise counsel his greatest stay in times of stress. Her death in 1884 was a blow from which Dr. Jones never recovered, although for eight years longer he successfully "carried on."

All who know the history of the south must concede to Dr. Jones a brave spirit and a persevering nature in holding on to the work to which he dedicated his life and heroically striving to place upon a high plane the oldest woman's college in the South during the ten years preceding the Civil War and the dark days of reconstruction which followed.

He was pre-eminently fitted for his life work. Refined by nature, gentle and courteous in manner and possessing a great sympathetic heart, his administration proved him a friend, a father and a wise counselor to the young women, as well as a born instructor and executive. He was a scholarly and cultured man and excelled in the higher literary and classical attainments.

Physically Dr. Jones was an unusual specimen of manhood. He was not a large man, but always carried himself with such dignity that one thought of him as rather a stately man. He was exquisitely neat in dress; his white hair, keen but kind eyes, a glowing complexion and white goatee looked like a clean cut cameo above the clerical collar and white tie that he always wore with the conventional Prince Albert.

In fact, his personal neatness was the complement of a painstaking, methodical mind that served him well in systematic handling of his stupendous duties. His study was indicative of the man—no matter the time one entered there, everything was in perfect order—his desk, his correspondence and his library denoting neatness and system in every detail.

The college was overflowing during his administration. He was fired by a great ambition in broadening the scope of learning, but was so handicapped financially that he had to go slow in carrying out his plans for the growth and culture of the institution.

There were two outstanding characteristics of this eminent educator which lent great power to his administration—a wonderful self-control born of a beautiful Christian spirit which unconsciously wielded a lasting influence upon all within the college walls, and a splendid memory—a rare and effective weapon to a man in his position.

So great was Dr. Jones' self-control that he never allowed temper to possess him. If he had a temper no girl ever came in contact with it, and his calm, gentle manner and kind, fatherly interest never failed. His very step measured self-control. No one ever saw him dawdle along, but he always walked with military precision and with the dignity of a well-balanced rhythm. No one ever heard his voice raised in derision. He simply went along in the ''even tenor of his way'', doing and planning for the advancement and happiness of his girls.

After a pupil came into personal touch with Dr. Jones all fear begotten by his dignified and courtly appearance vanished and he at once became the gentle, interested friend, extending fatherly advice in such a kind way that the girl would wonder why she had ever been afraid of approaching him.

Strange to say, his condemnation of rules broken or some unladylike behavior was administered in the same manner, as the writer had occasion to remember when standing before him on being questioned as to where the rising bell had been hidden when an Easter holiday had given rise to the desire to sleep late for once in her life. One always left his presence on such occasions chastened and repentant, with a great determination to become the grandest and strongest character in the school; however, she may afterward have fallen from grace when temptations arose.

His memory of names and faces was remarkable and gave him a hold upon all who knew him intimately. He seldom, if ever, forgot an old pupil or teacher, no matter how many years intervened 'ere he met them. This characteristic was indelibly impressed upon the writer when, as quite a young girl, she witnessed a scene at the station where Dr. Jones was aiding a pupil to take the train. He was some sixty-five years old at the time, when glancing down the length of the car and seeing a lady of some maturity who looked up in time to catch his eye, he went forward at once with outstretched hand, exclaiming: ''Why, Sallie, how little you have changed in the thirty-odd years since we have met!''

Thirty-odd years to remember the name and face of a pupil who spent one year at Greensboro College before it was burned—with forty-nine years plainly stamped upon that face—when in the years between thousands of faces and names had passed before him in review!

As a preacher Dr. Jones was appreciated for his scholarly discourses which were always uplifting as well as enlightening; in fact, to quote a contemporary, ''His sermons were gems of thought and diction,'' and when he accepted invitations to preach out of town he was heard by immense congregations.

There are very few of the thousands of young women who sat under his teaching and preaching but have carried in their hearts through life the beautiful lessons he taught and still more beautiful way he lived. For those lessons his name is loved and revered as a household word in the homes of old Greensboro College girls scattered throughout the land. The high standards of Christian living and education which he bequeathed to his pupils are the recognized standards of today.

The measure of the man is pictured in his last words, when on the morning of June 4, 1892, shortly before he breathed his last, with his family gathered around his bed, he said:

''I am ready, 'For I am persuaded that neither death, nor life, nor angels, nor principalities, nor powers, nor things present, nor things to come, nor height, nor depth, nor any other creature shall be able to separate us from the love of God which is in Christ Jesus our Lord'.''

The self-control taught by his daily life; the beautiful Christian influence brought to bear upon thousands of young women by his example and personal service; an utter lack of desire for applause; an ambition to build character for future generations and a noble effort for the higher education of women, were the attributes of this man whose life work was so closely identified with the fundamental growth of a great state in the making.

The work that Dr. Jones accomplished by indomitable courage and perseverance in the face of trying circumstances when there was little to build upon marked him as a success, and now that time and distance gives a clearer perspective of his achievements, he becomes a notable figure in the up-building of the educational and religious forces of the South and easily takes a high place in the galaxy of great men who were the builders of old Greensboro and whose visions included a ''greater Greensboro.''

CARRIE PELL GUNTER.

NEREUS MENDENHALL

NEREUS MENDENHALL
1819 - 1893

When the Carolinas were young and there was little or no thought of severing the tie which bound them to the Mother Country an emigrant from Pennsylvania settled on the banks of Deep River, Guilford County, North Carolina, and took up quite a large tract of land occupied by the present Jamestown and its vicinity. He built a homestead and a grist mill, the former of which is still standing and occupied. Desiring to go further south, the builder left his reservations to his son, George Mendenhall, and moved to Georgia.

George married Judith Gardner, of Nantucket, and remained on the domain left him, built houses and founded the village which from his father he named Jamestown. Sons and daughters were born and the war of the Revolution found them busily engaged tending the mill, tilling the fields, spinning and weaving, thus being almost sufficient unto themselves.

These children in their lifetime remembered the encampment of the British under Lord Cornwallis on the hill overlooking the mill, having seen the English general on the eve of the battle of Guilford Court House, and the family suffered some loss from the depredations of the soldiers. The children grew to manhood and womanhood, married and built for themselves homes on parts of their father's estate.

Richard Mendenhall married Mary Pegg, the prettiest girl in the country, as tradition relates. As an evidence that she was something more than pretty, it may be told that she spun and wove much cotton, flax and wool, and that with the fruits of her loom she purchased her wedding gown of changeable silk, riding on horseback all the way to Salem to make the exchange.

Richard took his bride to the quaint old house which still stands upon the slope of the hill opening directly from the street and built with numerous steps to suit the declivity of the ground. It is a rambling old house, but within its walls a generous hospitality was installed that the Mendenhall family never allowed to wane. Statesmen and philanthropists, men of almost every nationality and every phase of humanity, from a commodore to a street beggar, have been welcomed to its food and shelter.

Nereus Mendenhall, the fourth child in this home, was born in August, 1819. His father was a man of good education, reading the Latin authors easily and with great pleasure. His admiration for the Latin tongue is seen in the fact that to his sons he gave names terminating in *us* and to his daughters the Latin feminine.

As a boy Nereus was very bright and an apt pupil in the neighborhood school. In 1832, at the age of thirteen, he went to Greensboro to learn the printer's trade. While there he was closely associated with Lyndon Swaim, to whom ever after he was warmly attached. Although of different religious denominations, they were congenial to each other and in those deep or fundamental truths which actuate the lives of true manhood they walked in near sympathy for half a century or more.

He entered Haverford College in 1837 and showed rare mental power in his new surroundings, for although he entered the freshman class he completed the four years course in two years. Upon his graduation in 1839 he at once took the place as principal of the Friends Boarding School at New Garden, North Carolina. This school had been opened two years before and his entrance into its work was the beginning of an influence that really made it famous for sound scholarship and established a reputation which followed the institution when in the year 1888 it was changed to Guilford College.

His work in the school at New Garden was too arduous. He taught all day, even before breakfast, and his care did not end until every boy was in bed and the lights out. How he found time for study one cannot now very well see, but he always throughout a busy life found time to study. While thus occupied in teaching and governing the boys in this school he prepared for entering the Jefferson Medical College in Philadelphia. He won there the same high regard from medical professors that he had won before at Haverford, graduated in 1845, and returned to his native town to practice. As a practitioner he was successful, but his sympathy with those who were suffering wrought upon his sensitive nature.

He therefore gave up practice and returned to the New Garden School as superintendent.

In 1851 he was married to Orianna Wilson. She had been a student in the school during his first connection with it and was a cousin to his Aunt Delphina Mendenhall, the wife of his Uncle George. This marriage was happy and abounded in blessing to both husband and wife.

The long strain of constant study, teaching in the school and superintending at the same time threatened and impaired Dr. Mendenhall's health and he abandoned again the work of teaching to which he was devoted and became a civil engineer. This change proved most helpful to his health as well as more lucrative than teaching school. His work now was for many years railroad engineering, in which service his fine mathematical power found a useful field to display itself.

His father died in 1851, and while he was engaged on the North Carolina Central Railroad his home was for part of the time at Jamestown with his mother. The young couple later moved to High Point and afterwards to Florence, near Deep River Meeting House.

In 1860, at the urgent solicitation of the trustees of the New Garden School he again returned to take charge of the institution for another useful period of its history. The Civil War was coming on. While still in his home at Florence he had a foretaste of the spirit which threw North and South into battle array.

His home training, his Christian faith and his love of liberty combined to make him a strong abolitionist. In his father's home he received his first lessons in succoring the oppressed and assisting struggling human beings. While a young man he was threatened with the lash for trying to befriend a harmless negro who was about to be whipped in the streets of his native town. Though scoffed at and despised by some of his own associates for advocating the principles ''of justice and brotherhood,'' he never swerved from the truth nor attempted to conceal his convictions. He was a subscriber to anti-slavery papers, though every such subscriber was a marked man in those days. On principle he was opposed to all wars, and on account of his anti-slavery sentiments he was decidedly out of sympathy with his own section in the Civil War.

After the war had been in progress for a time but before the blockade was complete Dr. Mendenhall, being president of the Friends School at New Garden, was urged by his brother-in-law, Dr. Nathan Hill, to leave the South and with himself seek a home in the West. He had serious objections to rearing his family in slave territory, prospects of worldly advancement in the West were promising and the escape of the immediate effects of the war on him and his family enticing.

On the other hand, the school was full of young people and should he leave there was no one to take his place. The household goods were packed in boxes and homemade trunks and had been conveyed to the station at Jamestown and the family were ready to leave on the morrow. The conviction grew stronger in Dr. Mendenhall's mind that it was the will of the Lord for him to remain at New Garden and stand by the school come what might. He was obedient to the holy vision and after assuring himself that this course would meet the approval of his wife, he ordered the boxes brought back and went again to the old school room.

During this period—and always while teaching—he bound to himself in lasting friendship very many of the young men who were his pupils. Through his profound learning in almost all fields of scholarship and through a fine sense of justice and sympathy he attracted the thoughtful and never repelled by criticism the unthinking student. Though somewhat stern in discipline and exacting in teaching, his pupils recognized his loyalty to truth and righteousness. They remained deeply attached to him and were ever followed by his kindly interest.

Several of the Friends—Quakers as often called—were conscripted in the army who refused to fight or perform any military duty. These were punished in various ways and thrown into Castle Thunder at Richmond. Many attempts were made to obtain their release. Dr. Mendenhall was sent by the Friends Church to intercede with the Confederate government in their behalf. This was a somewhat perilous undertaking, but it was performed in the same courageous spirit in which his every duty was discharged. With his beloved friend, John B. Crenshaw, of Richmond, he visited the Friends in their jail and encouraged them. Together these two distinguished Friends—both striking in personality in form as well as in noble bearing—sought the release of the prisoners, appealing to President Davis, who treated them courteously, but had no power to grant their request.

These were times to make men's hearts quail, and to stand having done all that could be done was heroic. Dr. Mendenhall never shrank from avowing himself a Quaker and whenever he heard that sect abused or misrepresented he did not hesitate to maintain with vigor and in masterful manner the principles which the sect professed. On the streets, in railway trains, anywhere and everywhere, he would show the incompatibility of all war with the spirit and teaching of Christ.

During the years of arduous labor in the school and out of it he was active in the business of the Friends Yearly Meeting held near the school buildings. He served many years as presiding clerk, a position of large responsibilities. In the midst of all these duties he carried on, as previously stated, his own private study, Latin, Greek, German, Hebrew, natural science and mental philosophy, both ancient and modern. Neander's Life of Christ was almost his constant companion and from this source he obtained assistance in the solution of some questions that had long burdened his mind.

Two more daughters were born in the New Garden home, and aside from all other duties he took time to teach his children. Sometimes they recited at the school with the young men and sometimes by themselves at home. Never was any allowance made to them for lessons poorly learned because they were girls. This at a time when Vassar and Wellesley and Smith and Bryn Mawr were unthought of and long before even Cornell had opened her doors to women.

In 1867 his connection with the Boarding School was severed. He had in all given nine of the best years of his life to this institution and had been the main factor in preventing the closing of the school in the Civil War. Had this taken place it would in all likelihood have brought to an end the educational work of Friends in North Carolina. Such a terminus would have greatly weakened if it had not brought to extinction the North Carolina Yearly Meeting of Friends.

Upon leaving the New Garden School he removed his family to a farm which he owned one mile from the center of the Deep River Monthly Meeting of Friends to which all his life his membership belonged. For a time he took charge of a Monthly Meeting School at that place, which under the enthusiastic management of Ezra M. Meader, a New England Friend, had attained considerable note. Here many young people received instruction and were stimulated to pursue their studies elsewhere. Thus by doing what his hands found to do in this quiet community where his lot was cast he kindled a love for learning in the minds of boys and girls about him, the effects of which spread far and wide.

A little later Dr. Mendenhall again turned his attention to civil engineering, being employed upon the surveys in South Carolina, also upon the construction of the road extending from Greensboro to Winston-Salem.

Though an abolitionist before the Civil War and a Union man during the war, soon after its close he allied himself with the Democratic party in the state. The corruption and oppression of carpet-bag rule was so intolerable to one who had always stood for the rights of the oppressed that affiliation with it was to him impossible. He was twice elected to represent his county in the legislature. He regarded a campaign as an opportunity of speaking to the people and setting before them the truth as he saw it and allowed his name to stand on the ticket several times with little thought of election. He was always an earnest advocate of the cause of temperance although he never joined the prohibition party.

When it became necessary for our state to erect a new building for the care of the insane Dr. Mendenhall was appointed by the legislature one of the board of directors. He was active and highly useful in all the duties which this appointment imposed, selecting plans, buying materials and letting contracts and supervising the construction.

In 1876 he was elected a member of the Board of Teachers in the Penn Charter School in Philadelphia, under the management of Richard M. Jones, and was pleased to avail himself of the opportunity of spending sometime in Philadelphia. The elder children had returned home from extended school work at the Howland School on Lake Cayuga, in New York, and as Mrs. Mendenhall was loath to give up her home in the South, it was decided that the family should remain in North Carolina.

Later he was offered a place on the faculty of Haverford College, his Alma Mater, which he accepted. The work at Haverford was laborious and told upon his health and after two years he was compelled to return to North Carolina.

His interest in public education did not abate. He rendered great service to state and county. Mr. Jesse R. Wharton, of Greensboro, long time Superintendent of Guilford County Board of Education, Dr. Mendenhall being for many years chairman of said board, gave this testimony to the work of his friend: ''Dr. Mendenhall was not merely a scholar of wide and varied attainments, he was not simply a profound student, he was these and more. He was an intelligent, earnest and zealous lover of mankind. He made his extensive learning subservient to the cause of humanity; and his sympathies were as far reaching as the human race. Believing that true education was the great lever to lift up his fellowmen to higher and nobler views of life he was always a steady and ardent friend of universal education. As a political economist he believed that it was cheaper, and as a moral economist that it was far better to educate than to punish.''

As time went on home life changed rapidly. As four of the five daughters were at Guilford College, the husbands of two of them and the fourth daughter being members of the faculty and the fifth being a student, Dr. Mendenhall purchased a cottage nearby and moved into it in 1890. Soon thereafter his wife passed away and he subsequently spent his time in part with his sister Judith, in the old home in Jamestown, and in part with his eldest daughter Mary, the wife of L. L. Hobbs, the President of Guilford College. In August, 1893, he attended the Friends Yearly Meeting in High Point and took part in the discussions with much of his old time vigor. The end came in October following.

Dr. Mendenhall was a Friend, not because he had been born one, not because George Fox preached or the learned Barclay defended the doctrines of the Society of Friends, but because after studying almost all philosophies and all religions and constant and devout study of the Bible he came to the conclusions which the early Friends proclaimed. His opposition to many of the theories promulgated in those days was not the antagonism of ignorance or mere tradition, but the deliberate opinion of one who had studied the matter thoroughly and profoundly and knew it not only from the standpoint of a Friend, but that of a scientist and philosopher.

As a scholar he took high rank in almost all fields of learning. In mathematics he was easily among the foremost that our state has ever produced and always found himself at home in this department of learning anywhere his work as a teacher or civil engineer called him.

In medical science his fine work at the Jefferson Medical College in Philadelphia proved his capability. In ancient or modern languages he was equally among the best students of his time, making a life long study of the Bible, both of the Old Testament and the New, not only in English translation, but himself mastering the Hebrew for the special investigation of the Old Testament and the Greek for the New. In history he swept the entire field and he was one time introduced to President Gilman, of Johns Hopkins University, as the best read man in the Society of Friends in America. In religious philosophy he was a profound student. He embodied something of the fruit of his labors in this department of knowledge in an address to the alumni of Haverford College in 1879. For breadth of view, discriminating judgment and vigor of expression scarcely anything in brief survey can be found that gives a saner interpretation of some modern problems of science and religion than may be seen in this summary of human thought.

Dr. Mendenhall felt that his best work was done in the school room as a teacher. While he knew, it always seemed, almost everything, he was modest in his claims to mastery in scholarship and always gave you the greatest possible freedom to hold your own opinion, merely wishing in every case to know your reason for your conclusion. He was eminently Socratic in his methods both in teaching and learning. One of the finest lectures of his life, it would appear, was the one he made on Socrates based, of course, on "Plato's Apology and Crito," and upon the "Memorabilia of Xenophon," and included doubtless in its scope all that was or is known respecting the father of Greek philosophy.

The life of such a man was therefore very illuminating and invigorating to the young people of his day and he valued as Socrates valued, as every man should value, the privilege of living in the atmosphere of schools and colleges and stimulating inquiry.

His fine spirit meant much to New Garden School in which he spent nine years of his life in teaching. It also meant much, although this was coming to the end of a great life, to Guilford College, to the students of which he often lectured, and it meant much also all the way along his pilgrimage to North Carolina Yearly Meeting of Friends and to his native state.

L. L. HOBBS.

JOHN HENRY DILLARD

JOHN HENRY DILLARD

1819 - 1896

Judge John Henry Dillard was born in Rockingham County, North Carolina, near Leaksville, on the 30th day of November, 1819. He was sent to Patrick Henry Academy, in Henry County, Virginia, sometime in the thirties to a school then of great repute, under Professor Godfrey; after which he went to the University of North Carolina at Chapel Hill to enter the same class with Samuel P. Phillips. This was the class of 1841, but young Dillard did not graduate, since in 1840 he went to William and Mary College, Williamsburg, Virginia, to study law under Judge Beverly Tucker, having previously studied with Hon. James T. Morehead in Greensboro for a short time. Judge Tucker was the author of "Tucker's Blackstone."

When his law course was completed at William and Mary, Mr. Dillard located in Patrick County, Virginia, and soon became commonwealth attorney for that county, where he was busily engaged with the claims of his early practice until 1846.

Wentworth, in his native county of Rockingham, was the next home of the young lawyer and here he served as county attorney, clerk and master of equity for the county.

On July 13th, 1846, he was happily married to Miss Ann I. Martin, a daughter of Col. Joseph Martin, of Henry County, Virginia, a most estimable lady, who survived her husband several years. Of their children, Mrs. Pannell, the eldest daughter, died some years ago. The four surviving children are J. H. Dillard, of Murphy, N. C.; Mrs. Frank Hall, of Reidsville; Ruffin and Drewry Dillard, of Greensboro.

In the year 1848 Mr. Dillard formed a partnership in the practice of law with Colonel Thomas Ruffin, which continued until Colonel Ruffin was elected solicitor in the Fourth Judicial District in the year 1854.

When the War Between the States was declared this middle-aged lawyer, with twenty years' practice behind him, left home and office to serve his state. He organized a company known as Company G, of the 45th North Carolina Regiment, and served as its captain from February 27, 1862, till his resignation June 27th, 1863.

Greensboro was the next and last home of the Dillard family. This move was made in 1868 and Mr. Dillard practiced his profession here until he was elected in 1878 to a seat on the Supreme Court bench of the state.

In this high office he displayed great ability and learning, as shown in the many opinions which he wrote, and in aiding the Court in their deliberations in reaching proper conclusions on the many intricate questions which arose during his term on the bench. He resigned his seat in the spring of 1881 because of broken health.

Upon his release from the burden of state office Judge Dillard returned to his law practice in Greensboro, which was continued until his death in 1896.

In connection with Judge Robert P. Dick he conducted here the well-known Dick and Dillard Law School for fifteen years. Nearly three hundred young men were thus prepared to apply for license from the Supreme Court for the practice of law. Profiting by the example and instruction of these two eminent teachers they remembered both with gratitude in their various fields of honor and achievement.

Throughout his long life honor came to Judge Dillard as his due, yet he sought no honor for himself.

"He was not a born leader. He neither desired nor took a prominent part in political campaigns or in the various movements for social reforms and advancement. He was, however, interested in all such subjects and studied the principles involved, the objects sought to be achieved and the means and methods to be employed. By his counsel and learning he furnished many resources to his friends who were prominent leaders in such enterprises."

Judge Dick has said of his old friend and associate: "He was the best draftsman of legal papers and documents that I have ever met." Chief Justice Pearson said that "Judge Dillard was the best equity lawyer who appeared before the Supreme Court."

"In private life he was remarkable for his simplicity of taste and temperance of habits, for his uniform cheerfulness of disposition and freedom from envy, covetousness and selfishness. He diminished his wants by limiting his desires.

He had no grasping love of money and the security and contentment of his mind were not disquieted by the affluent indulgence and luxuries of abundant wealth.''

For more than twenty years he was an elder in the First Presbyterian Church of Greensboro, and for ten years before his death he taught in the Sunday school of that church a large class of warm-hearted young girls, instructing them with parental tenderness and possessed of their filial veneration and affection.

All Greensboro people of Judge Dillard's time knew of his great love for flowers. In the months that his garden bloomed it was his custom seven days in the week to leave his home on West Gaston Street with flowers in his hand for the young friends he was sure to meet on the way to his office or to his beloved church.

The writer of these sketches was present at the meeting of the Greensboro bar on May 26, 1896, to pay tribute to the memory and honor of Judge Dillard; the following is a portion of his address on the occasion:

''We have assembled at this hour and in this place to pay our tribute of respect to the memory of our distinguished friend and honored head of our bar, the Honorable John H. Dillard, who is now no more.

''The death of Judge Dillard on the 6th day of April, 1896, has created a void in this community and in the profession which he so much adorned and which it will be difficult ever to fill. He had lived among us for nearly a quarter of a century and our people had come to know and to esteem and love him. His praise was in every mouth and on every tongue.

''Well and truly it may be said of him, as was said of another:

'None knew him but to love,
None named him but to praise.'

''We shall miss him in the court circle; we shall miss him in the office, and upon our streets and in our social life. His familiar and pleasant face which has beamed upon us for so many years and his gifts of flowers shall be seen no more in our midst. His voice is silent; the mouth of wisdom is closed, but the memory of his many virtues shall linger with us as a rich and valued treasure during the continuance of our lives.

"His professional career, which was a distinguished one, extends over a period of half a century. Truly a long professional life. His early contemporaries in this state were such distinguished men as Hon. James T. Morehead, father of Col. Morehead; Hon. John A. Gilmer, father of Judge Gilmer; Hon. George C. Mendenhall, Hon. Ralph Gorrell, Hon. James R. McClean, Hon. Robert P. Dick, Hon. John Kerr, Hon. Robert B. Watts, Hon. Thomas Ruffin, Governor William A. Graham, Hon. Hugh Waddell, General John F. Poindexter, and others.

"Judge Dillard survived them all except our worthy and honored citizen, Judge Dick, and left a reputation behind him for learning, wisdom and ability in his profession second to none of his great contemporaries. 'Peace to his ashes'."

LEVI M. SCOTT.

Read before Guilford Historical Association December 12th, 1907.

FRANCES WEBB BUMPASS

FRANCES WEBB BUMPASS

1819 - 1898

As one searches the annals of the early days of Greensboro for names worthy of remembrance because of noble living and uplifting influence in the formative period of the community, there is none 'more to be revered than that of the subject of this sketch.

Among the forces to be taken into account in the building of society we must consider not only those which attract public attention through their performance in the eyes of the world, or through their value in contributing to the material prosperity of a community. Great as these may be, and are, the underlying spiritual power which emanates from some quiet unobstrusive life is no less potent in its influence upon the issues on which public life and true progress rest. It is indeed the sure foundation on which all may build with safety the structure of life.

Of the latter type of influence entering into the warp and woof of Greensboro life and ideals, we may point to Mrs. Frances Webb Bumpass, whose long life with more than fifty years in this city was a continual outpouring of her singularly pure and lofty spiritual aspirations which still enter into the best traditions of our religious life. So deeply was the life and character of this "elect lady" impressed upon the hearts of her fellow citizens that her memory is still as "precious ointment poured forth."

Mrs. Bumpass was descended from a long ancestral line of men and women of staunch character and sterling principles, and of loyalty in both church and state. On the paternal side this honorable ancestry traces its origin to Henry Webbe, of Doiset, a shire on the southern coast of Wales. This gentleman was a member of the household of Catherine Parr, the last queen of Henry VIII, and mention is made of him in connection with some grants and privileges, under the hand and signet of Catherine, then Queen Regent, in 1544. The settlement of the family in this country is connected with early colonial days. In 1640-1650 two Webb brothers came from Wales to America, one of whom settled in Massachusetts, and the other in Isle of Wight County, in Virginia, founding the southern branch of the family. It is to this branch that Isaac Webb, the father of Mrs. Bumpass, belonged.

On the maternal side the ancestry is honorable and noteworthy. Robert Dickens, the head of the family in this country, was a colonel of a cavalry regiment in the Continental Army. His eldest son, Jesse Dickens, married Frances Moore, and from this union was born Harriet Dickens, the mother of Mrs. Bumpass, who was the second child and eldest daughter of Isaac Webb and Harriet Dickens Webb.

In her early childhood the parents of Mrs. Bumpass moved from Mecklenburg County, Virginia, to Person County, North Carolina, and here in the simple, wholesome atmosphere of the farm life of ante bellum days, in the midst of a large family group of brothers and sisters, her childhood and young womanhood were passed. Though born in Virginia, she was through a long and useful life so identified with the religious, educational and social life of the state of her adoption that from one end of North Carolina to the other her name is honored and revered as that of few women has been.

Life in this excellent home was almost ideal, and could scarcely have been otherwise under the tender but firm guidance of such a father and mother. Not only were children of the household given the best obtainable advantages of that time, both in religious training and in educational opportunities, but domestic training was regarded as one of the prerequisites of useful living, and industry was one of the laws of the household. Like the model woman of the Scriptures, Mrs. Webb might have received the commendation: "She looketh well to the ways of her household, and eateth not the bread of idleness."

The head of the family was one of the best of men, enjoying the esteem and confidence of all with whom he was associated. His countenance was so illumined by his Christian character that one of the leading men of his day said of him: "If there is any truth in the human face, Isaac Webb is a good man." Always deeply interested in the moral and intellectual welfare of his community, many of his views were in advance of the sentiment of his day. In a time when nearly every family of position kept a decanter on the sideboard, and regarded it as a breach of hospitality not to offer liquor in some form to visitors in the home, Mr. Webb said to his wife:

"I fear some of our neighbors drop in a little oftener on account of the wine on our sideboard, and take more than is best for them." From that time these Christian people banished the tempter from their home, thus obeying the grand Pauline principle: "If meat make my brother to offend, I will eat no flesh while the world standeth."

Is it any wonder that with such heredity and such environment a daughter of that household should have developed a character of unswerving principle, always enlisted on the side of moral questions of her day and always exerting to the utmost her influence for the right?

As was to be expected Mrs. Bumpass was converted early in life. This great experience came to her at a camp-meeting in Person County at the age of fifteen, and soon after her conversion she was received into the Methodist Church by Rev. R. O. Burton, at Bethlehem, a church built mainly through the liberality of her father. It was not in accordance with her active earnest spirit to be an idler in her Master's vineyard, and she turned, as was her custom, to the duty nearest at hand, gathering into a Sunday school her younger brothers and sisters with other children of the neighborhood. She also gave religious instruction to the servants on her father's plantation, following a custom by no means rare in those days.

Mrs. Bumpass was fortunate in her educational advantages as in her home training. In childhood she attended a school in the family of her grandmother, Mrs. Amy Webb, under the instruction of Miss Caroline Patillo, a woman of fine culture and pronounced piety. Her last days in school were spent under the tutelage of Rev. D. G. Doak, a Presbyterian minister of Orange County, and a man of ripe scholarship. As a resident in his family and under his wise guidance she enjoyed advantages of mental training and discipline which tended greatly to broaden her mind and develop analytical power which she regarded as of special value and helpfulness when she was called to editorial work later in life.

Her school days finished, she herself became a teacher and spent four years teaching in two private schools in Granville County.

Thus glided by the active happy season of youth. But that event which marks an epoch in a woman's life, widening and deeping her happiness and influence if entered upon wisely and with a pure and holy love, was approaching to open to the young teacher a broader field of work as the companion of an itinerant preacher. An interesting and somewhat unique courtship is related among the family traditions. Though unusual, the method of the proposal was not entirely foreign to the spirit of the time nor out of harmony with the deeply spiritual nature of the lady herself.

The young aspirant for her favor was Rev. Sidney Bumpass, of the North Carolina Conference. This was no marriage made in haste to be repented at leisure, for Mr. Bumpass had met Fannie Webb while she was still a school girl. The first impression was made upon his mind when he was the examiner at a public oral examination, an ordeal much dreaded by youthful students of that day. The clear grasp of mind and poise of bearing of the school girl who answered so clearly and correctly the questions in natural philosophy and chemistry propounded by the scholarly young preacher, made an impression that never faded from his mind, but deepened as the years went by.

The object of his interest did not even guess his state of mind and heart until he determined to put the matter to the test by sending her a Reference Bible in which were some innocent looking little slips of white paper. On these slips were inscribed references to passages from the Second Epistle of John. These verses proved to be a declaration couched in these words: "The elder unto the elect lady whom I love in the truth for the truth's sake which dwelleth in me"; and "Now I beseech thee, lady, that we love one another." Was ever a marriage proposal proffered on a more lofty plane?

This being the first intimation of having awakened such a sentiment in the young man's heart she did not at first find a response in her own. However, as she pondered the words "for the truth's sake" she gradually realized that such a life companionship would conduce to her happiness through their very congeniality of religious sentiment. So it came to pass that in December, 1842, a happy marriage was consummated between Frances Moore Webb and Rev. Sidney Bumpass.

The young husband was at that time stationed in Raleigh, and here began the responsibilities that devolve upon the wife of a preacher. She proved herself equal to these new duties which were taken up with such sweetness and cheerfulness as ever characterized her in all the relations of life. After four years spent thus happily sharing the joys and sorrows, the lights and shadows of an itinerant preacher's life, she came to Greensboro, where Mr. Bumpass had been appointed presiding elder of that district in 1846.

Only a brief period of happiness in united service for this new field was vouchsafed to the devoted couple, but they proved a rich blessing to this community which they served together for five years and where Mrs. Bumpass continued to live during the long years of widowhood. In 1851, while attending Conference in Salisbury, Mr. Bumpass was called from labor here to his reward above. Crushed as was the heart of the wife 'neath this heavy blow, the child of God turned to her Heavenly Father as her refuge in this time of trouble, and relying on His sustaining grace, she returned to her home now darkened by the shadow of her great sorrow, taking up bravely the duties required at her hands in the care and training of her children, all of whom under her tender care and ministration of love grew to noble Christian manhood and womanhood and "rose up to call her blessed."

Among the tasks which seemed providentially placed in her hands and which she regarded as a sacred trust was the continuance of the publication of a religious newspaper, the first Methodist paper at that time in the state, which Mr. Bumpass had begun to publish a short time before his death under the title of "The Weekly Message." With some trepidation at entering upon a kind of work so unusual for woman in those days, she nevertheless complied with the known wish of her husband and took up the torch that had passed from his hand, trusting thereby to bring more of light and heart-warmth into a world that never has too much of either.

In this spirit, prompted by a desire for service and usefulness, she undertook this "labor of love," continuing it for twenty years, receiving from many sources assurance of the good she was doing with her pen.

Only after the North Carolina Advocate had appeared as the organ of the Methodist Church of North Carolina did Mrs. Bumpass discontinue in 1872 "The Weekly Message," which she had issued through so many years from her home, the printing and all mechanical details having been carried on under her supervision by young women trained and directed by her. This was no light task, but well and faithfully was it performed by this devoted woman, who never failed to answer the call of duty or an opportunity to do good.

After the discontinuance of "The Weekly Message" Mrs. Bumpass resumed an occupation in which she delighted in her earlier life, that of teaching, conducting in her own home for a number of years a prosperous day school, thus forging another link between herself and the community into which she brought much blessing through her beautiful Christian character and influence upon the young minds and hearts committed to her training.

The last years of this consecrated life were, if possible, enriched still further by an enlarged sphere of activity opened up to her through the Woman's Foreign Missionary Society which was inaugurated by the General Conference of the Southern Methodist Church in May, 1878. Mrs. Bumpass was the first corresponding secretary of the North Carolina Woman's Missionary Society and through this office she became a member of the Woman's Board of Missions. She filled this position most faithfully and acceptably until 1890, when on account of the division of the Conference she was elected to the same office in the Woman's Missionary Society of the Western North Carolina Conference. This relation to the woman's work of her beloved church she held with earnestness and zealous devotion until she "fell on sleep" May 8th, 1898.

The influence of such a life who can estimate? No life can be strong, gentle, pure and good without the world being better for it, without somebody being helped and comforted by the very existence of that goodness. How vast then must be the influence for good emanating from a character in which the purest and loftiest motives prevail over all that is low and earthborn; in which self is submerged in the greater good of humanity and the soul rises ever higher and higher on wings of aspiration toward the eternal source of purity and love.

Lucy H. Robertson.

J. HENRY SMITH

J. HENRY SMITH

1820 - 1897

The minister of the Gospel, like the doctor, the lawyer, and the teacher, is not what is technically known as a productive worker. He does not grow grain or vegetables or cotton, he does not make cloth or leather or iron; he does not manufacture garments or utensils or machinery. He is not a productive worker in the economic sense. And yet the most valuable member of any community is the true minister of the Gospel, because he is the representative of the spiritual ideal, he is the exponent of the highest things in life, the things that control the springs of action, the things that mould character, the things that determine the tone and trend of society and even the destiny of human souls. Therefore, the minister of gifts and consecration whose term of service runs through many years is rightly accorded a high place among the benefactors of his community. All this was signally illustrated in the life and work of Dr. Smith. He holds a unique position among the makers of Greensboro.

Jacob Henry Smith, the oldest son of Samuel Runckle Smith and Margaret Fuller, was born in Lexington, Rockbridge County, Va., August 13, 1820, and died in Greensboro, Guilford County, N. C., November 22, 1897. He was one of seven children, four of whom grew to manhood. Two, Alphonso and Charles, died in the Confederate service, and a third, Samuel Cunningham Smith, father of Professor W. C. Smith, now dean of the North Carolina College for Women, was for many years a teacher in Greensboro. At an early age Jacob Henry Smith joined the Presbyterian Church of Lexington, then under the pastorate of Dr. George A. Baxter —the church in which Stonewall Jackson was later a deacon.

He was prepared for college in his native town, and graduated with high distinction from Washington College— now Washington and Lee University—June 29, 1843. He had intended to practice law and for several years had devoted himself ardently to the study of it; but a sermon preached at this time by Dr. Archibald Alexander decided him in favor of the ministry. In the fall of 1843 he entered Union Theological Seminary in Virginia (then at Hampden-Sidney, now at Richmond), and taking the full course received his certificate in 1846. The most distinguished of his classmates in the seminary, the late Dr. Robert L. Dabney, pre-eminent as a theologian, said: ''It was difficult for me to avoid envying his gifts and habits as a student. He was compact in build, with perfect vigor and health, of a cordial and joyous temperament, with methodical habits, and the greatest capacity for labor. His classmates said that he studied fourteen solid hours out of the twenty-four. Hence his preparations were uniformly perfect, and his recitations and other exercises of the first grade.''

He was licensed August 24, 1846, by Lexington Presbytery and transferred to West Hanover Presbytery. In the following month he took charge of the church at Pittsylvania Court House, Va., and was ordained and installed there July 31, 1847. In 1850 he became principal and professor of Latin and Greek in Samuel Davies Institute, Halifax County, Va., and conducted the institution with marked success until 1854. During this period there were many indications of his growing favor with the church, his services being sought by congregations in Chicago, Richmond, Petersburg, Danville, Greensboro, and Charlottesville—indeed, as has been said, such overtures were frequent and urgent all through his life. Accepting the call to Charlottesville he preached there until 1859. One of the results of his ministry there was the conversion of a young man from New York by the name of Charles A. Briggs, who was then a student at the University of Virginia and who afterwards became widely known as a Biblical scholar and as the principal figure in a noted ecclesiastical trial. Another was the erection of a more spacious and commodious church for his congregation. Rev. Paul Whitehead, D. D., who was then pastor of the Methodist Church in Charlottesville, and who became one of Dr. Smith's intimate and life-long friends, has given a description of a Literary-Theological Club then flourishing in the town which had been organized largely through the influence of Dr. John A. Broadus and Dr. Smith and which included in its membership such men as James C. Southall, Judge Egbert R. Watson, Rev. William Dinwiddie, Mr. J. A. Latané (afterwards Bishop of the Reformed Episco-

pal Church) and others, and he says that in their discussions
Dr. Smith took a prominent part, he and Dr. Broadus and
Mr. Southall being "the life and glory of the exercises."

The call to Greensboro was renewed in 1859, and he began
his work there on the 20th of April of that year. From the
time of his coming the church grew steadily and rapidly. Two
other congregations were colonized from its membership and
are now large and flourishing organizations. The old house
of worship was eventually outgrown and in 1890 the present
attractive building was erected. A specially notable result
of his pastorate in Greensboro is that ten of the members of his
church became Presbyterian ministers.

Dr. Smith's activities were not confined to his own congregation and community. Being a powerful evangelistic
preacher he was often called on to conduct protracted services in destitute districts or in established churches needing
revival services. He was also an active and influential pres-
byter in the church courts. His counsel always carried
weight in Presbytery, Synod, or General Assembly. On June
16, 1861, shortly after the beginning of the War between the
States, he presented a paper in Orange Presbytery on the
"reported action of the General Assembly in relation to the
political crisis in the country." Dr. D. I. Craig, historian of
the Synod of North Carolina, says that the outcome of that
paper was one of the first leading and official steps, if not the
very first, towards the organization of the Southern General
Assembly. Dr. Smith headed important committees in the
Assemblies of 1870 at Louisville, and in 1888 at Baltimore, and
was unanimously selected by the Assembly of 1896 as chairman of the committee to prepare the program for the celebration at Charlotte, N. C., in 1897, of the two hundred
and fiftieth anniversary of the Westminster Assembly of
Divines—an honor all the more notable because he was not a
member of the Assembly that appointed him. The preparation of this program was his last official service to the church
at large. It was a matter of deep regret to all who attended
the celebration that failing health prevented Dr. Smith himself from being present.

He rendered valuable service to the cause of Christian
education as a member for many years of the Board of Directors of Davidson College, the largest of our Southern Pres-

byterian colleges, and as a member of the Board of Directors of Union Theological Seminary, the largest of our Southern Presbyterian seminaries.

Twice he received from institutions of learning the honorary degree of Doctor of Divinity, first from Hampden-Sidney College in 1872, and again from the University of North Carolina in 1877. How worthily the degree was bestowed in his case is well indicated by the estimate of his attainments expressed by the greatest of our Southern theologians: ''In theological learning he was an accurate scholar; in the Biblical languages an accomplished exegete. He was not only a profound theologian but kept abreast with the general literature of the day.''

The first time I ever saw Dr. Smith, as I have stated elsewhere*, was in a bookstore in my native town, Charlotte, N. C. If I had never seen him again I should have carried with me through life the memory of that compact frame with its decided and vigorous movements, the deep, rich tones of his voice, his genial and hearty greeting of the proprietor as he asked where the latest books were kept, and the intelligent sureness and authority of his manner as with shrewd and racy comments he took down and ran through with his eye one volume after another. Having some taste for reading myself, though then quite ignorant of the particular books he was handling, I felt drawn to a man who was evidently so much at home among books and lingered near him to hear his remarks, though I did not venture to speak to him, being only a lad of some thirteen years and very shy. He remained only a few minutes, but quite long enough to impress me with the fact that this was no ordinary man. I wished he had stayed longer.

It was therefore with uncommon pleasure that a few years later when I was a student at Davidson College I saw this same man walk up the aisle of the chapel one Sunday with his neat black sermon case under his arm and take his place reverently in the pulpit. I settled myself in the pew, confident we were going to hear something good, but thinking more perhaps, of the pleasure it would give me to listen to the

* See page 80 of In Memoriam: Rev. J. Henry Smith, D. D., a memorial volume prepared by the family and printed by the John Murphy Company, Baltimore, Md.

play of that strong and flexible voice, and of the vigor of
thought and the literary finish which must characterize
the sermons of such a man as I had heard talking in that
bookstore, than of the truth itself which he was commissioned
to deliver to us as an ambassador of Christ. That did not
last long, however, after he began. The voice did indeed roll
in rich volume through the house, crashing almost like artillery
in impassioned passages and seeming to shake the building;
and the style had indeed that unmistakable flavor of good
reading which results only from years of familiarity with the
master minds of the race. But attention to these things soon
gave place to absorbed interest in the subject itself, ''Turning
points in life.'' I can still see his hand follow with thumb
and forefinger the edge of the pulpit in a straight line till
it reached the corner and then turn sharply at right angles
to its former course. I can still hear the earnest tones
making the application to turning points in life. Hundreds
of sermons have faded from my memory. That one stands
out like a promontory on a flat and sandy shore. Perhaps
nothing that I could set down here would give a more vivid
impression of the force of his personality and the effectiveness
of his preaching. When I became a student in the seminary
I saw him every spring and from time to time heard him
preach or make addresses, being always struck with the thor-
oughness of his preparation, the richness of his matter, and
his soulful manner of speaking. It gave one a rare sense of
satisfaction to see him preside over public exercises as president of the board of directors; everything was done with so
much strength and fitness. None of the young men who
received from his hand their diplomas can ever forget the
earnest and tender words with which he sent them forth to
preach the everlasting gospel.

In the social circle his conversation flowed like a sparkling
stream, with innocent humor breaking over it ever and anon
like gleams of sunlight. He was a remarkable raconteur. I
have heard him entertain a group of gentlemen for hours
while riding in a lumbering hack over muddy roads and
through pouring rain. Nothing could dash the spirits of a
crowd listening to those irresistible stories, told as only he
could tell them—of the man who pronounced ''patriarchs''
partridges and who, the narrator said, was *making game* of

sacred things; of the ignorant preacher who read "badgers' skins" *beggars' skins* and commented on the severity of the old dispensation as compared with the new, saying that when a poor man died now he was given decent Christian burial, but then, whenever a beggar died, *they slapped his skin on the tabernacle;* of the darkey arraigned for stealing chickens, whom the judge asked if he didn't know it was a "reprehensible offense," and who replied that he "thought it wuz a plank fence, sah, but I found out it wuz a bob-wire, sah!"; of the colored woman whose infant he baptized and who, when asked what name he was to give the child, almost paralyzed him with the grave answer, "General Beauregard!"; of the ludicrous accidents which befell him and Dr. Pharr, or Mr. Doll, when they were preaching together, such as his attempt to raise the tune of "Blow ye the trumpet, blow," when, just as he uttered the first word "Blow," he inadvertently stepped off the high platform and found himself pitching forward with long strides down the aisle towards the door to keep from falling; of the Scotchman who wished to be made an elder, and when asked about his qualifications, said: "No, he could not pray in public, nor make pastoral visits to the afflicted," and so on, and when pressed to name his special qualification, said he could "raise an objection." The woods rang with unrestrained laughter—trustees, students, drivers, all alike— under the spell of his humor. Then, it might be, in a few moments, all would be moved well-nigh to tears as he related the story of the Scotch girl who applied for admission into the church, and, awed by the presence of the session, could give no clear answers to their questions, and who, as she withdrew, disappointed, found her voice at the door and said, "I canna talk for Jesus, but I cou'd die for him," and was immediately recalled and received into the communion of the church.

There was a wealth of affection in his nature. He specially loved children and they loved him. I recall the deep satisfaction with which he related the incident of his little grandson whose mother was trying to give him some idea of the happiness of heaven, and the little fellow asked, "Is it as nice as Dan'pa's?" And truly, there were few places this side of heaven that were "as nice as Dan'pa's." Dr. Smith was signally blessed in his home life: a gentle, wise, and godly wife, fully identified with him in all his work, and a troop of exceptionally active and gifted boys and girls, each of whom became early in life, under the influence of that home and pulpit, an intelligent, earnest and fruitful Christian— in nothing was God's goodness to him more manifest than in his family relations. He told me once that when one of his sons was about grown he heard him one afternoon through the open window of his study, as the youth passed through the yard towards the house, decline a companion's invitation to meet him uptown that night, adding that "he did not know how the streets of Greensboro looked by lamp light till he was eighteen years old." "Yes," said the listening and pleased father to himself, "and that's the reason you are what you are today." One of the secrets of his phenomenal success in bringing up such a family of sons and daughters was that he and Mrs. Smith made their own home the most attractive place to them in all the world. There was no temptation to go elsewhere. And those boys enjoyed all boyish things. They excelled in all games. They skated and fished and hunted and hiked, Dr. Smith himself sometimes going with them on their tramps through the woods and their camping trips to the mountains.

He was twice married: On March 15, 1848, to Miss Catherine Malvina Miller, daughter of Hon. Thomas Miller, of Powhatan County, Va. She died June 9, 1854. And on January 8, 1857, to Miss Mary Kelly Watson, daughter of Judge Egbert R. Watson, of Charlottesville, Va., who survives him. He left two daughters, Mrs. L. Richardson and Mrs. R. G. Vaughn, both residents of Greensboro; and five sons, Rev. Samuel M. Smith, D. D., who at the time of his death on January 10, 1910, was pastor of the First Presbyterian Church of Columbia, S. C.; Dr. Henry Louis Smith, President of Washington and Lee University, Lexington, Va.; Rev. Egbert W. Smith, D. D., Executive Secretary of the General Assembly's Committee of Foreign Missions, Nashville, Tenn.; Dr. C. Alphonso Smith, head of the Department of English in the United States Naval Academy, Annapolis, Md.; and Rev. Hay Watson Smith, D. D., pastor of the Second Presbyterian Church of Little Rock, Ark. One daughter, Elizabeth Clark, died in infancy, June 14, 1854; and one son, Norris Kelly, at the age of seven, November 23, 1882.

I have tried in this sketch to indicate various phases of Dr. Smith's character and work. He was, as has been said, not only a man of great native ability, wide, profound, and elegant scholarship, untiring industry, wise, loving and patient as a pastor, but more than this and above all he was a man of spiritual power. He had the force and fervor that come only from the unction of the Holy One. A thoughtful minister who knew him intimately for years has said he would rather have Dr. Smith's life work behind him than that of any man he had ever known. And where, indeed, could a more enviable work be found or one richer in benefit to the community in which he lived? His warm and tender sympathy with suffering made him an angel of God to the afflicted, his own deep experience of divine grace teaching him what to say for their comfort and making him a veritable Barnabas to the bereaved, the sick, and the dying. His firm grasp of the great doctrines of Scripture, his wide experience as teacher, pastor, counselor and evangelist, his robust preaching, kept fresh and rich to the very end by his diligence as a student, all combined to make him one of the most valuable community builders in the history of Greensboro and indeed one of the most notable benefactors of the state at large—for it must be remembered that he preached to a larger number of thoughtful and eminent public men than any other pastor that has ever lived in North Carolina, his church being for years the state's chief nursery of pure and learned lawyers, judges and governors. As we think of the thousands who were converted under his ministry and of the vast reach of his influence, and of the reward upon which he has entered, the Scripture that comes to mind is this: "They that be teachers shall shine as the brightness of the firmament; and they that turn many to righteousness as the stars for ever and ever."

WALTER W. MOORE.

ALEXANDER PERRY ECKEL

ALEXANDER PERRY ECKEL
1821 - 1906

The stage coach arriving in the little town of Greensboro one day in 1845, brought among its passengers a youth destined to devote to the life of the village his energy and love for more than half a century.

As was the custom, when the coach neared the village, the driver blew loudly on his horn, one blast for each passenger that the proprietor of the hostelry might know how many guests to expect.

Thus entered into the life of Greensboro Alexander Perry Eckel, who was of German descent, born in Jefferson County, Tenn., January 10, 1821. His ancestors came to the United States about the close of the Revolutionary War, landed in Baltimore, Maryland, and from there went forth locating in different parts of the country.

In childhood Alexander Eckel moved to Georgetown, now a part of Washington, D. C., where his early youth was spent. From Georgetown he came to Greensboro and was for sixty-two years one of her devoted and loyal sons. He was married in 1847 to Mary Hill, daughter of Matilda Boyd Hill and Wilson S. Hill, and to this union were born Matilda Hill (Mrs. M. H. Alford) and Charles Eugene, both now living in Greensboro. The Eckel home was located on a wooded knoll of ten acres, southeast corner of Washington and Davie Streets. A long curved walk of brick led up to the house, which was of Italian architecture, built in brick and stucco. Many roses bordered the walk. Magnolias and other ornamental trees interspersed with varied flower beds made the place known as one of the beauty spots of old Greensboro. It was called ''Rose Villa.''

In the troubled days of the sixties there came to Greensboro many interesting visitors and thrilling experiences. Among these was the visit of Commodore Forrest, of the Southern Navy, a man well past middle life, accompanied by his secretary, W. H. Chase. He asked permission to remain a few days as guest in the home of A. P. Eckel, then mayor of the town. His stay lengthened into two weeks and on leaving he gave his host as souvenir a southern sword, now treasured by the family.

Next came two members of the Confederate cabinet, whose mission was one of secret importance. When guests of only a few days, these officers confided to the host that they had in their possession gold belonging to the Confederacy which they wished to secrete, knowing they were closely followed by the Federal army. They deemed his private grounds studded with trees, shrubbery and flowers, a most suitable hiding place.

In the still hours of the night host and guests crept stealthily from the house, and deep at the foot of an old post which was covered with a heavy mantle of southern yellow jessamine, they buried a part of the South's treasure. None too soon was this commission performed, for with the coming day, a messenger brought the news of the approach of Federal cavalry, and hurriedly, but quietly, the guests took their departure.

Under the command of General Kilpatrick came the Federal soldiers. A knock at the door, and the Union officer sent in his card to the lady of the house. In a very courteous but decided way the General said: ''I wish this house for my headquarters.'' The hostess, belonging to the old school that was accustomed to hearing, ''By your leave,'' was very curt to the intruder and at once sent for her husband. He realized there was nothing to do but acquiesce; so the General and his staff occupied the house, leaving only two rooms for the use of the family, while on the ten-acre lawn the soldiers pitched their tents. General Kilpatrick made himself very agreeable, sending from his private table many delicacies to the family, and provided the lady of the house with her favorite beverage, genuine coffee.

When leaving he presented the young son of the family with a frolicsome colt of his beautiful thoroughbred saddler. Also when some of the negroes threatened to leave, saying ''the Yankees had come to free them,'' he ordered them to remain. He continued his camp several weeks then, just before leaving, without permission or explanation, he proceeded to have the grounds searched for hidden valuables. With quaking hearts the family watched the soldiers probe the ground in many places, and diligently search for treasure, but the fragrant gold of the yellow jessamine and the gold buried at its feet were undisturbed. After many months, when the south had laid down its arms, there came in code form telegraph messages concerning the buried treasure. The bags of gold were removed from their secure resting place and borne by express to the impoverished treasury of the Confederacy.

Few men were more prominently identified with the early history of Greensboro than was Mr. Eckel, known and loved as "Squire Eckel." He was active in every public enterprise and ever progressive. Among other things he was promoter of the first gas plant in Greensboro. Associated with him were the late Cyrus P. Mendenhall, Peter Adams and Charles Shober. He was one of the organizers and stockholders of the railroad to Winston or old Salem.

The grounds of Rose Villa and the beautiful grove surrounding the adjacent home of the Hon. Ralph Gorrell were both crossed by the first train that disturbed the quiet of the peaceful village of Greensboro, over what is now the Southern Railroad.

When Greensboro first felt the need of a mayor, before it had been chartered as a town, it was A. P. Eckel who was called to fill this place of honor, the first mayor of Greensboro. After Greensboro was incorporated he served twice again as mayor, thus directing the town's affairs before the War Between the States and twice afterwards, the last date being 1881. For more than forty years he was justice of the peace, a distinction that has probably not been equalled in the state. What he did was an open book; justice and fair dealing was his motto. His wisdom, his inborn sense of honor, and his unswerving integrity fitted him for a most capable public officer.

Like many another man noted for quiet and modest bearing, he had a record of personal courage of very high order. While Greensboro, with the rest of the South, was facing grave problems of reconstruction, an article, insulting the whole state, was published in a neighboring town. Greensboro was notified of this action through the Patriot, and an indignation meeting of citizens promptly followed.

The chairman selected for this meeting was A. P. Eckel, who held no municipal office then (for Greensboro was under military rule with leaders of General Canby's appointment), but he did hold on that trying day the absolute confidence of his town.

In the business enterprises of Greensboro Mr. Eckel took an active interest, being associated with W. C. Porter in the drug business, known as Porter and Eckel; also establishing what was probably the first jewelry store of Greensboro. In personal habits he was quiet, unassuming and remarkably methodical, of strong mind and steady purpose, as honest and upright as any citizen whose long life and usefulness has blessed our town. His extreme gentleness and courtesy marked him as a true gentleman of the old school. After eighty-six years of life and service he passed from us December 17th, 1906.

BESSIE ALFORD BALLANCE.

Robert Paine Dick

ROBERT PAINE DICK

1823 - 1898

Robert Paine Dick, the son of Judge John McClintock Dick (a sketch of whose life appears in this volume) and Parthenia (Williamson) Dick, was born in Greensboro, on October 5th, 1823.

He was prepared for college at the well known Caldwell Institute, and entered the University of North Carolina in 1840, from which he was graduated with second honors in 1843.

Returning home, he spent the next two years studying law under his father and Mr. George C. Mendenhall, a noted practitioner of that day. Obtaining his law license in 1845, he began practice in Wentworth and, as was the custom of those times, "rode the circuit" throughout several adjoining counties.

June 27th, 1848, he married Mary Eloise Adams, daughter of George Adams, of Pittsylvania County, Virginia, and moved back to Greensboro, which was thereafter his home until his death.

Like most young lawyers of those days, he took an active part in politics, and being an orator of exceptional natural ability, and a close student of public affairs, soon acquired as a speaker a reputation unusual for one of his age, being particularly gifted in the field of joint debate.

In the political division between the Whigs and the Democracy, he was an ardent Democrat; was a delegate to the National Democratic Convention of 1852, and made an active canvass of the state for its nominee.

In the spring of 1853, though only twenty-nine years of age, he was appointed United States District Attorney for the entire state, an office much sought by the members of the bar, and retained that office until February, 1861, when in view of the fast approaching political storm, he resigned to give himself greater freedom of action in any course he might see fit to take.

Always opposed to secession, but believing strongly in a large measure of states rights within the union, as a delegate to the National Democratic Convention, which met in Charleston, in 1860, he cast the vote which gave Douglas a majority of that convention, and was the only delegate from North Carolina who did not join the seceding minority which nominated Breckenridge.

In the spring of 1861, when a convention was called for the purpose of passing the ordinance of secession he was a candidate from Guilford County on a pronounced anti-secession platform and was elected with but little opposition. In the convention he opposed secession, but when the ordinance was finally passed, decided to accept the inevitable and help his state as best he could.

During the Civil War he was for a time a member of the Council of State, and together with Governor Vance, bitterly opposed what he regarded as the continual encroachments of the Confederate Government on the rights of the state.

He was never in the army, but so far as his official duties permitted, spent his time and energies in caring for the wounded soldiers in the various hospitals.

In 1864 he was elected State Senator from Guilford County, and seeing the futility of further resistance and useless bloodshed, joined that group in the legislature which favored the making of the best possible terms of peace.

In the spring of 1865, upon the collapse of the Confederacy, he, together with five other leading citizens of the state, was called to Washington by President Johnson to confer as to the best means of restoring the state to its former position in the Union. In this conference he, together with the majority of the delegation, took the position that the state being still in the Union, was entitled to all its former rights, and advised the restoration of its old constitution and government with certain necessary amendments, together with a general amnesty for all who had adhered to the Confederacy. This plan, though it had in substance been formerly approved by President Lincoln, was rejected by Johnson.

The President, however, offered Mr. Dick the position of United States District Judge for North Carolina, and a commission dated May 29th, 1865, was actually signed by the President and sent to him. The temptation was great. His slaves were free. His property was largely swept away. But he declined the office when he found that to accept it he would be obliged to take the "test oath" that he had never aided or abetted the Confederacy. The authorities in Washington ruled that never having held office, either civil or military, under the Confederate Government, he was eligible, but he still declined, saying that in a matter of conscience no one but himself had the right to decide.

He was a member of the State Convention of 1865 called by President Johnson and as such helped to formulate a new constitution and earnestly advocated the adoption of the measure known as the Howard Amendment, as he believed it contained the best terms that could be got from the National Congress. These measures were, however, rejected by a vote of the people, and the period known as "reconstruction" followed.

Prior to the Civil War Mr. Dick had been a Democrat in opposition to the Whigs. During the war there was a realignment in politics and Mr. Dick acted with the Conservative party of which Governor Vance was the leader. In 1867 there was another political realignment, and Mr. Dick, in company with a large number of other men who originally opposed secession but followed their state, assisted in the organization of the Republican party, of which he was ever afterwards a member, but by no means a violent partisan.

In April, 1868, he was elected an Associate Justice of the State Supreme Court and held that office until 1872. During these four years, perhaps the most trying through which our State Supreme Court ever passed, he took a prominent part in deciding many difficult and delicate questions growing out of the new constitution, the new code of civil procedure and the troublesome times of reconstruction.

The test oath having been abolished and the state divided into two Federal Judicial Districts, he was, while still a member of the State Supreme Court, on June 7th, 1872, appointed by President Grant Judge of the United States District Court for the Western District of North Carolina and held that position until his death.

In 1878, in conjunction with Judge John H. Dillard, he founded the Greensboro Law School, generally known among the lawyers of the state as the "Dick and Dillard Law

School'', and after the death of Judge Dillard continued it alone until shortly before his death. From this law school about three hundred students successfully passed their bar examination.

In early life Judge Dick became a member of the First Presbyterian Church and continued that membership until his death, for many years serving as superintendent of the Sunday school and as a ruling elder.

Always a close student, he made a life-long study of the Bible, not only as the inspired book of religion, but also from the viewpoint of history and literature and on this subject delivered a number of lectures before religious gatherings and at the University and other educational institutions. His lectures, afterwards printed in essay form, on ''Hebrew Poetry'' were perhaps the best known.

Though strong in his own convictions and firm and outspoken in expression, he was singularly free from intolerance and hatred, fully recognized the right of others to differ with him, as he claimed the right to his own opinions, and passed through the most stormy period of the history of our state with the respect of all and the personal friendship of those who differed with him in political and economic measures to an extent rarely equaled by men prominently before the public.

His mind was of an unusual character. Facts were not sufficient. There must be a reason for everything. He was fond of telling his law students that ''order was heaven's first law'', and though himself a constant reader of both legal and general subjects, often said that no amount of undigested information could take the place of clear and serious thinking. A natural gift, coupled with life-long mental discipline, gave his mind a power of absorption and analysis rarely equaled. A former Governor of North Carolina is authority for the statement that Judge Dick was the only man he had ever seen who could sit on the bench and at the same time read a law book and listen to a lawyer making an argument without either in the slightest distracting his full attention from the other.

About six months before his death, in his seventy-fifth year, failing health compelled him to retire from the bench and wait patiently for the end that he knew could not be far off, but which he did not fear.

Surrounded by his pastor, his wife, his five children and a number of grandchildren, he sank peacefully to sleep on September 12th, 1898.

Robert Dick Douglas.

MINNA RAVEN HILDESHEIMER

MINNA RAVEN HILDESHEIMER
1823 - 1901

A hundred years before this record there was born in the Province of Hanover, Germany, Minna Raven, a child dowered with a golden voice who, in coming years, was to bring a blessed ministry of music to the far distant village of Greensboro.

The Raven family were of gentle birth and superior culture. The three sons of the household became professional men of high rank in their day and the three daughters were educated for life work as teachers.

As a child the gifted Minna gave joy in the home by her songs. When an artist friend visited her parents she gladly obeyed the usual call to sing for a guest and the sweet German ballad was so exquisitely rendered that the great singer wept for joy, and kissing the surprised little one, she said: "Child you can bring the world to your feet with that voice."

In the years which followed every possible advantage in that land of trained musicians was provided to develop the young girl's talent, one of her instructors for a long period being Herr Klein, father of Oscar Bruno Klein, famous organist and composer, late of New York City. She became a brilliant concert and church singer, appearing many times in public in Germany during her girlhood. Her brothers, much older than herself, had already attained professional success and they united in opposing a life on the stage for their sister. For this reason she refused overtures from various opera managements, the natural result of her wonderful talent and great early success.

In 1852, Bertha Raven, who had married August Brockmann, sailed with her husband to make a home in new America, and her sister Minna, at twenty-nine, went with them. They were city people, but did not choose a city home in the new world, coming instead to the little town of Asheboro, North Carolina. Here there was a girl's academy, for which the singer was engaged as voice teacher, but very soon a rival school with a wider field was bidding earnestly for her services.

Edgeworth Seminary in Greensboro, founded by Governor John M. Morehead in 1840, with highly trained specialists from Europe in charge of art, music and language departments, was at that time drawing patronage from the entire south. Its founder and its able principal, Richard Sterling, were ever on the alert to strengthen an already exceptional faculty, and they succeeded in bringing Miss Raven to Greensboro as Edgeworth's voice teacher under Heinreich Schneider, a musical director highly esteemed in the seminary and also in the village.

Beautiful for situation as well as architecture, this seminary, now known only in Edgeworth Street, was then the pride of the town. Its campus, with shrubbery, rose bowers and many shade trees, extended from a point just west of Eugene Street to join the equally beautiful grounds of Greensboro College at the present intersection of Cedar, the two schools thus uniting to form a spacious park two blocks deep on the southern side of West Market, unbroken from Eugene to Mendenhall.

Directly south of Edgeworth stood stately Blandwood, the home of its generous founder, while just beyond the western boundary of Greensboro College, as an equally appropriate garrison, lived Peter Doub, early apostle of his faith in North Carolina, and Frances Webb Bumpass, "editress", then publishing, with a press operated in her own home, "The Weekly Message", state organ of the Methodist Episcopal Church.

Edgeworth was not at any time, we are told, a financial success. It seemed that Governor Morehead did not expect it to be. Five daughters of his own had turned his thoughts to the need of higher educational facilities for southern girls and he determined to build this seminary, "not for money", wrote one of his teachers, "but as a home for gentlewomen desiring to do earnest literary work."

For seven years Miss Raven was a vital factor in Edgeworth's training for southern girls, her influence for good music in the village growing stronger with each year.

One pipe organ only was the portion of Greensboro in that day. The organ had belonged to the Presbyterian church since 1849, and this congregation was thereby enabled to secure organists in the successive musical directors of both schools.   Thus the little village of the fifties was enriched by musical advantages of high order for the day.   Its daughters had training supplied by musical faculties of two schools. There was a glee club for the young people, through the generosity of Mr. Schneider and his colleague, Prof. Kern, of Greensboro College, and one pipe organ, with Mr. Schneider as organist, and Miss Raven's wonderful voice to lead his choir.

The singer's work for Edgeworth ended with her marriage just before the Civil War to Joseph Hildesheimer, a merchant in the town at that time.   Fortunately, however, for a people already indebted to her training, she resumed her work in private classes, teaching both vocal and instrumental music almost to the close of her long life.   Greensboro girls of two generations were thus privileged to be her pupils.

Mrs. J. E. Logan, to whom this paper is indebted for much of its data, knew Miss Raven perhaps best of all.   As Frances Sloan, she attended in childhood Edgeworth's primary school, which was taught in the building known in story as "Gum Castle".   Later she had a full course in the seminary, graduating—as maidens then were wont to do—at the early age of seventeen.   Her name is prominent in solo parts on the Edgeworth concert programs to be found in the files of the Greensboro Patriot, and it is known that in girlhood she often served her friend and instructor as substitute choir leader.

But neither Mrs. Logan nor her comrades among older women of the south today can recall their teacher in the face of the young concert singer, for it is a picture before their time.   Hundreds of us do remember with deep affection a gentle motherly face under a black lace headdress, a sweet voice with the accent of her Fatherland, unfailing patience and the high standards of a true teacher content with nothing less than the best for her pupils.

When called to her reward in December, 1901, the editor of a local paper wrote: "The greater part of her life has been spent in our midst and she has labored unceasingly to elevate the musical taste of our people.   Surely a life spent in the sweetest of arts is all the better fitted for the harmonies of Heaven.''

Soon after Edgeworth secured Miss Raven for its faculty the Brockmanns also moved to Greensboro, citizens of a sterling type always welcome in such a community.

Having no children of her own the aunt became a second mother to all her sister's sons and daughters and delighted in giving both inspiration and training to the three who chose her own profession: Prof. Ernest Brockmann, for twenty-five years Director of Music in the Methodist College of Columbia, S. C., Miss Laura Brockmann, now living in Lakeland, Fla., remembered and loved for her long service as organist and teacher in Greensboro and the State Normal College, and Prof. C. J. Brockmann, a leader in the establishment of orchestral music for both town and college.

Generous musicians have often given and are still giving unselfish service to Greensboro. The first of the long line we now know to have been Minna Raven Hildesheimer, golden voiced singer of the fifties. She did not ''bring the world to her feet'' as the great artist foretold. Instead she turned away from the great world's call, and when her lot was cast in a secluded village she won both love and gratitude from its people for the joy bestowed by her music.

We write her ''As one who loved her fellow men.''

BETTIE D. CALDWELL.

LETITIA HARPER WALKER

LETITIA HARPER WALKER

1823 - 1908

To a few now living, this article will recall some memories of a delightful and joyous past. And how pleasant it is to be thus reminded of the days when every incident is a priceless possession.

Mrs. Letitia Walker, the subject of this sketch, was the eldest child of Gov. John Motley Morehead and his wife Eliza Lindsay, to whom she was born at old Martinsville, in Guilford County, on September 26th, 1823. The site is now the Guilford Battle Ground. She was educated at Greensboro and Warrenton, N. C. On May 31st, 1848, she was united in marriage to William Richmond Walker, and by this union they were blessed with three children, Eliza Lindsay (or Lily as she was called), John and William Richmond, Jr.

Mrs. Walker lived a long and useful life, being more than 84 years of age at the time of her death, January 2nd, 1908. In 1855 she had the misfortune to lose her husband, and with her three young children continued her residence at her old home in Greensboro until 1875 when she went to Leaksville, North Carolina, to live with her son John. After his death she kept her home there with her son William and his wife, Minnie Faucette Walker. So with this brief interval her entire life was spent in her native county of Guilford in the town of Greensboro. It was here she spent the four years of the War Between the States, where as her timid and invalided mother's chief aid she was mistress of Blandwood and scintillated and radiated to friend and foe the splendors of the true southern woman and her home of that day.

Mrs. Walker was an extraordinary woman, distinguished by a tall figure, a firm carriage and an impressive and dignified bearing. She was gifted with intellectual qualities which elevated her in a striking manner above most of her sex of that day. Her life and nature were filled with benevolence, yet possessed of nerve and fortitude. Her name was spoken with gratitude by the poor and suffering. The children of the mill villages were ever on her sympathetic heart and mind, and for years she taught them in her home in the winter evenings the rudiments of an early education, the use of tooth brushes, soap and water and other sanitary methods of which they knew nothing.

She was instrumental in the erection of the First Presbyterian Church of her community and her pastor, Rev. W. T. Doggett, said of her in his "In Memoriam": "Those who knew her best and loved her most saw in the evening shadows the clearer splendors of those Gospel graces which enriched and adorned her character."

It is a source of sorrow and regret that one so gifted, so resourceful and so active should have to come to an end and lie idle forever. Again Mr. Doggett says: "Viewed from all its relations Mrs. Walker's life was the symmetrically developed—the well rounded—the beautiful life. It was beautiful in its simplicity. Of high social rank with many natural talents enlarged and beautified by education and association with the most cultured, she, with simple grace, adapted herself to every class and condition of life so that even the illiterate and obscure received and heard her gladly, while the more favored sought and enjoyed her society."

"Her conduct everywhere commended simplicity as a charming grace, and proved her power to have and to hold the entrance to the heart's life and needs." Among the many jewels in her crown of female excellencies and achievements the crowning work of Mrs. Walker's life, after the church she established, was her fifty years of real patriotic service at Mount Vernon, where the green banks and broad crystal waters of the Potomac were an inspiration to that Association to perpetuate the wonderful deeds and keep alive the memories of George and Martha Washington, the "Father" and "Mother" of this great republic.

In 1859 she was chosen by Miss Pamela Cunningham, of South Carolina, chairman of the "Mt. Vernon Ladies' Association of the Union" to represent the state of North Carolina as Vice-Regent; and so for fifty years she gave it her best thoughts and heartiest help at all times and in every effort was a great support to the Association. Her memory is among the most cherished and honored of all the notable women who met at Mt. Vernon every year.

Aunt Lettie—as all the girls in the family called her—was ever ready to chaperon them at Chapel Hill, and tell them the hows and whys and ins and outs of the different problems of the first season at "The Hill", where they found nothing but thrills and throbs of joy and gratitude for being alive. I might go on ad-infinitum and tell of her various talents as an artist, (some of her beautiful paintings are still possessed by descendants now in Greensboro) and of the landscape gardening still to be seen at "Old Blandwood", where she ordered and directed the laying out of the grounds and planting of evergreens and shrubs.

Mrs. Walker's mother, naturally a timid and shrinking woman, gradually allowed this gifted daughter to bear the social burdens of the home, as well as the household cares; and one of her nieces, Mrs. Johnston, of Alabama, in a recent letter, told of the lovely pictures she cut on melon rinds, more wonderful to her childish mind than her oil paintings; the marvelous cakes for the "marriage supper", the bowls of quivering jelly, and billowing mounds of "silly bub", the "piece de resistance", the "bride's cake" covered with wreaths of flowers and fret-work made of icing that flowed from her paper tube, all topped off by the miniature bride of Dan Cupid.

Realizing that she was not quite so beautiful as her four lovely sisters (Mrs. Avery, Mrs. Patterson, Mrs. Evans and Mrs. Gray), Mrs. Walker determined to make herself the most attractive in mental attainments. She was her father's helper in many ways and was thus thrown in close contact with the most distinguished men and women of that day.

Being a gifted raconteur, these men and women lived again as she painted in vivid words the pictures of the past—"Even when years said she was old" her heart was kept young, fragrant and fresh as the morn with the sympathy and interest and loving tenderness so strong in her youth and most beautiful was this life in its closing—"even as the sunset is the most beautiful part of the day".

MRS. JOS. M. MOREHEAD.

Memorial for Mrs. Walker published in 1908 report of Mount Vernon Ladies' Association of the Union:

"Beloved she was of the Heavenly Father who richly endowed her with the heavenly gifts of sympathy, love, purity, patience and intellect, a winning grace, an unfailing judgment and simplicity and integrity of character as rare as they are beautiful.

"He gave her also the blessing of a long life whereby her example should elevate all who came within her influence, teaching and transmitting to each and all a portion of these God-bestowed virtues, and finally without pain, in the fullness and ripeness of her faculties He called her away as she slept on the New Year's night, a call so quiet, so gentle, so secret in the darkness of the night, that she alone heard and answered the call to awake in the glorious dawn of an unending day. It is thus 'He Giveth His Beloved Sleep.'

"Beloved she was of all of us and hard it is to look upon the vacant chair and know her voice will be no more heard in its accents of loving advice, encouragement or warning, words which were never without weight, never disregarded.

"We have lost our beacon light which has so unerringly guided us through all the years since 1859, when Mrs. Walker became Vice-Regent for North Carolina. May the afterglow of this light, undimmed, still show us the way as years pass on.

"Mrs. Walker was the daughter of Governor Morehead, one of North Carolina's most distinguished sons, whose talents of infinite variety seem to have centered in this rare woman. Artist and musician as well as practical farmer and gardener, associated from childhood with all that was refined, cultured and intellectual, knowing as she reached womanhood and in after years those prominent in public life, her social education was perfected and with her adaptability, ready sympathy and remarkable conversational powers, rendered her a charming companion, scion of a race past and gone.

"Entering our Association at its inception she knew of its poverty, trials and discouragements; but, with other remarkable women whom our first Regent so wisely appointed, Mrs. Walker labored with unfailing courage and hope that never flagged. She lived to see all her prophecies fulfilled and to witness the success she had so helped to ensure."

SUSAN E. JOHNSON HUDSON.

JOHN CALVIN WHARTON

JOHN CALVIN WHARTON
1823 - 1915

On the night of February 22nd, 1906, a number of Greensboro citizens met informally at the home of Miss Bettie Caldwell, and the organization of a "Greensboro Historical Society" was had under advisement. From this preliminary meeting grew to decided proportions "The Guilford County Historical and Literary Association", organized at Greensboro, in the Smith Memorial Building, September 11th, 1906. Officers were elected, a constitution adopted, and committees appointed. It was my good fortune to serve with others on the "Committee on History", of which Mr. John Calvin Wharton was chairman. This was the beginning of a friendship lasting till his death in 1915, and now it is my pleasure to pay tribute to this venerable citizen, who so untiringly led us in the way of all truth about our county and town; for Mr. Wharton was a faithful recorder of Guilford's splendid past and was possessed of an optimistic faith in her future.

His ancestry was English. Born September 27th, 1823, the only child of James and Jane Rankin Wharton, grandson of Elisha Wharton, great-grandson of Nathan Wharton, who came to Maryland from England in 1767, and later moved with his family to Guilford County, North Carolina, settling in the North Buffalo section, and from Nathan Wharton the Whartons of North Carolina, as well as of other states, are descended.

Educational facilities were primitive and crude in the child John Wharton's time. Kindergarten and Montissori being undreamed of methods, he was taught his A B C's in the good old fashioned way by his mother, who held a small school for the little children of the neighborhood, this "school" being in a one-roomed house on the plantation.

Then he attended the "Old Field School" of Alamance, which he himself described so graphically. That you may more clearly visualize those times and manners, I quote Mr. Wharton:

"This old, red school house had a history in its day. Its location was about one mile southeast from Alamance Church, and its building, a single room, was of hewn logs, with the cracks chinked with split timber and daubed with red clay, hence its name. At one end was a chimney, with a large open fireplace; at the other end a window occupying the space of a displaced log extending from wall to wall, and beneath its light were a writing desk and the bench of the same length, upon which were seated pupils when taking practice lessons in penmanship. In one corner of the room and near the fireplace were the teacher's chair, desk, and only other window in the house. The benches were of sawed timber with sufficient thickness to support the weight placed upon them, and about 12 inches in width, with auger holes into which rude legs were inserted. These benches were without backs and the feet of the small children dangled beneath, but could not touch the floor. This was the furniture of the building.

"The teacher considered it necessary to have in readiness three implements: the birch, familiarly known as the switch, the ferule, and a small pocket knife. The first is not so long out of date as to need description. I suppose every child has heard there was such a thing in existence a generation or two back.

"The second had a double purpose, the flat side for inflicting blows upon the palm of the hand, the straight edge for marking lines upon unruled copy books. The pocket knife was for making pens from goose quills. Pens of any other description were unknown, hence the knife came to be designated 'penknife'.

"In favorable weather the larger pupils were permitted to prepare their lessons under the shade of the surrounding oaks.

"A thorough knowledge of Webster's Blue Back Spelling Book was considered the foundation stone of all future knowledge and the last exercise of each day was competitive spelling.

"This is the type of the common or old field school house of seventy or eighty years ago, and history would be incomplete should they be left unnoticed."

As a lad Mr. Wharton plodded through the simple curriculum required at old Alamance; later, as a young man, matriculating at "Caldwell Institute", this institute established by Orange Presbytery, in 1833, being the worthy child of "Caldwell Academy", taught by David Caldwell for a former generation. On account of ill health he was forced to give up a long-cherished hope of Princeton and instead went back to life in the open on the farm.

At twenty-one he married Rebecca Jane Rankin, the daughter of his neighbor, Mr. Robert Rankin, and in their happy farm home eleven children were born, eight of whom lived to maturity.

A type of the Guilford citizen of that day, Mr. Wharton was an ardent Whig in politics.

Keeping the even tenor of their way in the usual routine of farm life, the Whartons lived happily and uneventfully till the troublous years of sixty to sixty-five. During these terrible years, Mr. Wharton was from home most of the time in the service of his state, and serving also in the "Home Guards".

While he was of necessity away, his wife so ably conducted the affairs of the household and farm as to call forth repeated commendation from her husband, and constant surprise that "so frail" and "so little a body" could accomplish so much.

As illustrative of his high character and the confidence in which he was held by all men, this incident will be illuminating and interesting:

The Greensboro National Bank, the oldest in Greensboro, traces its succession through over half a century to the old "Bank of Cape Fear". Mr. Jesse H. Lindsay was its first president.

During the War Between the States, just prior to Johnson's surrender, fearing a Federal raid, Mr. Lindsay, in great perplexity, sent for Mr. Wharton, confiding to him that in the vault of the bank there was from ten to fifteen thousand dollars in gold and silver, and that it must be hidden at once, the hiding to be left to him.

Going carefully over the matter with the bank's president, Mr. Lindsay, Mr. Wharton consented to undertake this responsibility, and just here the fact that he was neither a director or a stockholder in the bank, nor had he aught to offer as security but his word, may be emphasized as further portraying his integrity.

Returning to town on horseback under cover of night, the bank's specie was carried by him to the Wharton farm and the secret of its possession and its hiding place confided to his mother and to his wife.

A hole was dug in the woods and the money buried, the spot indicated, as told me by his son, Mr. E. P. Wharton, by the peculiar location of certain trees. Then, that none might suspect its burial place a pen was built over it, and adjacent thereto several other pens, and the pigs turned in! Indeed, rare treasure to cast before swine! After the danger had passed the bank's gold and silver was returned and the panic averted.

In 1880, Mr. Wharton moved from his farm into town, living on Pearson Street, and from that time on he became actively interested in everything that pertained to the good of Greensboro.

A vital Christian, a Presbyterian of the "blue stocking" type, an elder in the First Presbyterian Church for years, until the building of Westminster Presbyterian Church in South Greensboro, transferred his membership and elder-ship there, Mr. Wharton was known of all men for his zeal in her activities, and his love for the church of his choice. He was faithful unto death in her tenets.

Possibly in this connection the following anecdote may not be altogether irrelevant:

A friend and classmate of the far-away Caldwell Institute days was Robert Beall, afterwards the Reverend Robert Beall.

The paths of these two friends had been widely divergent till, after the lapse of sixty years, they met once again in Greensboro, each the guest of a son who chanced to be next door neighbors. Many were the pleasant events coincident with their meeting, but this has a vigorous touch. Election day, 1912, preacher and elder, though with natural perturbation of spirit caused by the exigencies of the occasion, were still possessed of a wholesome belief that the "fervent prayer of the righteous man availeth much". So they met for a private prayer meeting of their own, asking the aid of an overruling Providence in making the calling and election of their candidate sure. Then further believing that "faith without works is dead", these two veteran Presbyterians arm in arm sallied forth to the polls, showed their "faith by their works" and cast a vote each for Woodrow Wilson!

After the marriage of his daughters and the removal of two sons to far distant states, Mr. Wharton, whose wife had died several years before, came to make his home with his son, Mr. E. P. Wharton. Here loving care was given him till, at the advanced age of ninety-two, he died June fifth, 1915.

His last years of peaceful leisure were spent in writing numerous articles for the local press reminiscent of other days and rich in the lore of those simple times.

During these latter days he was a diligent student of Latin and Greek, reading the classics in the original for his daily diversion. His granddaughter, relating this fact, said that "Latin was easy" for her as she "simply rode Grandfather's back" through the intricacies of Caesar and Virgil.

The last thing he did was a "Series of Tender Memories" of his wife, written for his grandchildren, in the gentlest strain, so that they who had never known her in the flesh might catch the reflection of her sweet spirit and know something of "the tender grace of a day that was dead."

REBECCA SCHENCK.

JOHN LAFAYETTE MICHAUX

JOHN LAFAYETTE MICHAUX

1824 - 1898

For more than thirty years Rev. J. L. Michaux was a familiar figure on the streets of Greensboro, known for his geniality, his hopefulness and ability to inspire hope in others. No record of the city's builders would be complete without mention of his faithful and unselfish service.

He was not a captain of industry as we know the term today, yet his spirit of optimism was contagious and by the influence of his personality a younger generation was moved to higher achievements. At this writing his visions for the town of his adoption have all been fulfilled, but it is well to remember that they were printed in days of poverty and discouragement and printed because of an editor's faith in Greensboro.

Mr. Michaux's paternal ancestors were French, as the name implies. Abraham Michaux and Susanne Rochet, his wife, came to Virginia in 1704 and settled in Henrico County. They were French Huguenots, who had left France in 1690 for Amsterdam, Holland, on account of religious persecution.

Quite a thrilling story was written and published a number of years ago by Dr. W. D. Morton, of the Presbyterian church, giving an account of the escape of Susanne Rochet from France to Holland. Members of her family in Holland wrote to relatives in France to "send the little night-cap (meaning Susanne) in a hogshead with other things being shipped to them", which was done, and by this ruse the young girl was carried safely across the French frontier to Holland where she later married Abraham Michaux on July 13th, 1692, twelve years before they sailed for America.

A grandson of Abraham and Susanne, Captain Joseph Michaux, served with distinction in the 14th Virginia Regiment during the Revolutionary War. A great grandson, another Joseph, married Anne Meade Randolph, and in the home this couple established near High Bridge, Cumberland County, their second son, John Lafayette Michaux, was born September 3rd, 1824.

No data is available as to the schools of that section in his childhood, but the mother had been carefully educated by her father, Brett Randolph, Jr., a graduate of Oxford University, and no doubt imparted to her son in early life the refining advantages she had received.

Upon the death of his parents the younger son, then only twelve years old, came to North Carolina to live with two sisters who had married in this state and settled in Guilford County. The outlook at this period of his life might well have discouraged a lad of less spirit, but with the courage of his ancestors young Michaux determined to win by his own efforts an education befitting a minister of the Gospel. After he succeeded we find him while a young pastor at Wilmington, still studying Hebrew in company with other young theologues under a private tutor.

In 1855, at the age of 31, he was married to Sarah MacLemore Macon, eldest daughter of George and Ellen Green Macon, of Franklin County, North Carolina, a wife who was both his helpmeet and inspiration during the thirty-nine years of this happy union. Her passing January 17th, 1894, was but four years before he joined her in the heavenly home July 6th, 1898.

Of their six children, five lived to maturity: L. M. Michaux, of Goldsboro, N. C.; Dr. E. R. and John S. Michaux, Mrs. Thomas M. McConnell and Mrs. Thomas H. Crocker, of Greensboro, N. C.

Among the names included in a book of this class we expect to find citizens who served the town in offices of public trust, others who established and maintained its business life and still others who taught the people from pulpit, press and school room. Mr. Michaux served Greensboro in this last class as editor, and served it well.

A successful minister of the Methodist Protestant Church, he was often honored by that body. Several times he was a member of the General Conference of his church. He served on the committee charged with preparation of a denominational hymn book, was a member of the Baltimore Convention of 1877, when union of the divided forces in the Northern and Southern churches was consummated. Eleven years before this date he had been sent to a conference of eminent representatives from both Methodist Episcopal and Methodist Protestant Churches, which met in Montgomery, Alabama, in 1866, to decide as to union of these two bodies. In the judgment of this conference union was deemed unwise and the plan was abandoned.

Thirty-five years a citizen of Greensboro, Mr. Michaux was for thirty years a Greensboro editor, but throughout this entire period he was frequently called to supply local pulpits of other denominations where his presence and discourses were always welcome.

The first of the three papers he edited in Greensboro was the "Watchman and Harbinger", published under the auspices of his church during the War Between the States when the national organ of that church at Baltimore could no longer serve the south. A publication committee had nominal charge of the enterprise, but there is abundant evidence that responsibility was carried entirely by the executive and that it was heavy even for that troubled day.

In a strong editorial he claimed adequate church support for his paper on its merits and because it was "the only journal of that faith in the bounds of the Confederacy". In a graphic picture of the situation he stated that "for the time being one man served as editor, bookkeeper and mailing clerk, with working hours which sometimes stretched from eight a. m. to five a. m. of the next day, too heavy a burden for one of such slender strength."

It was at this crisis that the editor made personal appeal to the War Department of the Confederacy, with the result that J. C. Roberts and W. O. Donnell, both Guilford men of ability, were temporarily released from arms and assigned in turn to service on the staff of the "Watchman and Harbinger".

This paper probably was published to the close of the war, though the exact date of discontinuance is not certain. The one copy known to be extant shows in its twenty-four columns editorial and typographical work both a distinct credit to the time. Church news covered less than five columns, advertisements (all of an educational nature), half a column more, all remaining space being given to secular news of the day with original and selected articles of a literary and religious character.

Evidently the Watchman and Harbinger was meant above everything else as an evangel of cheer, carrying its message from homes, churches and books to the camps of the Confederate Army. "Vox clemantis in deserto" was the significant line kept standing under the paper's title. The fair south in 1863 was indeed "a wilderness" and this editor in his post of trust bent every physical and mental effort to make his paper the "voice" of promise for a better day.

The Central Protestant, another weekly, was established in Greensboro as a state church organ in 1874, with Mr. Michaux in editorial control, a commission which he discharged with signal ability for the next eighteen years.

The Daily Workman, an afternoon paper, was the third and last publication edited by Mr. Michaux in Greensboro and the one by which he will be longest remembered. It was an unpretentious optimistic little paper, with the high standards of its editor and proprietor. Other dailies had appeared from time to time, always failing within a year, but the Daily Workman and Mr. Michaux came in 1883 to stay. Of financial prosperity there is no story, but doubtless this was not overwhelming. The Workman lived, however, proving that the town could have a daily paper and this fact inspired hope.

In 1890 the Daily Record appeared, with Reece and Elam editors, and the pioneer daily's task was done. It was absorbed by the Record in 1893.

The five remaining years of the editor's life were spent, partly in supplying calls to the pulpits of his church and partly in writing for the columns of various newspapers, his grasp of public questions and pleasing style of expression making these contributions always welcome. He left unfinished at death a story which was to have been published in book form, the faithful delineation of an old negro of high integrity who lived in north Guilford and had a very remarkable spiritual influence among his friends of both races.

In conducting the war paper, the state church organ and the Daily Workman, this editor was always the prophet of a better day and to those who knew him best in daily walk and conversation it seemed but a just meed of praise that at his passing July 6th, 1898, many Greensboro men, testifying to his tireless service for the community, declared that they were better citizens because they had known the Rev. J. L. Michaux.

J. F. McCulloch.

ALFRED MOORE SCALES

ALFRED MOORE SCALES
1827 - 1892

There is nothing, I think, in our Mother Country more distinctive or more impressive than the numerous memorials of her great men. Go where you will—whether through her mighty and ancient capitals, London and Edinburgh, or through rural Stratford and peaceful Ayr—in art galleries, museums, abbeys, palaces, cathedrals, ancient seats of learning, city halls, libraries and public buildings—the glory of the nation is before you in the portraits of the men and women who made England and Scotland what they are.

Soldiers, patriots, statesmen, jurists, rulers, churchmen, discoverers, artists, men of letters—they are an inseparable part of every public edifice and of each historic spot and hallowed shrine. It should be so with us.

In our midst lie ashes which make Guilford holier,
Dust which is even in itself an immortality.

The Caldwells, the Dicks, the Gilmers, the Gorrells, the Lindsays, the Mebanes, the Mendenhalls, the Moreheads, the Paisleys, the Worths, the Sloans, the Scales—there must be virtue in any community whose institutions and ideals are derived from a source and lineage so noble.

It was the watchword of one of the adopted sons of Guilford—the late Charles D. McIver—that "Each generation owes it to the past and to the future that no previous worthy attainment or achievement, whether of thought or deed or vision, shall be lost."

He counseled well. We owe it to ourselves, to those from whom we derived so goodly a heritage, and to those who shall come after us, that no one shall enter our public buildings and fail to find memorials of our noble sires.

Among those thus worthy of honor in our halls of fame, I can think of no finer type of manhood—citizen, soldier, statesman, Christian gentleman—than Alfred Moore Scales. Time permits me to give but a brief and most inadequate sketch of his career.

Born November 26, 1827, at "Ingleside", the old family homestead in Rockingham County, he received his preparatory education in the famous Caldwell Institute of this city, and in the fall of the year 1845 entered the University of North Carolina. He did not, as did two of his soldier classmates, Pettigrew and Ransom, remain to graduate, but with them received the anointing of Alma Mater, and going forth in a spirit of chivalrous service, linked his name immortally with theirs as part of the University's glorious contribution to the Commonwealth and the South. In grateful memory of this service, the University has recorded his name and achievements in marble and placed them upon the walls of her Memorial Hall.

After a few years spent in teaching, the excellence of which was a subject of frequent remarks by his pupils in their later years, Mr. Scales read law under Judge William H. Battle and was admitted to practice in 1852. His industry, his ability, his steady application to the demands of his profession, his zeal and devotion in behalf of his clients, won for him an honored place at a bar which counted among its members some of the illustrious names in our legal annals, namely: Dick, Dillard, the Gilmers, the Moreheads, the Ruffins and the Settles.

Called by his fellow citizens to represent them in a series of offices of honor and trust, he served them well and faithfully as county solicitor, clerk of the court, member of the General Assembly, and member of Congress. Mr. Scales was a Democrat in the truest and best sense of the word, and his political career began, continued and ended with the respect and esteem of the people whom he served. He held no position that he did not fill with honor to himself and to his constituents, and however strong the party opposition against which he had to contend, he used no means either to secure nomination or election or continuance in office that were not those of a gentleman.

His campaigns were models. In an age when passions were bitter and party strife ran high, candor, dignity and truth were his weapons. He indulged in no personalities, questioned neither the motives nor the integrity of his opponents, but intent upon a convincing presentation of the truth, met the issues fairly and squarely as one assured of the justice of his cause and the wisdom and integrity of the people.

Perhaps the title of respect most often given to Mr. Scales was that of General. As the breach gradually widened between North and South, he perhaps earlier than most of his associates, foresaw that the differences were irreconcilable save by an appeal to arms. He anticipated this, and while he did not glory in it, he met it face to face without fear and without hesitation. Yet he was a man of peace and in favor of using every earnest and honorable effort to reconcile the differences between the two sections. He favored reconciliation, but not compromise; fraternity and good will, but not a sacrifice of principle. He was by nature an advocate of harmony, but he believed it to be the duty of every loyal citizen to see that the rights secured to us by the fathers were kept sacred by ourselves and transmitted unimpaired to our children. He favored peace, if peace walked hand in hand with honor, but if war should follow as a result of secession (the right of which was by him unquestioned), then said he: "If I must shed my blood in battle, I will shed it for the South and my people and not against them". When the breach finally came, he was prompt to volunteer and was, by the vote of his comrades, elected captain of his company. His courage and ability won recognition from his fellow officers, who made him colonel. His military talent, his personal bravery, his resourcefulness, his care of his men, and their gallantry under his inspiring leadership, won for him the merited appointment of brigadier-general. Private, captain, colonel, general—in all stages of his career he was an ideal soldier. Loyal to his cause, prompt to obey, properly respectful toward authority, he was loved by his men and repeatedly praised by his officers. The noble Pender said of him: "He is as gallant a man as is to be found in the service"; and high words of praise were his and his command's from Longstreet and Lee. Struck down at Chancellorsville and again at Gettysburg, a kind Providence yet spared him for years of wide and rich usefulness in the trying days of reconstruction and rehabilitation. Such the record, all too meagerly told, of the splendid military services of Alfred Moore Scales!

In the constructive work that followed, as member of Congress for five consecutive terms, he proved himself a wise and faithful guardian of the people's interests, a progressive advocate of enlightened reform, an opponent of waste and extravagance, and an unalterable foe to corruption, selfishness and personal or party greed.

But the people of his state—his own people in a very true sense—felt that they must have him nearer home, and in 1884 he was called by them to the Governor's chair. The spirit in which he entered upon his new duties and the keynote of his administration is found in the opening words of his inaugural address: "Always remembering that duty and honor go hand in hand".

Four years of peaceful growth and development were ours under his safe and wise guidance. Hope and confidence returned, industries multiplied, wealth increased, and all about us were evidences of prosperity and good feeling. Reviewing the period, Governor Fowle said: "The administration of Governor Scales was so wise and conservative in its character that hardly a ripple disturbed the surface of public opinion during his entire term. The wisdom and justice of her Governor established peace and quiet through the length and breadth of the state".

Thus closed thirty-seven years of active public service, in peace and war, and this leader who was servant to us all, whose conception of public office was that of public trust, was, at his own earnest request, permitted to lay aside the cares of state and know some of the quiet joys of home life and simple citizenship.

For four more years, until February, 1892, it was our inestimable privilege to have him here in our midst, our foremost citizen, closely identified with our business life, interested in all that pertained to our welfare, and leading us all in good works. To meet and talk with Mr. Scales was an inspiration and a delight. Noble in appearance, engaging in manner, lovable in disposition, fervent in spirit

"None knew him but to love him
Nor named him but to praise".

I remember well the tone of affection and respect by which he was greeted by every person in Greensboro. In my home, as in others, his very name was spoken with love and reverence. I remember, too, how as boys we were drawn to him as steel to the magnet, happy to stand in the sunshine of his presence, and proud to be the recipients of his ever cordial greeting.

Mr. Scales was a soldier and ambassador of Christ, and in simple faith and loving obedience he lived the doctrines which he professed. As much as any man I ever knew, he was a living epistle known and read of all men. All the interests of the town and community were dear to his heart, but it was the church and the agencies for the spread of the Gospel that were his peculiar joy. An honored elder of the First Presbyterian Church of this city, he exercised a power for good, not simply in the local church, but throughout the entire state. As representative at the higher church courts, moderator of the Synod of North Carolina (the first layman to hold that important office), as founder of the Synodical Mission Work of his church in North Carolina, and as a devout and consecrated personal worker for Christ, he did a work in this community and in the state, the abiding influence of which is felt in our spiritual life today.

May the memory of this knightly gentleman be a perpetual benediction, inciting us to emulate his virtues and dedicate the first-fruits of all our physical and mental and spiritual powers to the uplift of humanity, the advancement of our state and nation, and the glory of our God.

W. C. SMITH.

Memorial address delivered on the presentation of the Scales Portrait to the Greensboro Public Library, June 6th, 1914.

NORTH CAROLINA
W.C.T.U.

ESSE QUAM VIDERI

Have not I commanded thee?
Be strong and of a good courage.

Josh.1.9.

1882 – 1902

CAROLINE C. GORRELL

CAROLINE C. GORRELL

1827 - 1905

Mrs. C. C. Gorrell was an outstanding character as a business woman, and as a philanthropist occupied a position of eminence. She was born October 23, 1827, at the old Gillespie homestead, now a part of South Greensboro. Her parents were Robert and Nancy Gillespie and as a descendant of Colonel Daniel Gillespie, of Revolutionary fame, she inherited great energy, resolution, deep religious fervor and undaunted courage which later characterized all her undertakings.

In 1871 Mrs. Gorrell, a widow with two sons, Robert and Frank, left Winston, the home of her late husband, Frank Gorrell, and moved to Greensboro. Being possessed of extraordinary executive and business ability she opened a millinery shop and soon became a conspicious figure in the business world, achieving a marked success, unusual to a pioneer woman. Meeting the keen competition of experienced business men she steadily and persistently conquered the difficulties and used obstacles only as stepping stones to enviable success.

For many years she was an invalid, but ill health did not conquer her brave spirit, and her great will power drove her on to the goal she had visualized as her part in God's great plan. The best business men consulted this woman of brilliant intellect and fine judgment, and numberless lives, particularly the young, were guided, stimulated and uplifted when privileged to come in contact with her. With her hard earned money she was most liberal to all deserving calls. She had a great tenderness and sympathy for the colored people, and perhaps no other death ever caused such widespread sorrow among their race, for she was ever their staunch and helpful friend. There is an amusing incident the older residents will recall, which illustrates how she even refused to hurt the feelings of old Pete Wagstaff, a noted negro of police court fame. Pete's repeated visits to "Old Missus" with his constant requests for "a little piece of money", finally became a nuisance. She with tactful firmness offered to pay him a larger sum just to stay away from her place, and this happily proved effective.

Mrs. Gorrell was prominently identified with the temperance cause and gave much time and financial aid in carrying on the great work of the Woman's Christian Temperance Union. A large room in her building on West Market Street was donated for state headquarters of the organization and for many years the large letters W. C. T. U. remained on the front of the building. She kept in closest contact with the work at home and abroad, being a personal friend of Frances Willard and others of national prominence in the work. Though herself possessing a genius for leadership she refused the public offices and insisted on quietly remaining at the obscure, but most necessary, helm of earning money, then making real but willing sacrifices that the prohibition cause, so uppermost in her heart, might spread. She had the joy of seeing every saloon in Greensboro closed during the last year of her life.

As a token of love and esteem the local W. C. T. U. erected a drinking fountain on Gorrell Street as a memorial to her. This is peculiarly appropriate as a symbol of a life which was a refreshing service to her toiling fellowmen.

For fifty years Mrs. Gorrell was a devout member of the First Presbyterian Church. She passed away January 27, 1905, and her burial was in Green Hill Cemetery. At her funeral her pastor, Dr. Egbert W. Smith, paid her this loving tribute:

"She saw much trouble in her life. Many and heavy shadows fell across her pathway. The loss of loved ones, the disappointment of cherished hopes, painful and long continued physical infirmities, she had to bear, but she came of gallant stock and God had given her in addition to His grace a brave and sunny spirit. Even when tied to her chair by crippling disease she was always bright and cheerful, full of humor and courage.

"She was willing to go and more than willing. The way had been very long and much of it very hard and the pilgrim's feet were tired, and the Master knew it, so he took her in His arms and bore her to that land where the old grow young again; where the Lamb which is in the midst of the throne doth feed her, and lead her unto living fountains of water, and God hath wiped all tears from her eyes.''

LILLIAN W. NOELL.

Thomas Settle

THOMAS SETTLE
1831 - 1888

Thomas Settle, the youngest judge who ever sat in the Supreme Court of North Carolina, was elevated to the bench at the age of thirty-seven. His term of service altogether was seven years and his qualities of mind and heart were such as to endear him throughout, not only to his associates on the bench, but to the bar generally, and won for him the admiration and affection of all who knew him.

The family to which he belonged is of pure English origin. Near the middle of the eighteenth century his great-grand-father, Josiah Settle, came from England and established a home in what is now Rockingham County. In that favored region among the hills of the Dan the Settle family lived for more than a hundred years—first Josiah, then David, then Thomas, father of him of whom I write.

The father, the first Judge Settle, was known and trusted as an able jurist and wise legislator of his day; sent as representative of his people to both state and national legis-latures, he served these bodies with conspicuous ability and was chosen as Speaker for the House of Commons in 1829. He was Judge of the Superior Court from 1832 till his death in 1857. An ardent advocate of education he served as trustee both for Wake Forest, his own Alma Mater, and the State University, where his sons were educated.

Thomas Settle, the second of that name and fourth of the seven children of Thomas and Henrietta Graves Settle, was born in Rockingham County, January 23, 1831, and was equally fortunate in home training received from both par-ents, his gifted mother being a sister of the distinguished Calvin Graves. He received his academic training at the excellent school of Samuel Smith, near Madison, and at Dr. Wilson's school at Hawfields, Orange County. He was edu-cated at the University where he was graduated with distinc-tion in 1850 at the age of nineteen. The year of his gradua-tion his brother-in-law, David S. Reid, was elected governor of the state, and the young graduate made his entrance into political life as the private secretary to the Governor.

The Whig party, to which his father belonged, had won its last victory in the election of General Taylor three years before, and was already showing signs of early disintegration. In this situation Mr. Settle, like many southern young men of that day, allied himself with the Democratic party.

At the age of twenty-three he received his license to practice law. He had studied under Judge Pearson, at Richmond Hill, and it was during those days that he first met Mary Glenn, who afterwards became his wife. The same year he was elected to the House of Commons from Rockingham County, and for five successive years, 1854 to 1859, was an accomplished member of that body and the last year was chosen its speaker. In 1856 he was placed on the National Democratic ticket as elector for his district, and cast the electoral vote of the state for Mr. Buchanan.

A Democrat, born and reared in the South, firm in his advocacy of southern rights, Mr. Settle was an ardent supporter of the Constitution, a staunch believer in the Union, and opposed to secession in any form so long as the Constitution and laws enacted by its authority could be upheld and obeyed. Consequently when later the expediency of withdrawing from the Union became involved in the presidential contest of 1860, he wisely advocated the election of Mr. Douglas as the surest way to forestall the calamity. But the controversy between the North and the South could not be settled by the ballot. The cause of it was too deep-seated to be reached by that peaceful remedy. Mr. Lincoln's election alarmed and angered the South. Despite his majority in the electoral college he had received little more than one-third of the votes cast by the people and they came entirely from the northern states.

South Carolina took the first step, in December, following the election, and Mississippi, Florida, Alabama, Georgia and Louisiana followed in the order named. By February, 1861, the Confederate government had been formed at Montgomery and its president and vice-president inaugurated amid scenes of the wildest enthusiasm. On April 12th, Fort Sumter was bombarded and in two days it surrendered. The President of the United States issued his call for troops and the President of the Confederate States prepared to meet them. North Carolina, Virginia, Arkansas and Tennessee still remained in the Union, but their Governors refused to respond to Mr. Lincoln's call, holding that a state had the right to withdraw from the Union and could not rightfully be compelled to return. Virginia yielded to her southern sympathies in April, Arkansas early in May, and both promptly joined the Confederacy, leaving North Carolina and Tennessee still in the Union and still hoping that the united efforts of patriotic men in every part of the nation might avert the dangers threatening it and again unite the states in a common bond of fraternal and perpetual union.

The real question was not so much the right of secession that had time and again been conceded North and South. It was rather the expediency of withdrawing from the Union so long as there was hope of remaining in it with peace and honor. Like Morehead, Graham, Badger, Ruffin, Gilmer and others of this state, and Stephens, Johnson and Hill, of Georgia, Mr. Settle believed that secession at that time was premature and that our troubles might and should be settled within the Union rather than out of it. On May 20, 1861, a convention in Raleigh assembled ratified the Constitution of the provisional government of the Confederate States, and thus North Carolina, next to the last of the original states to enter the Union, was the last to leave it.

The popularity of Mr. Settle during this period was strikingly illustrated by the fact that though a Union man and opposed to Mr. Breckenridge's election to the Presidency, he was elected, early in 1861, Solicitor of the Fourth Judicial Circuit by a legislature the majority of whose members were Breckenridge Democrats.

On Monday, April 12th, he was prosecuting for the state at Danbury, in Stokes County, Judge Howard presiding. He joined James Madison Leach, a Union Whig, in a request for the use of the courtroom for political speaking during the noon recess. The request was granted and between Mr. Settle, Mr. Leach and the Hon. John A. Gilmer as Unionists on the one side, and Mr. A. M. Scales and Mr. Robert McLean as Secessionists on the other, there followed a political debate of intense feeling and marked ability. In a few days the court adjourned and the judge and solicitor left for the latter's home in Rockingham—the one as strong for immediate secession as the other was against it. On the way as they approached Madison, a strong Union town, they discerned a flag floating from a building in the village. They saw at once that it was not the flag of the Union. Several persons were riding toward them reading newspapers. Hailing one of them the solicitor inquired what was the matter. Promptly the answer came: "Haven't you heard the news? Sumter has been attacked. President Lincoln has called for 75,000 troops. Everybody is for war. Governor Reid is speaking in Madison and volunteers are enlisting." The solicitor turned to the judge and exclaimed: "They are right! I must go to Madison and go with them." They turned out of their way and drove to the village. As they approached they heard the voice of Governor Reid speaking in an upper room of a building, while a large crowd was gathered in and around it. The solicitor sprang up and waving his hand aloft declared that they were right, and leaping from the buggy mounted a doorstep and poured forth a passionate appeal for every man to stand by the South.

The next Monday at Rockingham soon after court met the sound of fife and drum was heard from several directions and soon there marched into Wentworth one hundred and fifty volunteers, with both Scales and Settle in the ranks. Two companies were formed, Scales was elected captain of one and Settle of the other. Mr. Settle and Mr. Scales, late antagonists on the stump, were now enlisted as comrades in a common cause, and as captains were placed with their respective companies in the Third, afterward the Thirteenth Regiment of North Carolina troops, which earned a proud record in the subsequent struggle.

Upon the expiration of his enlistment Mr. Settle was again elected solicitor of his district and held that office until his election to the Reconstruction Convention of 1865. He was among the younger members of that convention, but was active in the discussion of all matters of public interest that came before it. He was chairman of the committee on the abolition of slavery and the author of the ordinance forever abolishing slavery in this state. He was described as he appeared in this convention by a spectator as "a man of about six feet in height, 190 pounds in weight and thirty-four years of age; erect broad-shouldered, with full face, firm mouth, bronzed and rosy cheeks, large brown eyes, dark brown hair and whiskers. He speaks with force and unmistakable emphasis, gesticulates with a full sweep from the shoulder, and adds a sincere love of the Union to a hearty hatred of secession."

Sixty days after General Lee's surrender there was not a Confederate soldier in arms. They had fought to the point of exhaustion and when they gave their parole the war indeed was over. Throughout the Confederacy the surrender was complete. The southern people were anxious to renew their allegiance to the United States and submit to its authority. There was no law on the statute books providing a way for their return to the Union. They could not resume their old relations of their own accord; their state governments had been destroyed or abandoned and they were compelled to look to Washington for the manner, the terms and conditions of their restorations. There the trouble arose. In the absence of law, both Lincoln and Johnson did substantially right when they adopted a plan of their own and endeavored to carry it into execution.

A definite and certain way of return having at last been prepared the practical question was the acceptance or rejection of it. To accept it meant immediate readmission with all the rights of an American state; to reject it continued military rule. Mr. Settle, like many of his friends, acquiesced in the stern measures prescribed by Congress. He was deeply convinced that the interest of the state required prompt acceptance of these terms with the resolute purpose on the part of the people of making the best they could of the dark troublesome situation. Accordingly, on March 27, 1867, he attended a convention at Raleigh, whose object was the organization of a party with that end in view. Upon his motion it assumed the name of the Republican party and allied itself with that political organization. Its cardinal principles were Liberty, Union and Equality before the law and it advocated the acceptance of the plan of reconstruction proposed by Congress. Shortly afterwards, by request of his neighbors and friends, he set forth his views on public affairs in a speech at Spring Garden, Rockingham County. He had participated in the war and had held a judicial office under a Confederate state government and was himself disfranchised under the recent act. His audience was composed of both white and colored people. He had no arguments for one that could not properly be addressed to the other.

He strongly urged the necessity of industrial education for both races and that machinery and educated labor were especially needed at that time, and discouraged the denunciation of northern men and northern notions. "We want their capital," said he, "to build factories and workshops and railroads and to develop our magnificent water powers. We want their intelligence, their energy, and enterprise to operate the factories and to teach us how to operate them. Let hate and prejudice have no place here," he said. "Elevate yourselves, but pull nobody down. Go for the education and progress of mankind without regard to race or color and invite all to come forward and assist in the development of our common country. These principles are founded upon a rock and cannot be moved."

Except the time he served in the war and in the convention and legislature of 1865-'66, Mr. Settle was solicitor of his district continuously from 1861 to 1868. In April, 1868, he was elected Associate Justice of the Supreme Court of North Carolina, and served till his appointment as Minister to Peru, 1871, when he was succeeded by Nathaniel Boyden. The climate of Peru severely threatened his health. Besides his heart was with his family and his friends in North Carolina, and he was not satisfied to remain away. In the spring of 1872 he resigned and came home. The same year he was chosen president of the National Republican Convention at Philadelphia, which nominated General Grant for his second term, the only southern Republican ever honored with the presidency of a National Convention of his party. The same year he also became unwillingly the candidate of his party for Congress from the Greensboro district against General James M. Leach, the incumbent, and after a joint canvass of great ability was defeated by the narrow majority of 268. Associate Justice Dick having resigned his membership of this court in the summer of 1872, Judge Settle, on the 5th of December of that year, was reappointed to this Court, where he served as Associate Justice until June, 1876, when he resigned to accept the nomination of his party for Governor of the state.

Judge Settle was nominated for Governor on the 12th of July, 1876. Governor Vance had already been nominated as the Democratic candidate. The candidates agreed on a joint canvass of the state. Their debates are historical in North Carolina. They were conducted with splendid dignity, each candidate treating the other with fine courtesy throughout the discussions. It was a return of the spirit of older times when such men as Graham and Hoke, Gilmer and Bragg, Badger and Miller led the opposing force in the field of political contest. In all that makes political speaking instructive, impressive and convincing, these discussions were in no respect less masterful than the debates between Lincoln and Douglas in 1858. No braver, fairer, manlier political battle was over fought on American soil than that which was fought by Judge Settle in 1876. After his defeat for Governor, President Grant, on the 30th of January, 1877, tendered Judge Settle the appointment of United States Judge for the Northern District of Florida, which he accepted and filled with great distinction until his tragic death in the judge's room in the government building in the city of Greensboro December 1, 1888.

Judge Settle possessed in an eminent degree the qualities of courage and independence of character. Though his official stations were occupied for the most part in trying and troublesome times when men's feelings were most bitter, such were the dignity of his presence and manner, the firmness of his resolutions and the magnanimity of his actions that whether sitting as a judge or presiding over the deliberations of the legislature or conventions unquestioning obedience was rendered to his authority. So good a heart had he, so kind and benignant were his words and deeds, that even his enemies at last became his friends. At the time of his death he was the foremost man of his party in the South and the end came when his fine abilities were in their prime. Many eyes all over the country were looking for him to be called to Washington as a member of the cabinet in the new administration.

Personally Judge Settle was unusually magnetic and lovable. In public life his generosity, courage and intellectual force made him easily a leader among men. As a politician he was valiant in advocating the principles and policies in which he believed.

His reputation was not confined to this state. He was as well known and as well loved in other states as in North Carolina. Experience of the past had not caused him to distrust the patriotism and wise conservation of the American people and his faith in the advancement and glory of the Republic was unfaltering and sublime.

The greatness of men is usually estimated from their public career and services. This is not always a true test. It was in the family and among his intimate friends that the shining qualities of Judge Settle's character were most apparent. His social traits were beyond compare. A more upright, lovable, chivalric gentleman never lived in this land. He had a pleasant word and a kind look for every one. He was benevolent to the poor. His generosity usually outstripped his means. The lowly and humble venerated him for his tender heart. He loved little children and was patient with them. He had gathered around him his children and grandchildren and they all looked up to him with pride and affection as their leader and adviser. To them indeed:

"He lived
Considerate to his kind. His love bestowed
Was not a thing of fractions, half-way done,
But with a mellow goodness like the sun
He showed o'er mortal hearts, and brought their buds
To blossom early—thence to fruits and seeds."

W. P. BYNUM.

Condensed from address delivered upon presentation of Settle portrait to Supreme Court of North Carolina, November 7, 1905.

JUNIUS IRVING SCALES

JUNIUS IRVING SCALES

1832 - 1880

It is unusual for a son to write a sketch of his father's life, but it seems to the writer that nothing could be more fitting, provided he refrains from undue laudation on the one hand, and on the other hand provided he does not, from a feeling of delicacy, fail to do the subject justice. Although the son was only a child at the time of his father's death, yet no one now living probably understood or knew him better than the son, and to no one now living would it be more a labor of love to sketch briefly an outline of this noble life.

Junius Irving Scales was born on June 1, 1832, in Rockingham County, North Carolina. He was the son of Dr. Robert H. Scales and Jane Bethell Scales, both of Rockingham County.

The Scales family, formerly spelled D'Escaler, was originally Norman, coming over with William the Conqueror. The companion of the Conqueror was known as Hardwin D'Escaler, and upon him William conferred many estates in Hertfordshire, Warwickshire, and other shires in England. The family continued in the possession of its estates and titles until the time of the War of the Roses, when Lord Scales was captured and executed. The records in the British Museum say that the family then remained for some years as landed gentry and then disappeared from England. It was at this time that they emigrated to the new world and settled in Virginia. Nathaniel Scales, the grandfather of young Junius, moved into North Carolina and settled about seven miles from Reidsville. His son Robert, although a doctor of medicine, soon returned to the plantation and lived the life of a country gentlemen, being a great fox hunter and enjoying the other sports common to those days. In later life he moved to Reidsville, and was the first elder of the Presbyterian Church there. He died when he was about 83 years of age.

Robert had seven sons and three daughters—Robert, who moved to Mississippi; Nathaniel, who died of wounds in prison during the Civil War; Wallace, who was killed when he was twenty years of age, in one of the battles around Richmond, during the Civil War; Alfred Moore, who was a brigadier-general in the Confederate States War and afterwards Governor of North Carolina; James Pinckney, who moved to Mississippi, was speaker of the House of Representatives of that state, and served brilliantly as a captain during the Civil War; E. D. Scales, commonly known as Dick Scales, who although just a boy, served in the Confederate States Army, and who afterwards moved to Texas and left a large number of children, including Col. Wallace Scales, of the United States Army; and Junius Irving, the subject of this sketch.

The daughters were Emma J. Scales, a famous school teacher of Reidsville, who conducted a private academy for years; Sarah Scales, who married Col. Alexander H. Galloway, and Anne Scales, who married Alvis D. Montgomery.

Junius Irving Scales was educated at the University of North Carolina, and was graduated with the class of 1853, with high honors. He was a brilliant student, and even while at the University, showed rare gifts of speaking, having a place with the debaters of the University. After graduation he taught for a short while and then read law with Judge Pearson. He moved to Graham, Alamance County, and began to practice law, representing that county in the House of Representatives in 1857. At that time it was necessary for a member of the legislature to be a freeholder, and some of the friends of young Scales, in order to make him eligible, gave him 300 acres of land.

He was married to Effie Hamilton Henderson, the daughter of Archibald Henderson, and granddaughter of Chief Justice Leonard Henderson, of Granville County.

He decided to move to Mississippi, where several of his brothers were residing, and in 1861 went to that state, carrying with him sixty negro slaves, the property of his young wife. He settled near the Yazoo River, in a little town called Carrollton, the home of Mr. George, who afterwards became Senator George, and who was imprisoned with him on Johnson's Island.

He had been in Carrollton only a few months before the War Between the States began, and he at once enlisted as a private in the Carrollton Company. Before the company left the town he was elected as its captain and immediately began the active and gallant service that ended so disastrously for him at the battle of Chicamauga. His company was assigned to the western army and was in a number of engagements and battles and he was wounded four or five times.

The battle of Chicamauga commenced on Friday, September 18, 1863. By this time Captain Scales had been promoted successively to major, lieutenant-colonel, and was now full colonel and had been suggested for election as a brigadier-general. At the battle of Chicamauga he was in command of the 30th Mississippi Regiment, which fought bravely and gallantly throughout the three days of this bloody battle. On the second day of the battle, the 30th Mississippi suffered peculiarly heavy losses. General Anderson in his official report, speaking of the 30th Mississippi, says: "Most gallantly did they perform their part. In moving across an open field in short range of grape, canister and shrapnel, sixty-two officers and men were killed and 139 wounded, of this regiment alone, all within a very short space of time and upon an area not greater than an acre of ground."

On Sunday, September 20th, the third day of the battle, the fight raged with undiminished ferocity. The 30th, along with other regiments, had been ordered to advance across an open field. Hardly had they begun to execute this order when concealed batteries from three positions opened upon them and in ten or fifteen minutes had done such deadly execution that the men were ordered to lie down to escape being exterminated. Col. Scales' horse was killed under him and his hat and garments were riddled with bullets. At four o'clock in the afternoon after the line had been reformed and was advancing, the line on the left of the 30th regiment gave way as the enemy charged in a flank movement and the whole line was ordered to withdraw. So rapid was the charge of the enemy, however, that before Col. Scales could withdraw his sharp shooters, who were two or three hundred yards ahead of the line, the enemy were upon him and captured him and twenty of his sharp shooters. The rest of the regiment withdrew to the line of battle as reformed and escaped capture. Col. Scales was sent to the Federal War Prison at Johnson's Island, on Lake Erie, where he was confined until after the close of the war. Such were the privations suffered that life at this camp was unendurable. The rations consisted of a portion of corn bread and fat meat served in the morning, which the prisoners usually ate for breakfast and had to starve the rest of the day.

It was a prison for officers and many were the attempts at escape. On one occasion the officers dug a tunnel from the room of one of the prisoners and a number escaped through this tunnel until a prisoner unusually stout blocked the passage and was discovered. Some of the prisoners escaped over the ice to Canada and finally found their way south, but many were killed, some died of exposure, and some were recaptured.

On one occasion Col. Scales and Col. George were elected generals of the camp to lead the other prisoners in revolt. The plan was to overpower the troops guarding the prison and escape over the ice into Canada. All the preparations had been made and were to have been carried into effect on a certain night. Providentially no doubt that very afternoon a storm blew down the stockade and additional troops were sent to guard the prison, and thus the plan was frustrated. Col. Scales always thought that the attack would have been unsuccessful and that God preserved his life for some useful purpose.

At the close of the war Col. Scales returned to North Carolina and for two years engaged in farming at the Henderson home place, in Granville County. He decided to return to his profession of law and moved to Greensboro about 1869 or 1870. Later he was joined by his brother, Gen. Alfred Moore Scales, and the two built up a remunerative practice under the name of Scales and Scales. In 1876 Col. Scales was elected alderman of the City of Greensboro, and in 1877 and 1879 he represented this senatorial district in the General Assembly of North Carolina. In the General Assembly he was regarded as a wise counselor, a safe legislator and an eloquent advocate.

On April 29, 1873, he was elected a ruling elder of the First Presbyterian Church, Greensboro, N. C., and served his church with rare zeal and ability.

Col. Scales made friends easily, being of a genial and happy nature. He was a painstaking and successful lawyer and had in a high degree the gift of real oratory. He was a devoted husband and father and a strict and at times a stern disciplinarian. He was always stern against any evil and any dereliction in the matter of veracity always brought sure and swift retribution. The boys might fight by the hour without punishment, but one hint of falsehood was enough to secure for them vigorous punishment.

At the age of 48, while still a young man, his heart, weakened by the privations of imprisonment on Johnson's Island, gave way and he died in the Presbyterian Hospital in New York City on July 11, 1880. He left eight children, and one was born two weeks after his death. The children were: Annie Bullock, who never married, but who spent many years teaching in the public schools of Greensboro and in a private school of her own; Jennie Bethell, who married H. W. Cobb; Wallace Nathaniel, who moved to Idaho, and for a number of years served as Judge of the District Court of that state, and who died in December, 1923; Archibald Henderson, Rear Admiral United States Navy; Alfred Moore, of Greensboro, N. C.; Effie Irving, who married Zebulon V. Taylor, one time mayor of Greensboro and later connected with the Southern Power Company as president of a number of its subsidiaries; Katherine Henderson, the second wife of H. W. Cobb; Junius Irving, a lawyer, who died in Greensboro, on January 1, 1924; and James Pinckney, of Greensboro, N. C.

So lived and died Junius Irving Scales, leaving to his children a sense of everlasting obligation, a fair and honorable name in which they take pride and an abiding devotion to his memory as man and father.

ALFRED MOORE SCALES.

JESSE A. CUNINGGIM

JESSE A. CUNINGGIM
1832 - 1899

Dr. Jesse Anderson Cuninggim was born in Greene County, North Carolina, January 28th, 1832. He enjoyed the advantages of a truly Christian home, in which love, work and worship played their respective parts in the formation of character, culminating in a consecrated and sympathetic ministry. His father, Rev. W. H. Cuninggim, was a local elder in the Methodist Episcopal Church, South. His mother was Edith Gibbons, a daughter of Rev. J. H. Gibbons, an itinerant minister in the same church.

Dr. Cuninggim was the fifth of eleven children, three sons and eight daughters. Only one of these died in childhood; all the others reached a comparatively old age. One of the daughters is still living and is almost eighty-five years old. Of the children from this humble farm home two sons became preachers and one daughter married a local preacher. Among the grandchildren four sons became preachers and four daughters married preachers. At the time of this writing one of the great-grandsons is a preacher and one of the great-granddaughters is preparing for foreign mission work.

Under the influence of religious example and instruction which surrounded Dr. Cuninggim in his early days it is not surprising that at the age of eleven years he joined the church at Ormond's Chapel, where he was attending a Methodist camp meeting. Rainbow Methodist Church was the place where the family usually worshiped.

Among the experiences of his early days which helped to prepare him for the proper choice of the life work was his narrow escape from drowning in a swollen stream into which he fell from a boat on a winter day. When he came first to the surface he was under the boat, but the second time the rushing stream had swept him near the shore, where he involuntarily caught hold of a hanging branch of a tree. Holding to this small limb he was able to remain on top till he was rescued. In this deliverance he saw very clearly the hand of Providence and was constrained to make final decision to become a minister.

In 1853, after due consideration of his duties to the family, Dr. Cuninggim, under a deep conviction of God's call to service, applied for and received license to preach. He spent one year at Normal College, in Randolph County. Being unable to remain longer in college he joined the North Carolina Annual Conference in session at Wilmington, N. C., 1855.

On January 2nd, 1862, he was married to Miss Lucy Armfield, of Statesville, N. C., and took his bride to Wilson, N. C., where he was just beginning a pastorate in that city. These two souls were joined together in what seemed to be a true spiritual union. No husband and wife ever appeared to be more congenial and more helpful to each other. No children were born into this home, but during their happy and useful ministry they were the genuine friends of hundreds of children whom they loved, counseled and inspired to high ideals of service. This love for young people led them both to become widely interested in the young women at Greensboro Female College and the young men at Trinity College. Young preachers and missionaries had a large share of the love of this devoted couple. It was not thus unnatural for these loved young people to regard them as "Uncle Jesse" and "Aunt Lucy", which terms of endearment came to be used widely by all their friends.

Dr. Cuninggim gave forty-three years of consecrated and efficient service to his church and state—twenty-three of these years as a pastor, sixteen of them as presiding elder and four of them as agent for Greensboro Female College. Twelve of these years were spent in Greensboro. In addition to the time given to the college he was four years pastor and four years presiding elder of the Greensboro District. By these varied and wide relationships to the people of Greensboro he became closely attached to the city. He wielded a wide influence in the city's life and loved it with a genuine devotion. It was perfectly natural for him to turn back to this loved place to spend the hours of life's twilight when he discovered that his physical condition would no longer permit him to render effective service in the Conference. This was a short twilight, for on the seventh of January after superannuation at the Annual Conference which met the 30th of November, 1898, he came to the close of a useful life. Though he knew death was near he was calm and unafraid. How fitting it was that he should have died in Greensboro and with his devoted wife by his side.

One who knew him well writes thus: "Dr. Cuninggim was pre-eminently a great man; great in character and purpose." He certainly was a rare combination. Some men have genius cropping out at one point and are able to achieve much in one field of activity. Dr. Cuninggim had such a combination of capabilities that no one stood out pre-eminent, but they all made contributions to his well-rounded and strong personality. His energies were always directed toward practical ends. This was evident in his ministry of preaching as well as in his ministry of service. His emphasis in preaching was to strengthen and soothe instead of to raise questions or arouse fears. His personality gave nobility to his work, he received no greatness from his work. Of this man Bishop John C. Kilgo said: "Some men have special facilities for the destruction of men; others a genius for making men. Dr. Cuninggim belonged to the latter class. The young men of his Conference will suffer the greatest loss by his death."

Here then, was a man who loved much and gave much to bless the world in which he lived. His was a sympathetic ministry, seeking those who needed service and bestowed lavishly upon them such as he had to give. Silver and gold he had very little to give, but of this small amount he gave liberally. Among the contributions which he made was a gift of one thousand dollars to Trinity College as a scholarship for worthy young men seeking an education. His life as a pastor was a most helpful one. Not only did he visit his parishoners or the preachers' homes on his district, but he made yearly visits to his kin scattered over many sections of the state. His visits always carried benediction and comfort. He respected the opinions of his contemporaries, though he had strong convictions. He was greatly loved by the ministers and laymen of his Conference and his judgments were reliable.   He was sent by his Annual Conference to represent it in the legislative body of the church.   Trinity College, of which institution he was for many years a trustee, honored him with the degree of Doctor of Divinity.   A great man lived among us here in the world and is gone, but although he is not here in person to continue his ministry, the influences of his life will remain to bless and to guide those who carry on the ministry of love and sympathy.

J. M. ORMOND.

DeWitt Clinton Benbow

DEWITT CLINTON BENBOW
1832 - 1902

It is for county historical societies to preserve the local folk lore and traditions, which, in many cases, are more to be relied upon to "keep a history straight" then the many more imposing efforts of historians and biographers.

Guilford has been fortunate in having among her citizens statesmen, professional men, divines, and teachers, who have added to her reputation and placed her in the forefront of the counties of the state—among them Calvin H. Wiley, the first State Superintendent of Education—and whose memories are cherished, not only by the citizens of Guilford, but by the people of the state. A few of their portraits adorn the walls of the Public Library, and it is well that statues and busts and portraits should remind us, and especially those of later generations who have no personal recollections of them, of our obligation to them.

There died in Greensboro, in 1902, one citizen of whom it is not exaggeration to say the City of Greensboro is more indebted than to any other of her citizens for his activities since the War Between the States in the upbuilding of her business and industrial life, and no one surpassed him in his efforts in behalf of the educational advantages she now possesses. For many years he was foremost among the leading spirits of enterprise. He never sought popularity. He was a thinker, not a talker, unless he was approached for information and advice by those who contemplated entering upon some untried venture, when he always gave the results of his investigations and meditations. While he had visions, he was never visionary. He had the greatest faith in the possibilities and probabilities of the uplift and improvement of his native county, and Greensboro—DeWitt Clinton Benbow.

In the rush and hurry of later years and the great growth and improvement of both city and county, we are prone to ignore, or not revert to simple beginnings. I have often said that the genesis of the City of Greensboro was the building of the original Benbow Hotel—the present Guilford—and I have not changed my idea. This will doubtless strike as extravagant those who did not know Greensboro just before, and for half a decade after, the War Between the States—a straggling village of less than two thousand people, white and black; a wayside station on the North Carolina Railroad and the Piedmont Railroad; visited by few outsiders, who tarried only long enough to transact their business which called them there; known only for its educational advantages—Edgeworth and Greensboro Female College—and as being the residence town of a few state notables.

At the time Dr. Benbow began the erection of his hotel Greensboro had three hostelries, such as they were, not very inviting, whose patronage did not exceed upon the average three strangers a day, one for each day during twelve months. When the walls of the Benbow Hotel were about three stories high, some one said to Dr. Benbow: "Doctor, why are you spending so much time and money in erecting such a large building for a hotel? Do you not know that very few strangers stop here over night?" Dr. Benbow's reply was: "Where would they stop? I will give them a place to stop."

Dr. Benbow had a dairy and vegetable garden in connection with the hotel, but he did not have the hotel "bar" which was so great an inducement to patronize other hotels in the "good old days." The Benbow Hotel had a good send-off in the very beginning. The day it was opened to the public David B. Hill, afterwards Governor of New York, made a political speech from the veranda, and among the names appearing on its register, the name of Zebulon B. Vance stands first.

This hotel, I had almost said, to use an expression very common, "placed Greensboro on the map." The change in the number of visitors was marvelous. The fame of the house was spread over the state, especially by commercial traveling men, "drummers" as we used to call them, many of whom, attracted by the appointment of the hotel and its service, made it their headquarters. The hotel had not been open many months when a great number of commercial travelers who, on Saturday night were within one hundred miles of Greensboro, would come to the Benbow Hotel to spend Sunday. One evidence of the great influx of visitors as a result of Dr. Benbow's foresight and faith is that the average number of daily patrons for five years was ninety-three, as shown by the hotel register. Contrast that with the average combined daily patronage of all the Greensboro hostelries of only three.

When Dr. Benbow returned to Greensboro from Fayetteville in 1862, where he had resided for several years practicing dentistry and operating a cotton mill, he acquired property on South Elm Street, south of Sycamore, and soon built a brick storehouse on the corner now occupied by Meyer's store, and conducted a retail business for some while. Soon thereafter he built quite a block of buildings on South Elm, adjoining the storehouse. In this block was the Benbow Hall, which for many years supplied the place of a town hall, used by theatrical and concert companies, and as a dance hall; in fact, it was a theatre, opera house, and dance hall. Not long thereafter he built the Crown Mills, on East Washington Street.

While in failing health and after he began to feel advancing age, and under some great difficulties, he superintended the building of the New Benbow (Meyer's site), having sold the original to Capt. Fisher, the present Guilford—"his ruling passion strong in death."

Dr. Benbow's efforts were not confined to the upbuilding of the city. He was among the foremost advocates of the "stock law," or "no fence law," which encountered strong opposition and created unfriendly feelings toward him personally, but he lived to know that some of the bitterest opposers came to be its staunchest friends. He was also among the earliest advocates of good roads, and showed his faith by his work. As an object lesson, at his own expense he built two sections of paved, or macadam road, on roads leading to the city.

Having seen a vineyard near Fayetteville he determined to give the Guilford people an object lesson in the cultivation of grapes, and established a vineyard in Oak Ridge Township, and through the Agricultural Departments, Federal and State, and the Federal Immigration Bureau, he obtained the services of a native of Holland, an expert in grape culture.

He was among the first to devote attention to the improvement of the cattle and stock of the country, and to that end purchased a number of registered cattle of improved breeds.

He was also among the first to invest in new farming machinery and dairy improvements.

But Dr. Benbow's activities were not confined to the material, commercial, and manufacturing developments of the city and county. While a member of the Board of Aldermen he advocated the establishment of graded schools, and by having the charter of the city amended, he succeeded in giving Greensboro the credit of having the first graded school in the state, and as a trustee of Guilford College, he participated in establishing the first rural graded school in the state at that college village.

When the work of rebuilding Greensboro Female College, after it was burned in 1863, was in danger of being stopped, at least temporarily, owing to the death of Rev. Mr. Barringer, who had been superintending the work, Dr. Benbow took upon himself the financing and completion of the building, and at once notified all contractors and laborers to proceed with the work and to look to him for their pay, which they did.

At one time, as is well known, the state conducted its normal institutes at stated periods and limited terms in the several sections of the state under the supervision of Dr. Chas. D. McIver and Edward A. Alderman. Dr. Benbow and a few others, especially a lady connected with Guilford College, conceived the idea of having a permanent school for women, and with the aid of Professors McIver and Alderman, succeeded in getting the North Carolina Teachers' Association interested, and finally at the annual meeting at Black Mountain that assembly recommended the necessary legislation. It is said that some of the most ardent friends of the measure were so fearful of the result at that meeting that there was a prospect of deferring the matter for another year. When Dr. Benbow was advised of the status he at once wired to the friends of the measure to force a vote at that session, which was done and the recommendation was adopted by a small majority. The idea of Dr. Benbow and his coadjutors was to have a state institution for women on the order of the University. As a matter of policy, to disarm opposition, the name proposed was "Normal and Industrial School for Girls". After the success of the institution became established and had met with pronounced popular favor, the title was amended as we have it now.

After the act of the Assembly incorporating the school, its location became the subject of active competition between different localities, and donations of land and funds were offered by several cities. The trustees of the school met in Greensboro to open the bids and to settle the question of location. In order to locate the college or school at Greensboro, in addition to other inducements, a subscription by the city of $30,000 in money was necessary to give Greensboro a living chance. Before the city could subscribe the proposition had to be submitted to the voters, for which election some time would be required. Dr. Benbow and other citizens got together and signed an obligation to personally pay the amount in case the city did not subscribe it. This action gave Greensboro the location. Of course the voters approved the subscription. Dr. Benbow and some other citizens also guaranteed an amount sufficient to have the colored A. and M. College located here.

Another evidence of the foresight and accuracy of his calculation is the Mt. Airy Granite Company, the stone from which is being used in the erection of our new court house. While the C. F. and Y. V. Railway was being built, Dr. Benbow and another citizen had occasion to visit Mt. Airy, and while there inspected the large area of granite and the local structures built with it. They at once contracted to purchase, and for awhile developed the property, and organized a company, and now the output is shipped annually to sections of this state, to several other states, and the District of Columbia.

Of course Dr. Benbow was not the only citizen who has largely contributed to the growth of the city and county, as is well known. My object is writing this is "lest we forget" that he was a prime mover in many of the causes of our prosperity and reputation, and an adviser and co-worker in nearly all of them.

I had almost neglected to call attention to the fact that he was one of the original five who foresaw the great advantage of a public park at the old battle field for the city and county, and who purchased the property and organized the Guilford Battle Ground Company.

Dr. Benbow came of one of the oldest families in the county, a family noted for industry, honesty, and public spirit. His great, great grandfather, Charles Benbow, came from Wales in 1718, to Pennsylvania, when a lad of fifteen years of age, and to pay for passage across the seas was bound to a Quaker gentleman named Carver. Soon thereafter Mr. Carver moved to Bladen County, North Carolina, bringing the lad with him. In the course of time Charles married the daughter of Carver and moved to Guilford, first to the southern part of the county, and then to the northwestern section, where so many Quakers lived. One of his sons, Thomas, who had a blacksmith shop not far from New Garden (now Guilford College) wrought the nails, hinges, and latches used in the building of the old New Garden Meeting House. He also had one of the few tanneries in this section of the state.

One of Thomas's sons, Charles, married a Miss Saunders, in 1787, daughter of the man who built the famous old Saunders Mill, in what is now Oak Ridge Township, which was patronized by farmers of adjoining counties. Dr. Benbow was the youngest child of this marriage, born in 1832, was educated in the common schools of Guilford, and at a college in Providence, R. I., where he also studied dentistry. He married in 1857 Miss Mary Scott, of Greensboro, daughter of David Scott, a merchant. She proved to be a helpmeet indeed. He died at the age of 70 and was buried at Green Hill.

Our Guilford Benbows were of the family of Admiral Benbow, of the British Navy, who earned great reputation for himself and the navy in Britain's war with Spain at the time of the great Spanish Armada's threatened invasion. Comparatively recently the British have named one of their finest ships in his honor, as was done many years ago, and the silver service presented to the original Benbow Man of War was again presented to the last named ship.

At the time of Dr. Benbow's death many newspapers of the state took note of the loss to Greensboro and the state, but these were of but passing notice, so I have prepared

hastily this sketch that our Historical Society might preserve among its records the name of a citizen whose memory
every citizen of Guilford should delight to honor, thus carrying out one of the purposes for which it was organized. I
was acquainted with him since the summer of 1865, and,
knowing him well during the last twenty years of his life,
I have personal knowledge of many of his activities I have
mentioned.

JAMES T. MOREHEAD.

Written for Guilford Historical Association November
19th, 1911.

JULIUS A. GRAY

JULIUS A. GRAY
1833 - 1891

Julius A. Gray was born in the County of Randolph, on the 6th of September, 1833, and the force of heredity, or the truth of the terse Anglo-Saxon axiom that "blood will tell", was notably portrayed in the moral and intellectual qualities which characterized his childhood and youth, and shone in the maturity of active manhood. His maternal grandfather, Jeduthan Harper, was a gallant officer of the Revolution, and his mother was a direct descendant of Robert Goodloe Harper, the erudite scholar and learned jurist; his father, General Alexander Gray, was an officer of the war of 1812, and his long life of nearly one hundred years was spent in the service of his state, for 22 years being a member of the legislature, and before Tennessee became a state, a commissioner to treat with the Indians of that region.

Col. Julius A. Gray was a man of clear, vigorous intellect, unbending will, indomitable energy and unsullied integrity. He graduated at Davidson College and commenced his business training as an officer of the Bank of Greensboro, of which Mr. Jesse H. Lindsay was president. In 1858, at the age of 25, he married Emma Victoria Morehead, youngest daughter of the late Gov. John M. Morehead, and "Blandwood", the old homestead of the Morehead family, famous for its hospitality through several generations, became his home, and there he reared a family of six—two sons and four daughters. During his life, "Blandwood" continued to be the center of the social life of Greensboro, and many distinguished persons were entertained within its portals.

At the annual meeting, in 1879, of the stockholders of the Western Railway Co., when its reorganization was effected, Col. Gray was elected president, the name was changed to the Cape Fear and Yadkin Valley Railway Co., and from a short line of but forty-two miles, commencing at Fayetteville, without connections, and stopping in the woods, a road without credit, impoverished, and in debt, Col. Gray, by his tireless energy, financial skill and faultless judgment, built up a great system of more than 400 miles, extending transversely across North Carolina from the seaboard to the mountains—a North Carolina road in truth and in fact—building up waste places, revivifying our own territory, and putting new life into our own people. This road is truly a monument to his memory, more lasting than marble column or adamantine shaft.

While the building of the Cape Fear Road was the crowning achievement of Col. Gray's life, still he was deeply interested in the development of the industrial wealth of the state, and the development of the towns along the railroad. His chief interest centered in his home town of Greensboro, and it never had a more loyal citizen. He gave lavishly of his time and means to develop its educational and industrial facilities. From a geographical standpoint, the city being near the center of the state, and because of its splendid railway connections, he steadfastly maintained that Greensboro would one day become a large and prosperous city. This prophecy has happily come true, though he did not live to see the completion of many of his enterprises.

Col. Gray was also a director in the Greensboro Female College, an honorary colonel of the Guilford Grays, a promoter of the North Carolina Steel and Iron Co., director of the Central Land Co., president of the Greensboro National Bank, president of the Mt Airy Granite Co., director of the Guilford Battle Ground Co., and other civic and state wide developments.

He was a devoted member of the First Presbyterian Church, of Greensboro, and on April 14, 1891, as the sun sank in the west, the tide of life ebbed out, and he passed into the Great Beyond in the 58th year of his life. The many beautiful floral tributes and resolutions of sympathy sent to the family by various business and social organizations from all sections, attested the high esteem in which he was held, not only by the community in which he lived, but the state at large. As stated in one of the resolutions of sympathy received: ''Col. Gray combined, in rare symmetry, the qualities that ennoble and dignify a man. In form, feature and manner he was attractive and impressive; in

council, wise; in judgment, accurate; in business, diligent;
in leadership, brave and aggressive; undismayed by obstacles;
calm and self-poised in the face of danger, kind and sympathetic in disposition, considerate of the feelings of others,
courteous to all of every station and degree in life, charitable
to the poor and erring, true to his friends, loyal to his word,
clean-handed, honest and honorable''.

J. H. MYROVER.

Adapted by the family from Myrover Memorial of 1891.

JESSE RANKIN WHARTON

JESSE RANKIN WHARTON
1833 - 1904

The subject of this sketch was born September 2nd, 1833, on what was then known as the Watson Wharton farm, lying one mile north of the city limits at that time, but today it constitutes northern Greensboro.

His parents were Watson and Melinda Wharton. In early boyhood be labored on his father's farm, but his parents being ambitious for his future career, used every available means to secure for him an adequate education. His academic training was acquired through the male academies of Greensboro under the tutorship of different men. He entered the State University at Chapel Hill at an early age, graduating from that institution at the age of twenty-three with distinction and honors. Soon after his graduation he went to Hertford County, in eastern Carolina, and engaged in teaching.

While located there he met and married Mattie Turner. Of that union, dating from August 3rd, 1859, two children were born, a son and a daughter. The daughter, Minnie, died at the age of 16. The son, the Rev. T. A. Wharton, D. D., is pastor of the First Presbyterian Church, of Sherman, Texas, today.

In 1862 Mr. Wharton brought his young family to his father's home, and accompanied by an early chum, James Albright, he went to Richmond, Va., entering the affray between the states, by volunteering in the 12th Battalion of Virginia Artillery on May 3rd, 1862. This battalion was commanded by Rev. Taylor Bolling, of Petersburg, Va. As a member of this battalion he rendered many courageous and valorous deeds in the interest of his country in the battles of Drewry's Bluff, Seven Pines, and many other points in Virginia. He also served his comrades in various ways as a non-commissioned officer in a courteous and a commendable manner, thus showing his genuine manhood.

He remained with this command of the Confederate Army
until General Lee surrendered at Appomattox Courthouse.
After the war he returned to Greensboro.

His wife died soon after, leaving him the care of two
small children. Feeling that his life work was along the
educational line, he entered Edgeworth Female Seminary as
professor of mathematics. Here he remained for several
years, rendering very efficient service as a teacher, living at
his father's homestead.

On May 16th, 1867, he married as his second wife Mary
Rankin, of this county. To this union were born four sons,
Henry Watson, Ernest Rankin, Lee Gilmer and Robert Hall,
two of whom still survive, Henry W. and Robert H. The
value of this home to the community is attested by the fact
that of its five sons one (Turner) became a minister of the
Gospel and three (Henry, Lee and Robert) were made ruling elders in the church of their fathers.

Soon after his second marriage he went to Statesville and
entered a partnership with Rev. W. W. Pharr in a female
school, but after teaching one year Mr. Wharton severed his
connection with this school. A few months later he took
charge of a male school in Salisbury, where he remained for
two years. While here he prepared several boys for college,
among whom was our worthy Senator Hon. Lee S. Overman.

At the end of two years Mr. Wharton was called to his
old home on account of his father's illness, where he remained
after his father's death to care for his invalid mother and his
father's farm. Here he spent the remainder of his years,
occupying a part of his time on the farm, but to a greater
extent in matters pertaining to the educational interest of
his county.

In 1892 he was elected on the Board of Commissioners
for the town; he also served on the Board of County Commissioners for a term or two.

When the first graded system of school in Greensboro was
inaugurated Mr. Wharton was chosen as the first superintendent and principal. He also constituted one of the board
of examiners for common school teachers of the county.
Later on he was elected Superintendent of County Public
Schools. Here he did a noble work. He visited the schools
of the county in person, traveling all over the county on

horseback, over all sorts of roads in all kinds of weather. His work in this capacity has never been properly estimated and appreciated. The writer knows from personal association with Mr. Wharton that he gave this work the greater part of his time, the best of his intellectual talents. His whole heart was in this work. As County Superintendent of Public Schools for nearly a quarter of a century he developed a school system in Guilford that is unexcelled in any county of the state. Few there were in the city or county that did not know the familiar face of Mr. Wharton, his long connection with the public school system bringing him into close touch with two generations of his fellowmen.

Walking constantly upright in the sight of God and man, his life was an inspiration and an example to the youth of the county in which his interest seemed to center. This work stands today as a monument to his ability, his energy and his untiring philanthropic zeal. From early manhood his pure character, his intellectual endowments, his lofty ideals, his integrity, his fidelity to every worthy cause were all marked characteristics and the impress of his character on the county is indelibly fixed.

J. R. Wharton's name will go down with the annals of Guilford County history as one of her most intellectual sons and one of her leading educators. As a citizen he was thoroughly democratic, always standing for and advocating any measure that looked toward the advancement of the public interest of his town or county. He was genial and social with his fellowmen and while he was not a sportsman, yet one of his greatest delights during his idle hours was to engage in a game of chess, at which game he was a champion player.

He was a staunch Presbyterian and loyal to his church and pastor. His life reflects the Christian principles for which he stood. His own motive in life was the uplift of his fellowmen and the advancement of public interest. He was faithful in every trust and shrank from no duty, however disagreeable it might be. He had to face many cares and perplexities, but he met them with manly courage and fidelity.

W. C. RANKIN.

WILLIAM FRANKLIN ALDERMAN

WILLIAM FRANKLIN ALDERMAN

1833 - 1911

A generation ago a new girl entered Greensboro Female College just before the mid-winter examinations. It happened that she had an unusual liking for mathematics. With the freedom that was given pupils in those days she had traveled rapidly over the ground of her easiest study and had given too little time to other subjcts, therefore she found herself ill-prepared for general work when she was classed according to her mathematics.

Lonely, homesick, depressed, because she saw herself in an almost impossible situation, she was ready to give up, go home and wait for the fall term when things might better adjust themselves.

Among the influences which held her to the college and thus changed her subsequent life was the kindness of the mathematics teacher, Professor W. F. Alderman.

How the memory of him strikes through the years and emphasizes Matthew Arnold's words in regard to Emerson: "He was a friend and aider of the spirit."

Professor Alderman was essentially this for any girl who was searching for the finer things of life, for intellectual development, for spiritual beauty. Only the shallower pupils failed to recognize this quality in the quiet Christian gentleman who led us with unfailing courtesy and patience.

Among the upbuilders of Greensboro Professor Alderman should stand out as the man who builded better than he knew because of his love for the less material things of life. He founded no great business by which money might be drawn to the town. He simply went his modest way, loving music, poetry, all those immaterial things which have been dear to the seers of visions, but Greensboro is today a better Greensboro because W. F. Alderman held such high place in its beginnings. The town is now a music loving one partly on account of the Woodroffe-Alderman Orchestra, which used to delight Greensboro College girls and, at the same time, was helping to form the musical taste of Greensboro itself.

So unassuming was Professor Alderman he would not have classed himself with the makers of the town, and for this reason, I stress the fact of his influence as teacher along with that unconscious influence exerted by every fine personality.

We of America have such a passion for bigness we are belittling the small college in our educational system. The highest mountains and longest rivers, the biggest schools and richest men impress us so greatly we sometimes lose sight of the landscape's beauty or the real worth of men.

Your lecturer who knows nothing of his hearers can never be the teacher that Arnold of Rugby was, or Sawney Webb of Bellbuckle. The student may accumulate all possible facts under the broader system, but for pure joy in learning a thing, for that inspiration which comes from thought kindling at the fire of living thought you must have the direct human touch. It is just here that the smaller school gets in its best work. There is no possible way of measuring the good that Professor Alderman accomplished in his dealings with girls at old Greensboro College. Mothers and grandmothers scattered far and wide would gladly give voice, with me, to the love and appreciation inspired by this teacher whose heart was in his chosen work.

When I consider that our great colleges and universities are sometimes manned by teachers whose brilliance overshadows their moral force I am distressed for the pupils. "Character teaches above our wills." In the long years of a strenuous life, happy the man or woman who can look back to a real friendship with teachers whose strength of character, whose whole moral fiber, helped their students into right paths.

Professor Alderman was possessed of a catholic taste. Though much of his work was in the field of mathematics, he had a profound love for literature. He had read widely, and always the best held its appeal for him. His familiarity with the English classics was remarkable, and along this line I owe him much because of his wise leading and his fine discrimination.

In later years, and during my own teaching days, I spoke to him of the fact that poetry had lost its power over me. He disapproved of this and cautioned me about allowing that side of my nature to become dwarfed. I remember that he spoke very seriously, and not once did he make me feel that his humor might bestir itself (what girl does not recall that glint of humor which sometimes brightened those deep seeing eyes), but this time he was not making fun.

I took him at his word and once more began to cultivate my love for pure beauty, such beauty as one finds in Keats and Shelley, and others of the great lyric poets; and now, almost daily I have cause to thank my teacher for helping me to save that quality of one's being whose loss is irreparble—a recognition of beauty and joy in its expression.

Professor Alderman's religious life was so much a part of the man you could not differentiate it from his life as a teacher. You might speak of his connection with West Market Church, his loyalty to that organization, his long service as treasurer there, but when you have stated these facts you have not given any idea of the gentleman who walked in his Master's footsteps, wearing always the white flower of a blameless life, but wearing it without ostentation —a Christian gentleman in deed and in truth.

Now that I have given my tribute as pupil to teacher, I shall speak of the outstanding facts of William Franklin Alderman's life. He was the son of Daniel Alderman, of New Hanover County, N. C. The Aldermans were of English ancestry, having come to America from London in the middle of the eighteenth century. Professor Alderman was born in New Hanover County, January 8, 1833. He was educated at Randolph-Macon College, Va., and the University of North Carolina, graduating with distinction from the last named institution on June 19, 1856.

He had chosen the profession of teaching as his life work, and immediately after graduation he entered upon his life pursuit.

He commenced teaching in Goldsboro Female College, in the summer of 1857, under the presidency of Dr. S. Milton Frost. In the year 1860 he accepted a position in Greensboro Female College, where he continued to labor until the college was burned in 1863.

This great blow to the college left it prostrate for the space of ten years. Meanwhile, in the fall of 1863, he accepted a position in Spartanburg Female College, where he continued until the winding up of the war, which also wound up the affairs of that institution. The college suspended, the faculty disbanded and students retired to their homes.

Eight months after the surrender at Appomattox Dr. Turner M. Jones opened up the Louisburg Female College and Mr. Alderman accepted a position in that school. He remained there for four years, when this institution was suspended. One can hardly imagine a more heroic fight than southern educators were making in the heart-breaking days of reconstruction.

After the suspension of Louisburg College, Professor Alderman went to the village of Maysville, N. C., and taught until 1873.

In the fall of that year Greensboro Female College again opened its doors for the reception of pupils with Dr. Jones as president.

Professor Alderman accepted a position in the school a second time and taught there till 1892.

During this period Dr. Jones and Professor Alderman, working unitedly, made their impress for good on the lives of girls from different states in the south. Greensboro College was a pioneer in the cause of woman's education, and the loyalty of the alumnae of an older day speaks profoundly for the work of the faculty at that time.

Professor Alderman's influence for good in college and community was doubtless due in a great measure to his very happy home. He was married February 1st, 1859, to Miss Anna Maria Love, also of New Hanover County, and the well known names of their eight children which follow testify both to inherited ability and Christian training of that home: A. Haywood, Sidney L., William F., and Jesse E. Alderman, Mrs. Charles Ireland, Mrs. Myra Albright, Mrs. Norman Wills and Mrs. Richard Wills, all of Greensboro, and all living in 1924 save the eldest son, A. Haywood Alderman.

The first break in this happy circle was the mother's death July 11th, 1888. The father lived on till June 8th, 1911, and, fortunately for the youth of that day, continued his beloved work till physical strength failed. His spirit never grew old, for encompassed by the love of his children and cheered by books, music and religion, his last days were filled with sunshine and almost to the end his trained mind gave glad service in solving student problems of a third generation.

Of such lives a prophet of old has written: "They that be teachers shall shine as the brightness of the firmament".

METTA FOLGER TOWNDSEND.

DAVID SCHENCK

DAVID SCHENCK

1835 - 1902

The ancestors of David Schenck came to this country from England, having originally lived in the mountains of Switzerland, where they had been exiled on account of religious convictions. In 1708, they came to Pennsylvania. There, in 1737, was born to Michael Schenck, a son, who was also named Michael, and to this second Michael, there was born, in 1771, in Lancaster County, a son, likewise named Michael.

In 1790, Michael Schenck, the third of his name, settled in the village of Lincolnton, North Carolina, engaging in the mercantile business. He prospered, and is known to history as being the founder of the first cotton mill established in the south. This mill, erected in 1813, was located on Mill Branch, a short distance east of Lincolnton. The mill was six years later removed to the South Fork (Catawba) River, and continued in operation until 1863. Thus was made the modest beginning of cotton milling in that section, which now leads the United States in the manufacture of cotton.

A son of this founder of cotton milling in the south, David Warlick Schenck, was born at Lincolnton, in 1809. He studied medicine at Jefferson Medical College, in Philadelphia, and won distinction in his profession, particularly for surgical skill. He married Susan Rebecca Bevens, of Charleston, S. C., named for her grandmother, Susan Rebecca Folker, who was the wife of James Folker, a captain in the English Navy, who married in Charleston and settled there.

On the 24th of March, 1835, David Schenck was born. He was educated in the high school of Silas C. Lindsley, read law under Hon. Haywood C. Guion, then attended and was graduated from the famous "Log Town" law school of the distinguished Chief Justice Richmond Pearson.

He began the practice of law in 1857 at Dallas, Gaston County, N. C., and his promising abilities were almost immediately recognized by the County of Gaston, which made him its solicitor in the following year. On the 25th of August, 1859, he was married to Sallie Wilfong Ramseur, sister of the distinguished Major-General Stephen Dodson Ramseur, who was mortally wounded while gallantly leading his troops in the battle of Cedar Creek (1864).

Returning in 1860 to his native town, the County of Lincoln made him its solicitor, and in 1861, he was elected a delegate to the Secession Convention, which comprised in its membership the state's leading men. He was the youngest delegate in that body, but actively participated in its momentous and important deliberations.

He was later appointed Confederate States Receiver, in which capacity he collected large sums of money for the Confederate Government.

Being under political disabilities, he did not, after the war, immediately enter political life, but devoted himself to the practice of his profession, to studious reading over a wide range of subjects, and took an active interest in public movements, looking to the moral and material reconstruction and upbuilding of his community and section.

He served as Alderman and Mayor of Lincolnton, as Master of his Masonic Lodge, as a ruling elder in the Presbyterian Church, of which he was then a member, and as a trustee of Davidson College. He took an enthusiastic and effective interest in better school facilities—an interest in education which was maintained throughout his life. It would be gratifying to him that there now stands on the site of his beautiful old homeplace, "Evergreen," the Lincolnton High School.

At this time, he was particularly concerned in better railroad facilities for his section, interesting himself in the extension of the Wilmington, Charlotte and Rutherfordton (now Seaboard Air Line) Railroad, and later was one of the organizers and a member of the original board of directors of the Chester and Lenoir Railroad.

During this period, he enjoyed a rapidly growing legal practice in Lincoln and the surrounding counties, and his reputation as a lawyer and advocate was being constantly extended and enhanced.

The election of 1868 had given North Carolina a set of Superior Court judges whose administration of justice had brought the courts into disrepute. In 1874, when new elections were to be held, great public interest was manifested in the elevation to the bench of men who would restore the courts to the respect and confidence of the people. In the Ninth Judicial District, both Hon. William M. Shipp and Col. John F. Hoke were brought forward by their respective friends, but when the convention assembled, May 13, 1874, Schenck was nominated by the Democrats over these two prominent and distinguished opponents. He was then just thirty-nine.

Conforming his action to the constructive requirements of the time, Mr. Schenck made an extended and exciting canvass, not discussing politics or parties, men or measures, but insisting upon the supremacy of the law and the restoration of justice and equity as essential elements in our daily life. In the campaign, he urged for North Carolinians the restoration of those rights which had been abused—the rights to full citizenship and impartial justice.

He won a notable victory, doubling previous Democratic majorities, and it was his task and fortune to rehabilitate, in his district, the administration of justice.

In 1875 the Constitution was so amended that the judges rode all the circuits of the state. Wherever he held courts, Judge Schenck made a profoundly favorable impression, and was universally regarded as one of North Carolina's truly great judges. Typical of many editorial comments of the press at this time are two short extracts:

"Judge Schenck is one of the best lawyers, and is indeed, in all respects, one of the leading men of the state, and the manner in which he has discharged the duties of his high office since his election places him at once by the side of Gaston. Ruffin, Mangum and others whose names are immortal in North Carolina." (Concord Register, 1875.)

"Judge Schenck is an honor to the state, winning all who know him, as much by his genial bearing and admirable social qualities as by his distinguished abilities as a jurist and the sacredness in which he holds the ermine he wears so honorably." (Raleigh News, February, 1877.)

In recognition of his erudition, the University of North Carolina, in 1880, conferred upon Judge Schenck the honorary degree of LL. D.

One of the outstanding incidents of his life as a judge was the conflict of authority between the Federal Courts and the

North Carolina Courts. Judge Schenck was the first state judge to test this issue; he believed that the rights of the State Courts had been invaded, and he instructed the Clerk of the Court of one of the counties not to obey a writ issued by the Federal Court. This legal controversy was one of important significance, and attracted the attention of the entire state. The correspondence between Judge Schenck and Judge R. P. Dick, of the Federal Court, the discussion of the legal points involved, and the elaborate "opinion" of Judge Schenck, constitute one of the most interesting legal controversies that the state has known in its entire history. (The first case was that of State vs. Young, Polk County, 1876. Later cases: State vs. Ray, et al.; State vs. Hoskins.)

As far back as 1881, prohibition was an issue in North Carolina, and Judge Schenck canvassed his section in favor of prohibition. In an editorial written at the time of his death, in 1902, the North Carolina Christian Advocate referred to this campaign:

". . . The writer recalls with great satisfaction his first opportunity of seeing and hearing Judge Schenck. It was during the summer of 1881, in the court square, in the town of Newton, in the celebrated prohibition campaign. He was then in the zenith of his power, and he threw himself with all the force of a matchless oratory into earnest contention for the adoption of the Constitutional Amendment.

"There were thousands of sturdy men of Catawba and adjoining counties in the great throng, many of them strenuously opposed to the measure, but they swayed and melted under the burning words which came as from a tongue of fire, and there is hardly a doubt, if the election had followed immediately, that almost the whole audience would have voted for the adoption of the amendment."

At an earlier time he had taken a leading part in a town election in Lincolnton, which resulted in closing the saloons, then called "grog shops".

In 1881, the Richmond and Danville Railroad tendered him the position of General Counsel, and the compensation being so much greater than that attached to his office, in view of the growing demands of his large family, Judge Schenck felt constrained to resign his judicial position and return to the practice of law. The position of General Counsel of the

Richmond and Danville Railroad (now Southern Railway) was, at that time, regarded as probably the outstanding corporation legal position in the state, and paid what was then considered a large salary and carried with it great responsibility.

His new position caused him to move to Greensboro in May, 1882.

In 1883, Governor Jarvis tendered to Judge Schenck the appointment as Associate Justice of North Carolina Supreme Court, which he felt compelled to reluctantly decline, largely for pecuniary reasons.

In Greensboro, his new home, he became a leader in all that tended to its moral and material progress.

In 1887, Greensboro began to awaken from a sleepy village to a more progressive town, and an election for a one hundred thousand dollar bond issue was to really determine whether the town should continue to stand still or go forward. Judge Schenck threw himself into the campaign for bonds with energy and determination, and the bond issue carried. A one hundred thousand dollar bond issue then was considered a stupendous sum for Greensboro, and one hundred thousand dollars then went a long way—for this bond issue was to be expended for opening new streets, for paving, water works, sewer, electric lights, schools, and for the cemetery!

Judge Schenck, a member of the Board of Town Commissioners, was made chairman of the three important committees that were to handle matters in which he was most interested and active: the committees on schools, on extending North Elm Street, and on improving and extending the cemetery.

At that time, Elm (Main) Street terminated at what is now the O. Henry Hotel site, and the residence of Judge Gilmer was directly in the course of the further extension of the street. As chairman of the committee, Judge Schenck carried forward to a successful and satisfactory conclusion the negotiations with Judge Gilmer for the removal of his house and for the right of way for the new street, the Elm Street extension. The street was soon built, marking an epoch in the growth of the town; for the extension of this street also carried with it the construction of a number of other streets and the opening of a large new section for the growth of the town.   One of these streets was named by the Commissioners "Schenck" Street, in appreciation of his great public service in this matter.

A keeper was employed for the cemetery, and it was soon made larger and more beautiful.

But Judge Schenck was most interested in better schools, and after a hard fight in the board, was authorized to expend ten thousand dollars for a new *brick* school.   The first brick was laid August 1, 1887, and at a public gathering celebrating the cornerstone laying, on August 17th, he delivered the dedicatory address, a plea for better popular education.   This school, still in use (1924), is known today as the Lindsay Street School.

Also while a member of the board, he sponsored an ordinance providing that no saloon should be licensed to do business within four hundred feet of the public square, the market house, or graded school.

When he resigned from the Board of Commissioners, the leading paper of Greensboro, commenting editorially, said:

"The beautiful City of Greensboro of today—the paved streets and sidewalks, the fine public schools, the superb fire department, the beautiful cemetery, the waterworks and electric lights, and the grand progressive spirit and public energy of our citizens, are as much the fruit of the mental and physical labors of Judge Schenck, and the result of his tireless energy and force of character, as are all the evidences of industry and devotion shown by the restoration of the Guilford Battle Ground".

About this same time, Judge Schenck became deeply interested in rescuing from oblivion the Revolutionary Battlefield of Guilford Court House, which is about four and one-half miles northwest of Greensboro.   In his personal journal, he wrote (May 7, 1887):

"The Guilford Battle Ground Company was organized today.   Last fall (1886), I visited Mr. Hoskins, who lives on part of the Battle Ground, and as I drove over the sacred spot on my return home, I suddenly conceived the idea of purchasing it and improving it and endeavoring to persuade the United States or the state, or wealthy individuals, to erect suitable monuments thereon to preserve the memory of the men who here crippled Cornwallis, so that he began the race of escape which ended in his capture at Yorktown.''

This vision of his purpose, written in 1887, through succeeding years, became a reality in every particular. He did immediately interest a number of public-spirited men in this work. At the organization meeting, May 7, 1887, the five original directors of the Company elected were J. W. Scott, D. W. C. Benbow, Julius A. Gray, Thomas B. Keogh and David Schenck. Later, making a telling and powerful appeal before the legislature, he obtained the passage, by a majority of one, of a bill providing a small annual appropriation for the maintenance of the battlefield. After he and his associates had time and again introduced bills in the National Congress, the United States erected several splendid monuments, and it was finally, some years after his death, made, by Congressional Act, a National Park (1917). The entire property was deeded, free of cost, to the United States Government, and is today one of the most unique and attractive spots in North Carolina. The battlefield has been reclaimed and beautified, and is adorned with many monuments and markers erected by individuals, by the State of North Carolina, and particularly by the magnificent equestrian statue erected by the National Government to the memory of Major-General Nathanael Greene, the Commander of the American forces in this battle, and for whom the City of Greensboro is named. Judge Schenck continued as president of the Guilford Battle Ground Company until his death in 1902, devoting his energies, his studies, his means, his thought and his time to this work.

However, his interest in preserving history—and preserving it accurately—did not end with the reclamation of this battlefield. He believed that a gross injustice had been done the North Carolina troops at Guilford by most historians, and his painstaking researches converted this belief into firm conviction. He determined to find out the truth, to publish it, and to vindicate these North Carolina troops, and, as well, to establish the importance, of the battle of Guilford as the turning point of the Revolution.

At a patriotic celebration on this battlefield, May 5, 1888, Judge Schenck delivered the address devoted to the battle of Guilford, and to a vindication of the North Carolina troops.

At the close of his address, he received a great ovation, and the Governor of the state, Hon. Alfred M. Scales, arose and said:

"The battleground itself has been neglected and left without a monument to mark the spot, save its desolation. It has been reserved for my distinguished friend, Judge Schenck, the orator of the day, more distinguished than ever before, to uncover the truth of history and tell the tale of this battle as it was actually fought. He it was that, while a comparative stranger to our people, though a native of North Carolina, conceived the idea of forming the Guilford Battle Ground Company, to purchase and adorn the grounds. He it was who raised the money that was necessary, contributing a large share thereof himself, to investigate the truth of history; and he it is that, by patient and wide research, and months of incessant labor, collected the evidence from friends and foes, at home and abroad, which has enabled him to wipe out forever the stain that rested upon our home militia. In the name of the descendants of these great men, in the name of our great state, I thank him for this great work."

Continuing his historical researches, Judge Schenck extended the scope of his labors, and published, in 1889, his history, "North Carolina, 1780-81," a thorough treatise, with much new and hitherto unpublished data, of the Revolutionary campaign in the Carolinas. At this time little attention was being given to North Carolina history, and he was, in many respects, a pioneer in searching out and publishing a true history of North Carolina's glorious part in the stirring and far-reaching events of that time, and in stimulating others who were to follow him to carry forward historical research and publication.

Guilford Court House today is being given its rightful place in history—here Cornwallis's pursuit was turned into a retreat, and the surrender at Yorktown and the independence of the colonies was made an assured and logical result.

His historical work brought him wide recognition, and he was elected to many literary and historical societies.

During these years of active interest in the civic affairs of Greensboro and the Guilford Battle Ground, and in the writing of his history, Judge Schenck carried on his very large law practice. He was Division Counsel of the Richmond and

Danville Railroad, was General Counsel for the Charleston, Cincinnati and Chicago Railroad, and enjoyed a large private law practice, taking part in many of the principal trials of that time.

One of the many victories in the courts, in which he played a leading role, was the case of Patrick vs. Richmond and Danville Railroad, tried in Charlotte. The case attracted considerable attention, as it was a very difficult and seemingly hopeless one for Judge Schenck's client. Commenting on his winning and conduct of the case, the Charlotte News (March, 1889) said:

"The verdict in favor of the Richmond and Danville Railroad in the Patrick case is due, in a great measure, to the great learning, ability and thorough preparation of Judge Schenck. His masterly presentation of the law has never been excelled at this bar."

Judge Schenck was a man of tremendous industry and unflagging energy and zeal. It was his custom to rise early in morning, and his historical researches and writings were done principally in the early morning hours between six and eight o'clock. But with all of his capacity and love for work, he found time for those recreations which were congenial to him. He was well versed in the lore of birds and trees and plant culture. In early life he was an enthusiastic fox hunter, and maintained a small plantation and fish pond for recreation, and both at his old home in Lincolnton, as at his home in Greensboro, he cared for and planted many trees and personally superintended the care of his orchard, garden and vineyard. Many of the beautiful maples at Guilford Battle Ground were planted under his personal direction, notably along the road leading to "the lake." Even in his latter days, he was an exceptionally fine quail shot, and while riding the circuit as judge, found occasion for hunting turkey, deer and duck, and fishing for mountain trout.

He loved and enjoyed his home life, and it was a home typical of the traditions of the old South, with a simple, cordial and generous hospitality, often full of welcome guests, and brightened by frequent social gatherings.

His extensive library indicated his dominant tastes. His law library was one of the finest in the state. His historical library was extensive and contained many rare volumes.

And there were books on ornithology, plant and tree culture, and a large number of volumes of Bible commentaries and treatises.

Failing health, brought on largely by over-work, made him practically an invalid during the last six years of his life, and he died in Greensboro, August 26, 1902.

Throughout his life he was a devout and faithful Christian, and was recognized as a deep student of the Bible. He was warden and vestryman of the Episcopal Church up to a short time before his death.

In addition to his history, he published several other historical volumes and a number of pamphlets, and was the author of the pamphlet "Railroad Law in North Carolina."

At his death, in 1902, the City of Greensboro and the State of North Carolina mourned his passing:

". . . the funeral services . . . . were conducted by Bishop Joseph Blount Cheshire, a warm personal friend, from the West Market M. E. Church, which had been tendered for the occasion, and accepted for the reason of the inadequacy of Saint Barnabas (Episcopal) Church. A great many prominent men from other points were present." (Greensboro Telegram.)

He was buried in Greene Hill Cemetery, which he had done so much to extend and beautify during his life.

Selected from a number of editorials are a few extracts from the state's leading papers:

"Few outside of those immediately connected with him can appreciate the magnitude and extent of his efforts. None can measure the benefits that have come to his adopted city through his Herculean efforts. It is therefore natural that Greensboro and Guilford County should feel deeply and keenly the loss of him who has done so much for both and shed such luster upon their annals. . . .

"He was the peer of any man who has ever appeared in the courts in this county, whose bar has ever been noted for its learning and ability.

"He was a man of wonderful attainments outside of his profession. He had read widely and thoroughly and explored every field of literature. His energy was boundless. When one considers the amount of work he accomplished in a few short years here, prior to his failing health, he no longer wonders that his strong and robust physical powers were broken and shattered. . . .

"Whilst he was as brave as a lion, he was a man of kindly heart and generous soul, a loving and devoted father, a tender and affectionate husband, a neighbor of kindliest impulses, a gentleman of noble soul, knightly instinct and heroic mould. Greensboro may well mourn. He was her benefactor. She consigns to the grave her most distinguished citizen. (Greensboro Daily Record)

Under the editorial caption, "Greatest Man In The State," the News and Observer, of Raleigh, said:

"Not many years ago when North Carolina's delegation embraced such men as Ransom, Vance, Davis, Waddell, Steele, Armfield, Scales and R. B. Vance, there was an informal discussion in Washington by most of the delegation and some visiting North Carolinians. Someone asked the question: "Who is the biggest man in North Carolina?" The concensus of opinion was that David Schenck and Braxton Craven came nearer being the two biggest men then living in the state. . . .

"As historian, as lawyer, as jurist, as public-spirited and unselfish citizen, he stands among the greatest men North Carolina has produced."

The Charlotte Observer commented editorially in part as follows:

"The state loses one of her great men in the death of Judge David Schenck in Greensboro. Leonine in cast of countenance and masterful in purpose, he was a born leader. In his long and successful legal career, he was a power before the jury. As a judge, he was able and just. His greatest and really inestimable service to North Carolina, and through her, to the Nation, is his magnificent defense and vindication of the North Carolina troops at the battle of Guilford Court House, and his rescue from Time's obliterating hand, of the Battle Ground of Guilford".

A number of the courts in the state adjourned a day in respect to his memory, and resolutions were passed by quite a number of the bar associations.

The resolutions of the Greensboro bar read in part:

"The State of North Carolina has lost one of her most beloved, illustrious and deserving citizens. Devoted to her honor and renown, he attempted no labor too arduous, no difficulty too great, no sacrifice too costly, if her welfare and glory demanded his service. To him belonged preeminently, above all men who lived in the same era, unstinted praise of vindicating the truth of the Revolutionary history of the state.

"A learned and upright judge, a brilliant and eloquent advocate, an accomplished scholar, a devoted husband and affectionate father, and above all, a sincere Christian, he has gone to his rest."

The Guilford Battle Ground Company, March 16, 1903, adopted resolutions in commemoration of "its distinguished and beloved president, who was its originator and creator, to whose active brain, tireless energy and ardent patriotism, this company is largely indebted, for the grand work already accomplished in vindicating the truth of history and the fair name of North Carolina, and in reclaiming and perpetuating the historical spot on which she fought the pivotal battle of the Revolution." And after paying tribute to his distinguished abilities, it was further resolved:

"That this company desires to record in permanent form its indebtedness for and its appreciation of his great and unselfish services, and to proclaim itself the crowning work of his life and an undying monument to his ability;

"That it is the sense of this company that a monument be erected to his memory on the field of the Battle of Guilford Court House."

In pursuance of these resolutions, a monument, substantial, and simple in design, was erected and unveiled at the Battle Ground, July 4, 1904, when an address was delivered by the late Chief Justice James E. Shepherd, a long time friend of Judge Schenck's.

The inscription reads:

"David Schenck. The projector of this battlefield's reclamation and organizer and first president of the Guilford Battle Ground Company."

The legislature of North Carolina passed a resolution of respect to his memory and in appreciation of his work.

At the Home-Coming Celebration in Greensboro, in 1903, the distinguished and venerable United States Senator Ransom, who was presiding over one of the meetings held at the Guilford Battle Ground, begged the attention of the audience to what he had to say:

" . . . The truth of history must be spoken. For nearly a century, the battle of Guilford Court House had been shrouded in ignorance, prejudice and blunder. A worthy North Carolinian, with great labor, and much expense and trouble, has rescued the name of his countrymen from doubt and misrepresentation. He has developed and demonstrated that the militia of North Carolina did its whole duty on that day, in obedience to the order of the Commander-in-Chief. He has vindicated their title to honor and immortal gratitude, and I ask this great audience to resolve that its thanks are eminently due the late Honorable David Schenck for his patriotic, diligent and successful labors in presenting the true history of the battle, and I would ask for a rising vote on this resolution: 'Resolved, that this convention puts upon record its profound conviction of the inestimable service which the late Honorable David Schenck has rendered to historical truth in vindicating and establishing by incontrovertible evidence and unanswerable argument, that the soldiers of North Carolina did their whole duty in the battle of Guilford Court House; that we will cherish all gratitude and honor to the memory of this devoted patriot' ".

The resolution was unanimously adopted by a rising vote of the assemblage.

Chief Justice Walter Clark, in an address at Guilford battlefield, in paying a tribute to Judge Schenck, said:

"He redeemed this battlefield from oblivion and the names of its defenders from obloquy."

PAUL W. SCHENCK.

JAMES W. ALBRIGHT

JAMES W. ALBRIGHT
1835 - 1917

No record available to the writers of these sketches has been used so frequently as "Albright's Greensboro", a little volume of town reminiscenses, compiled as a labor of love, in 1904, by a veteran newspaper man around whose familiar name cluster stories of the Greensboro press for more than forty years.

From 1892, when he followed his only daughter to an Asheville home, to 1917, when he was brought back to sleep in Green Hill, Mr. Albright never forgot, nor allowed others to forget, the welfare of his native town. He wrote the Greensboro book in Asheville as well as an unpublished volume of personal reminiscenses for his grandchildren. He also contributed various local sketches to the columns of his brother editors here, and while at work on the Asheville press his business cards were inscribed: "J. W. Albright, Press Agent, formerly of Greensboro."

In the latter part of the eighteenth century Jacob Albrecht and his wife Catherine, left Wurtenburg, Germany, for America and settled in Philadelphia. Daniel Albrecht, one of their eight children, came in early manhood with his young wife—another Catherine—to live in that part of Orange County, North Carolina, now known as Alamance. Seven from his family of eight founded new homes in western states, but the remaining son, George, cast in his lot with the neighboring village of Greensboro, going back in 1818 for a bride from the Orange settlement.

The German name had softened with Carolina usage so that it was George and Martha Albright, not Albrecht, who kept a hostelry which bore their name, at 113 East Market Street, for more than forty years, and "Landlord Albright" was a familiar appellation of the fathers, by whom he was held in high esteem. The fifth child in this East Market family of six, James Washington Albright, was born August 16th, 1835.

The memories of this son's childhood, as recorded for his family, give many interesting glimpses of early Greensboro, the limits of this paper allowing mention of only two. First of all he remembered clearly the historic Harrison and Morehead parade, with its gorgeous banners, picturesque floats, military music and patriotic Whig forces en route from Greensboro to Salisbury at 6 a. m. July 4th, 1840.

The other story selected is his graphic account of a disastrous Greensboro fire January 2nd, 1849. The alarm found all lads of the village gathered in a meeting of the "Cadets of Temperance" held in the Lindsay corner, present site of American Exchange Bank. This organization was the Boy Scout movement of that day, pledging its membership to abstinence from tobacco as well as alcohol, and its constitution was counted worthy of a place in the famous court house corner stone of 1858.

Young Albright left the hall with his comrades to find three East Market houses belonging to his father in flames and great excitement among the people, for the village was then entirely without fire protection. A citizens' meeting held within the next few days resulted in the prompt purchase of Greensboro's first fire engine, "General Greene." It was a hand engine made in Baltimore at a cost of $600.00, with three hundred feet of hose. The water supply was provided by a cistern at each of the four town pumps on Market and Elm Streets.

At the age of fourteen Mr. Albright's health failed and he was taken from the village school and sent to live for a time with an older sister in the bracing climate of Mt. Airy. At the end of two years he came home fully restored and obtained a printer's apprenticeship in the Patriot office under Swaim and Sherwood, disappointing his parents, who wanted him to be a physician.

Enthusiasm grew with knowledge of the press and during his fourth and last year as apprentice he published under an assumed name and entirely on his own responsibility a little weekly paper, "The Town Squib", filled with jokes and delineations of the foibles of that day as they appeared to a youth of nineteen. When the wrath of offended citizens was in evidence his identity was loyally shielded by the Patriot staff and the one bound volume of "The Squib" was a cherished treasure of its editor's old age, second only to the German Bible of his fathers.

The close of his apprenticeship was followed by a journey to northern cities to study the work of the largest American newspapers. A Philadelphia offer was attractive and he almost decided to locate there, but changing his plans, returned to the Old North State. He went to Mt. Airy for another term in the schools of that town, then came home to form a partnership with E. W. Ogburn and C. C. Cole as publishers of The Greensboro Times, called "an independent literary weekly newspaper." The date of this venture was January, 1856, eight months before Mr. Albright's majority. On September 16th of the same year he married Miss Celestia Crowson, and in the five happy years of their union two sons were born, one only living to maturity.

In his paper, as well as his home, the very young editor was fortunate. The Times won early recognition on its merits, such writers as John Esten Cooke, Mrs. Sigourney and William Gilmore Simms being among its frequent contributors.

Mr. Ogburn died in 1860 and the state's call for troops cut short the service of the Times in 1861. Mr. Cole went into the army as captain of a local company—the Minute Men, Company E, 22nd North Carolina Regiment—and had risen to the rank of lieutenant-colonel when his young life was sacrificed for the south at Chancellorsville May 3rd, 1863.

Mr. Albright was a charter member of the village military company, the Guilford Grays, which had been organized in 1860 to succeed the Greensboro Guards of the past generation. The Grays—Company B, 27th North Carolina Regiment—being already equipped were first of Guilford's ten companies to leave for the front, but so brief was the struggle then expected to be that the three married men in the ranks (Lamb, Pritchett and Albright) were excused from service with the proviso that their uniforms be loaned to younger volunteers.

Not entering the army until 1862 Mr. Albright gave the Confederacy in this waiting year a service for which he was peculiarly fitted. Southern schools were confronted with a dearth of textbooks; various publishing concerns strove to meet this need as recorded in "Week's Bibliography of Confederate Textbooks". Three Greensboro men, Richard Ster-

ling, principal of Edgeworth Seminary; J. D. Campbell, a
member of his faculty, and J. W. Albright, editor, organized
the Confederate publishing house of "Sterling, Campbell and
Albright", operating in the office of the suspended Greensboro Times, a small brick building which stood till 1924 at
218 West Market Street.

Messrs. Sterling and Campbell prepared a primer, a
speller and a series of readers; an arithmetic and English
grammar were contributed respectively by C. W. Smyth and S.
Lander. These books were called "Our Own" school books
and copyrighted in the clerk's office of the District Court of
the Confederate States for the District of Pamlico, North
Carolina. Thousands of volumes were printed and sold, Richmond and Columbia firms serving as distributing agents for
Greensboro.

A small Washington hand press proved unequal to the
demand, and the junior partner, being a practical printer,
was sent on a tour of southern cities in search of improved
equipment. He brought back a small job press with supplies
of good ink and paper from New Orleans and an Adams book
press from Columbia. This last purchase, the finest book
press of that day, was put together with difficulty, only to
find that it was too heavy to be operated by hand, but the
use of a horse power, patented by A. P. Boren, of Pomona,
for grinding sugar cane and threshing wheat, saved the day,
and C. F. Thomas, then a young lad, acted as motorman.

Later in the life of this firm its books were stereotyped in
Liverpool, England, the cost being paid in cotton. J. J. Ayers,
a Frenchman (another member of Edgeworth faculty), was
entrusted with this commission and brought the plates home
safely on the blockade runner Ad-Vance. When Stoneman
circled the town early in 1865, burning several railroad stations, these plates were buried in the basement of the office.
On April 20th, 1865, Federal soldiers entered Greensboro,
30,000 strong, and soon afterward the publishing house was
closed and sale of its books stopped by military law.

Mr. Albright served his firm only in its first year. His
young wife died in August, 1861. His purchase of the
Adams press was in February, 1862. Two months later he
was recruiting soldiers, and with twenty other Guilford men,
he met Capt. G. H. Gregory, of Greensboro, in Richmond, on

May 1st. He enlisted as a private in the 12th Battalion of Virginia Light Artillery and was soon made its Ordnance Sergeant, a position he held during the three remaining years of the war. His diary records the service of his battalion at Richmond, Drury's Bluff, Petersburg, Franklin on Blackwater river, with Longstreet near Suffolk, Wilmington, Wrightsville, Smithfield, Lockwood's Folly, and return to Petersburg in successful attack on Canby's celebrated cavalry.

When the southern cause was lost and the tragedy of Appomattox on April 10th had been followed by Johnston's surrender on April 26th, 1865, Greensboro was filled with Sherman's soldiers. Sergeant Albright, now once more a practical printer, made application to the Federal commandant, Major Worth, for permission to open his shop for job printing, which was granted, and so it came to pass that the Confederate press of "Sterling, Campbell and Albright" was used to print the paroles of Johnston's gallant army.

His daily bread once more assured, the ex-soldier returned to Virginia to wed Miss Mattie Purvis, of the Isle of Wight County. Four years of the young bride's life had been spent amid the deepest shadows of the conflict and a cherished possession, long afterward bequeathed to her granddaughter, was a pistol presented for her patriotic service in 1863 by General Longstreet.

Reconstruction days were gloomy in Greensboro as elsewhere, but newspapers are needed to tell of weal or woe and the editor did not lack for work. He published, in part with his brother Robert and in part alone, The Patriot and Patriot and Times from 1868-1876. In the eighties, as the clouds began to lift, he published The Beacon, a Democratic Greenback weekly, 1880-'81, and The Daily Bugle, organ of the new tobacco interests, 1883-'84. He served for a brief period as city editor of the North State, and when Reece and Elam established the Daily Record in 1890 he became their city editor, retaining this office till he left Greensboro in 1892.

Mr. Albright was long a faithful steward of West Market Street Methodist Church and an enthusiastic Odd Fellow since early manhood, having held every office in the gift of Buena Vista Lodge No. 21. He gave loyal support to every temperance movement, served as clerk for the two progressive town boards headed by Mayors Sloan and Mendenhall, was exceedingly proud of Greensboro's leadership in the taxation for public schools, and loaned his books to the State Normal College, and others later in life to the Greensboro Public Library. He was an earnest and valued friend in the work of the West End King's Daughters, a band of young girls led by his daughter Clara, the only surviving child of his second marriage, now Mrs. E. C. Chambers, of Asheville.

In his adopted home, the newspaper man found work, first as city editor of the Morning Gazette in 1892, later as publisher of a prohibition paper, The Ballot Box, 1894-'95. While health permitted he spent some working hours of each day in the printing concerns of Asheville, while the Zeb Vance Camp of Confederate Veterans and the writing of his memoirs afforded him pleasure as a pastime.

A long invalidism preceded his passing December 5th, 1917, and his last journey home. On February 3rd, 1923, he was followed by his gentle wife, and younger brother-printers of his own day reverently carried her to rest beside him in Green Hill.

The town the old editor so loved is rapidly changing to a little city of varied and highly organized activities, yet those who serve its educational needs note the increase of local history study in each new year, so that in the records bequeathed to his old home James W. Albright in a very real sense is still serving Greensboro.

                                        BETTIE D. CALDWELL.

JOHN ALEXANDER GILMER

JOHN ALEXANDER GILMER

1838 - 1892

Few of the makers of Greensboro come back to me with more vividness or distinction than Judge Gilmer. Everybody knew him, everybody revered him, and everybody loved him. You could not talk with him even casually without noting his gentleness, his gracious smile, the play of humor in his conversation, and, underlying all, the sterling and disciplined manhood that gave substance and force to all that he said or did. To my boyish mind his crutches testified more eloquently than words to his valor in battle; and a large canebrake on the Gilmer premises, to which the Judge welcomed all boys in search of fishing poles, bespoke a nature that never lost its sympathy with youth or youthfulness.

John A. Gilmer, jurist, soldier, statesman, was born in Greensboro, April 22, 1838, and died in his home on North Elm and Church Streets, March 17, 1892. His great grandfather, William Gilmer, of the masterful Scotch-Irish stock, fought in Captain Arthur Forbis's Company at the Battle of Guilford Courthouse, and his father, Congressman John Adams Gilmer, typified the best citizenship of the state in his sturdy opposition to disunion and in his loyal support of the Confederacy when war became inevitable. The effort to secure John Adams Gilmer for Lincoln's cabinet is interestingly related in the third volume of Nicolay and Hay's "Life of Abraham Lincoln." It was an effort that attested Lincoln's insight into character as well as the elder Gilmer's influence in national affairs. Judge Gilmer's mother was Julianna Paisley, daughter of the Rev. William D. Paisley, pastor of the first Presbyterian Church organized in Greensboro.

With such ancestry it is not surprising that young Gilmer was given the best education obtainable in the state. After thorough preparation in Greensboro he was sent to the University of North Carolina, then presided over by ex-Governor David L. Swain, from which he graduated with distinction in 1858. He at once began the study of law under his father, but the fame of John B. Minor drew him to the University of Virginia, where he completed the law course and returned to enter into law partnership with his father in 1860. At the University of Virginia, Gilmer was a close student, but a social favorite, his voice and guitar being still remembered in the homes that he visited. The partnership with his father was to continue until the death of the latter in 1868.

But the crisis came in 1861, and Gilmer was ready for it. North Carolina was wholeheartedly for the Union and one cannot help wondering what might have happened if Lincoln, instead of summoning the South to fight the South, had followed the urgent admonition of John Adams Gilmer. He had advised Lincoln to take the South into his confidence, to publish frankly his views and intentions, and thus to disarm the hostile criticism which, as Gilmer thought, was due chiefly to prejudice and ignorance. Lincoln declined, saying that his views had already been proclaimed in the debates with Douglas, that he had nothing to add or alter, that the South had refused to give him a hearing, that repetition would be futile, and that, so far as he knew, there was only one fundamental difference between Gilmer and himself: "You think slavery is right; I think it is wrong."

To Lincoln's call for southern soldiers, Governor John W. Ellis, of North Carolina, responded on April 15, 1861: "You can get no troops from North Carolina." The Guilford Grays had already organized and the flag of the Confederacy had been entrusted to their keeping at old Edgeworth Female Seminary when Miss Mary Morehead, handing the sacred banner to their leader, had said: "Strength, energy, and decision mark the character of the sons of Guilford whose noble sires have taught their sons to know no fear save that of doing wrong." Not one of the Guilford Grays was ever to betray the confidence thus imposed, but not one of them was to vindicate the valor of their Guilford ancestors with a finer loyalty or a firmer constancy than John A. Gilmer.

The little company was drilling at Fort Macon, near Beaufort, when war was declared. They were soon organized into the Ninth and later into Company B of the Twenty-Seventh Regiment of North Carolina State Troops. Gilmer was at first second junior lieutenant, but was promoted in

September, 1861, to adjutant. In December, of the same year, he was elected major and was in command at the battle of Newbern on March 14, 1862. Newbern was then the second largest city in the state, but the loss of Roanoke Island a few weeks before made it impossible for the diminished Confederates to hold their own against the augmented forces of Burnside. Six months later after the bloody but indecisive battle of Sharpsburg or Antietam, where Lee faced McClellan, Major Gilmer was promoted for gallant conduct to the rank of lieutenant-colonel, and in November, 1862, to the rank of colonel, a position that he held until wounds compelled his resignation three months before the surrender.

His first wound was received at the battle of Fredericksburg, a ball striking him in the left knee. Though he fell and could not move, he called to the litter-bearers who were pushing their way through the dead and wounded to rescue their beloved colonel: "Remove these poor fellows first; I can wait." Among those who leaped forward to rescue Colonel Gilmer was Samuel Weir, who was instantly killed. He was the son of Dr. David P. Weir, of Greensboro, and was a student at the Union Theological Seminary of Virginia when the Guilford Grays organized. Fredericksburg was a glorious Confederate victory, but the shadow of it hangs still over Greensboro and Guilford.

Though limping slightly, Colonel Gilmer continued in active service until after the battle of Bristoe Station in Virginia. Into this battle, fought on October 14, 1863, fifty of the Guilford Grays went. Seven came out alive and only three of these were uninjured. Colonel Gilmer was not among the uninjured. He was wounded in the thigh and limped and suffered the rest of his life.

As soon as he was able to leave the hospital Colonel Gilmer reported again for duty and was assigned to the invalid corps in Salisbury. But a malignant attack of fever incapacitated him from active service and he returned to Greensboro. Here on July 14, 1864, was consummated the happiest event of his life, his marriage to Miss Sallie L. Lindsay, daughter of Jesse H. Lindsay, who had served with distinction in the House and Senate of North Carolina, and who at the time of his death was the honored and revered president of the

National Bank of Greensboro. "I saw them married," writes my mother, "he on two crutches and she standing by his side. Never were two more devoted lovers." Of the three children born of this union—Ellison L., Julia P., and John A. Gilmer, Jr.—only the two sons survive. Mrs. Gilmer died on December 18, 1920.

In 1866 Governor Jonathan Worth appointed Colonel Gilmer Adjutant General of North Carolina, a position which, in the turmoil of reconstruction, he was permitted to hold for only one year. When General E. R. S. Canby, leader of the carpet-baggers, called a convention to meet in Raleigh in January, 1868, to form the New Constitution, Colonel Gilmer was nominated by the Conservative Party to oppose the radical measures that the carpet-baggers and recently enfranchised negroes were bent on introducing. He was elected, but counted out. In accepting the nomination Colonel Gilmer had written: "Although in no sense a politician, my professional business at this time requiring my closest attention. I do not feel at liberty to decline your flattering and unsolicited request. I will therefore become a candidate and canvass the county, hoping at least to convince some of the people that hear me that their self-respect and security from degradation and contempt depends upon their rejection of the 'New Constitution'."

When Colonel Gilmer was elected State Senator in 1870, The Patriot of August 11, hailed the event as the first victory of the Conservative Party and as a sure indication that a better day was at last dawning upon a sorely stricken commonwealth. "May his star," continued the editor, Mr. Robert H. Albright, "that has so rapidly risen, burn brighter and brighter as it rises higher and higher, and when at the full meridian of his fame, may he always be assured of the grateful remembrance of those whom he so ably served." It was at this session of the senate that W. W. Holden, Republican Governor since 1868, was impeached, convicted, and forbidden ever again to hold office under the state government.

Colonel Gilmer returned now to the active practice of law in Greensboro. In 1879 he and Judge Robert P. Dick and Professor Samuel C. Smith were chosen as ruling elders of the First Presbyterian Church. In the same year Governor

T. J. Jarvis appointed Colonel Gilmer Judge of the Superior Court of the Fifth Judicial District to fill out the unexpired term of Judge Kerr. The appointment was endorsed by popular election in 1880 and in 1882 he was elected to the full term. This high office Judge Gilmer filled at a crisis in our history with increasing acceptance to the bench and bar and people of the state. His happy faculty of making loyal friends wherever he went, his native kindliness, his judicial temperament, his ability to detect fallacy or evasion in argument, his skill in shredding away technicalities wherever they obscured the underlying principles of simple justice, and the Christian character of the man that shone through his demeanor on the bench as well as in the home, made Judge Gilmer one of the great constructive forces in rebuilding a commonwealth that was struggling painfully back to stability and prosperity. When in January, 1891, he resigned his judgeship to attend more closely to his law practice, everyone felt that though the bench was the poorer for his loss, the social and civic and moral life of the state had been permanently enriched by his ministrations. His death followed only a year after his resignation.

Judge Gilmer's character and career were so well rounded that it is difficult to characterize him by a selection of distinctive and individualizing traits. He was never an office-seeker. When, in 1884, his comrades in battle were urging his nomination for Governor, when the newspapers were hailing him as one who "would instill such enthusiasm into the Democratic ranks as no other but the illustrious Vance could do," Judge Gilmer refused to let his name come before the convention. Positions of responsibility came unsolicited to him because men saw in him those qualities of head and heart that stabilize a state in its hour of need and that belong of right to the trained leader.

As a citizen of Greensboro he had faith in the growth of the city and was a co-worker in all constructive causes. As a student of financial problems, as a stockholder in the National Bank of Greensboro and in the North Carolina Railroad Company, and especially as a member of the board of aldermen of Greensboro in 1870, the new Greensboro of today reflects the permanence of his influence. It was in 1870 that our city aldermen established in Greensboro "the first system of public schools in the state supported by special taxation."

As a speaker Judge Gilmer was not only forceful and effective. His language was at times touched with a grace and beauty that blended the appeal of the orator with the charm of the poet. On May 10, 1873, at the celebration of the third Memorial Day in Greensboro, he delivered an address, a brief selection from which seems to me to summarize both the greatness of his character and the patriotic worth of his example: "The arbitrament of the sword has long ago decided our sectional differences and as true Americans we abide today implicitly by its decisions. But the ties that bound us to a common cause and the sense of honor that forbade the desertion of a comrade on the field are not severed by disaster, reverses, or death. I am unable to read the heart of any American who sees not beauty in devotion to the dead, who feels not sympathy for the wounded heart and desolate home, and who recognizes not in the sacred ashes of the Confederate dead an added honor to the soil that gave them birth."

C. ALPHONSO SMITH.

JAMES TURNER MOREHEAD

JAMES TURNER MOREHEAD

1838 - 1919

James Turner Morehead, the subject of this sketch, was born in Greensboro, North Carolina, on May 28th, 1838, and died there on the 11th day of April, 1919. He was the son of James Turner Morehead and Mary Lindsay Morehead, and was never married.

His father, an eminent lawyer, did a large and lucrative practice in Guilford and adjoining counties, and at the time of his death was and had been for many years recognized as a leader in his profession at every bar at which he practiced. He realized to the full the maxim that "the law is a jealous mistress and he who would serve her must serve no other." Guilford sent him to the State Senate for five consecutive times, 1835-1842, and he represented his district in Congress one term (1851-'53), but could not be prevailed upon to accept another and so retired from politics.

Colonel Morehead's mother was a woman of many virtues and of strong character and intellect. The Lindsay family, to which she belonged, was prominent in business and socially in Piedmont North Carolina. His father was a younger brother of John M. Morehead, Governor of North Carolina, 1840-1844, and pioneer in internal improvements for this state. It was under his wise leadership that the North Carolina Railroad was built and in the long list of Governors of our state he is generally recognized as the most distinguished, far-seeing and useful.

Colonel Morehead was educated at the private school of Dr. Alexander Wilson, of Alamance County, and at the University of North Carolina, from which he graduated in 1858, a first honor man of his class. Having chosen the law as his profession, he next became a pupil of Judge Richmond M. Pearson in his famous law school at Richmond Hill. He was admitted to practice in all the courts of this state in 1860.

When in 1861 the great Civil War burst upon a divided and distracted country and North Carolina had cast in her lot with the Confederacy, James T. Morehead was among the first to respond to the call of duty. He began his military service with the rank of lieutenant in the Guilford Grays, a

Greensboro company, which, having been organized in 1860, was the first company sent to the front from this county. The company was known later as Company B, Twenty-seventh North Carolina Regiment.

Lieutenant Morehead was rapidly promoted and before the close of the war was colonel of the Fifty-third North Carolina Regiment. He was wounded three times during his gallant leadership of this brave regiment, and March 25, 1865, was captured at Hare's Hill, near Petersburg, Virginia, during a raid within the enemy's lines. He was then a prisoner till the end of the war.

When peace was declared Colonel Morehead returned to his native town where he resumed the practice of his profession. He became deeply interested in the vital political problems of that day and was a leader among those who were devoting their lives and energies to the redemption of his state from corruption and oppression, conditions which had resulted from the enfranchisement of the ignorant negroes, led in large part by unprincipled adventurers from other states.

In the dark days of 1868-1870 he was a valiant leader in the ranks of those who waged an unrelenting and finally successful fight against these forces of evil. Never an extremist, he was at all times a sane, conservative leader and counselor. His fine courage, sane judgment and appealing personality were such that his people soon after his return home elected him, in 1866, as a member of the last House of Commons which ever met in North Carolina and he became a prominent member of that body.

After the so-called reconstruction of the state he was elected a member of the State Senate, serving in 1872 and in 1875. After the successful impeachment of W. W. Holden as Governor, Colonel Morehead was elected president of the senate. In 1883 he was again sent to the senate and served one more term.

While he was entrusted with many offices, this favorite son of Guilford was no office seeker and political life had few attractions for him. When such preferment was offered he accepted it only when he thought he could be of real service to his section and his state.

Colonel Morehead was devoted to his profession and as a trial lawyer he had few equals and no superiors. With great natural aptitude for the law he had a strong analytical mind and an effective, unique and taking address especially in the arguments of issues of facts before juries. He was a man of striking appearance and personality, more than six feet tall. Spare and erect, his soldierly bearing and quiet dignity of manner attracted and held attention in any gathering. He was kindly and approachable, considerate of the feelings of others and no man ever had more of the milk of human kindness in his disposition.

The professional life of Colonel Morehead is a story of upright dealing and support of law and justice and was an inspiration to younger members of the bar. His character as a man and a lawyer was above reproach. As has been well said by another writer: "His place in the esteem of his profession was an exalted one and he was generally accredited as being one of the ablest lawyers in the entire state until failing health compelled him to give up his more active practice, though he continued his practice in a limited way to the very end. His practice had been an extended one and he appeared in nearly all the important litigations of the circuit during the past forty years."

"As a citizen he was ever ready to support any movement that had for its purpose the development of the city and county. His consistency, his simple faith, his sterling integrity, his simple aims, his fine poise of character, his charity, his generous deeds and kindly words, were read in the daily walk of his daily life."

For many years Colonel Morehead had been a consistent member of the Presbyterian church.

He achieved distinction as a soldier and as a lawyer, but his chief triumph was the place which he held during a long and useful life in the affection and esteem of all who knew him. When the news of his serious illness first became known the city was impressed by a sense of impending loss and sorrow, and when it was learned that he was dead the sense of bereavement was universal. It was felt that "a prince and a great man had fallen upon sleep."

> "And thus he bears without abuse
> The grand old name of gentleman,
> Defamed by every charlatan
> And soiled with all ignoble use."

R. C. STRUDWICK.

JOSEPH MOTLEY MOREHEAD

JOSEPH MOTLEY MOREHEAD

1840 - 1911

"Joseph Motley Morehead, of Greensboro, N. C., was a member of the distinguished family of that name, and has himself been associated from the beginning with the highly patriotic work of establishing, maintaining and adorning the famous Guilford Battle Ground. The Moreheads are of Scotch descent, Charles Morehead, their ancestor, coming from Scotland to Virginia in 1620, but earlier than the Revolution they had located in North Carolina."—Ashe's History of North Carolina.

Major Joseph M. Morehead, the subject of this sketch, was the son of the late James T. Morehead, a distinguished man and a great lawyer. He was the nephew of the late Governor John Motley Morehead. Hon. Cyrus B. Watson, a life long friend of Major Morehead's, in a memorial address delivered on July 4th, 1911, at the Guilford Battle Ground, gave appreciation of the life and character of Major Morehead, which cannot be improved upon, for discriminating judgment and beauty and vigor of expression. Speaking of his ancestry, he said: "Mr. Joseph M. Morehead was of splendid stock, both on the paternal and maternal side. His mother was Mary T. Lindsay, of Guilford County. He received his preparatory education at the school of that king of teachers, Dr. Alexander Wilson, in the County of Alamance, near the historic Presbyterian Church of Hawfield's. He entered the State University at the age of 17; and while in college, was among those of his class who won first distinction. He was a fine classical scholar. His health giving away, he did not remain at the University to graduate. After returning home and after recuperating his health, he entered the great law school of Chief Justice Pearson, at Logtown, Yadkin County; but while there pursuing his studies, the war clouds began to gather, and in April, 1861, he put aside his law books, hurried to Fort Macon, on the North Carolina coast, and joined the "Guilford Grays," who had been sent to garrison this fort by the Governor of the state. He entered this company as a private soldier. After remaining with the "Guilford Grays" for a time he was offered a lieutenancy in Company E of the Second North Carolina Regiment. This he accepted, and served as first lieutenant until his never too robust health failed and he was compelled to resign his commission and return to his home. After resting for a period, he again took up his studies at the Pearson Law School. He finished the law course, and was admitted to the bar shortly before the close of the War Between the States. It was said of him that he was one of the best equipped young men that ever finished the law course. Soon after he obtained his license, he was appointed clerk and master in equity, a very responsible position, which he held until the change of procedure in the courts in the year 1868. Having large land interests, he now turned his attention to farming, and with the wholesome outdoor life he recovered his health. He then resumed the practice of his profession. As a lawyer, he was painstaking and thorough in all things; as a man he was honest, truthful, faithful and just. He was a straightforward man in his life. He never saw the time when he was willing to bend the knee to the great and powerful. He never saw the day when, with haughty head, he passed by the poor, the weak, the needy. He sternly walked the path of rectitude and no power could have swerved him from its well drawn line. He was much of a philosopher; was always cheerful, full of humor and mirth. He never looked upon this God-built world, with its flowing rivers, lofty mountains, and beautiful landscapes as a 'low-ground of sorrow,' nor as a 'vale of tears.' He enjoyed a clean sprightly joke, and he regarded a good hearty laugh as one of nature's tonics.''

In 1883 he was happily married to Miss Mary Christian Jones, of Bachelors Hall, Virginia, who survives him, with their son, James T. Morehead, the third, of Greensboro.

Major Morehead will be remembered and honored longest and most highly by those who love our country's history; who honor our heroes of the past; and who prize as priceless possessions the achievements, principles, traditions and institutions which are distinctively American, which mark us as a peculiar people among the nations of the world, and which furnish the bed-rock upon which our national greatness and glory have been builded. To perpetuate the memory of the heroes and the heroic deeds of those who lived and died during the century which immediately preceded his own period of active life, was the great absorbing ambition of this patriotic poet-historian.

The Battle Ground Park, now inseparably associated with his name, contains one hundred acres, has twenty-three monuments, and one of the most interesting museums of Revolutionary relics and autographs in the Union, and five pieces of statuary. As it stands today, it is the result of the patriotic work of private individuals, aided by the Legislature of North Carolina and the Congress of the United States. But behind this record of extraordinary achievement, which as time passes will be of increasing pride to the men and women of North Carolina, stood two personalities, and it is safe to say that but for these two there would be little of anything in Guilford Battle Ground to stir pride in the breast of North Carolinians. Judge David Schenck and Major Joseph M. Morehead made "Guilford Battle Ground," as seen today, both possible and real.

After the death of Judge Schenck, Major Morehead assumed leadership and carried on the work. His conception of the extent of the task was great. He met adverse opinions, criticisms, and some ridicule. But with all of his great heart he was committed to the undertaking. There were devoted and loyal friends who were ever ready to uphold his hands; but much of his journey to success was of necessity along a path of loneliness, for he only could then visualize the task as it stands to be seen by all today.

Upon him fell the burden of convincing the Legislature at Raleigh that it was wise and just to have the state expend money that Guilford Battle Ground, stained with the blood of heroes, might be made beautiful. With unfaltering faith and high courage he dared go further, and against strong opposition he undertook to convince the Congress of the United States that the nation owed much to General Greene, and the brave but untrained soldier-citizens of North Carolina who faced the seasoned veterans of England and by their valor broke the power of the proud Cornwallis.

To this task Major Morehead gave himself. He lived to see his vision a certainty, but was taken before it materialized in majestic and monumental marble.

To such men who look beyond the material things of today, and forgetting things of sense and sight, conceive of tasks pronounced impossible by some, and unnecessary by others, but seen by them to be needful, and therefore possible—to such the world owes a debt of appreciation and gratitude.

His voice is silenced, but the message of his life will be proclaimed through the coming years, and to succeeding generations.

MELTON CLARK.

DR. HALL

DR. LOGAN

DR. BEALL

W. C. PORTER

DR. WILSON

DR. MICNAUX

O. HENRY

CLARK PORTER AND HIS DRUG STORE

1842 - 1902

The most hopeless dullard understands that the most interesting and most important records of a city are never written in the minute books of its governing body, and that its greatest builders are not necessarily the men who put together the brick and stone and steel of its monumental structures. It is less obvious, but equally true, that sometimes notable institutions lurk under strange guises, and are not recognized for what they were until long years after they have disappeared. A strange generation, looking back through the perspective of decades, can see the picturesque in what passed for the commonplace of its day; time, like autumn haze, settles over the institutions of years long past, blotting out the trifling and ephemeral, but leaving those that were really significant standing bold and plain enough, yet touched with the enchantment of distance, veiled ever so lightly in romance.

Such an institution existed once in Greensboro in a building that still stands as this is written, forty years after the time. It existed in a disguise as commonplace, surely, as any that ever masked a shrine, namely, a drug store. Yet a notable institution it was; and, after all, the assertion will not be incredible to anyone who has lived in a village of two thousand souls, such as Greensboro was in the eighties of the last century, and who is able to remember how the life of a village often centers around the drug store. This drug store differs from others mainly in that it was its fortune to house for a while a genius so great that his fame has spread throughout the earth, and made of every place in which any considerable part of his life was spent a literary shrine. As long as men continue to delight in the work of the sometime drug clerk who called himself O. Henry, that spot will remain famous. Yet, while the renown of Greensboro's most illustrious son naturally overshadows all else, it was not for O.

Henry alone that the older citizens of the city, after forty years, still remembered Clark Porter's drug store as an institution to be recalled with affectionate delight.

Let it be admitted in the beginning that this story of Clark Porter and his drug store comes at second hand. On an October afternoon in 1923, Dr. W. P. Beall essayed a service, not of a professional kind, to an old friend long since gone beyond reach of the ills that flesh is heir to. In order that this book might include some recognition of the influence in forming the traditions and historic background of the city exerted by Clark Porter and the group that surrounded him, Dr. Beall took an afternoon off to turn his mind back to the days when, a fledgling physician just out of a Philadelphia medical college, he came to try his fortunes in the village of Greensboro. It was at Porter's drug store that he made his headquarters. As he spoke, the identical building still stood on the east side of Elm Street, halfway down the block between Market and Sycamore Streets; but under the magic spell of memory it was transformed. The strident roar of traffic that fills Elm Street from day's end to day's end dwindled into silence. Street car tracks and asphalt dissolved and vanished, leaving an ordinary earth road, deep in summer's dust or winter's mire. Granite curbs and concrete sidewalks disappeared to be replaced by a path beaten smooth by the feet of pedestrians, but owing nothing to construction engineers. On the edge of the sidewalk, directly in front of the door of the establishment a tall sycamore sprang up, under whose shade habitues of the place sat all summer long, discussing interminably every subject that interests the freeborn American in his hours of ease.

The building itself lost a story, coming down to one, for the upstairs offices had not yet been added when Dr. Beall first saw the place. The show windows bore the style of decoration as inevitably a part of a drug store then as a wooden Indian was a part of a tobacconist's shop, or a red and white striped sign is part of a barber shop today, namely, monstrous bottles filled with liquids tinted in strange and enticing hues. Entering, one faced the partition that cut off the prescription counter in the rear and had on his right the cigar case, while on his left was the soda fountain, which assumed the shape of an onyx cube of some thirty inches edge sitting at one end of a marble slab. These various appurtenances were, however, but the Gentiles' court; the temple itself lay behind the barrier of the prescription counter. The center of this inner apartment was occupied by a tall, fat-bellied stove, of the sort ludicrously reminiscent of an obese old dame giddily arrayed in those fashions of a by-gone day, a picture hat and a hobble skirt. Around the stove were scattered half a dozen chairs, generally decrepit, but nevertheless much to the taste of the frequenters of the place, a quartet of whom arrived so consistently with the kindling in the morning, there to remain until the lights were put out at night, as to gain from the ironic junior clerk the name of The Fire Brigade.

At the rear of the brick building, in a wooden addition, were two more rooms, one theoretically the proprietor's office, the other sacred to the use of the doctors and a few lawyers and others who gathered there for a quiet game of checkers or dominoes—if anything else Dr. Beall, whether by accident or design, forgets. Back of this, where today is a tangle of warehouses, shops, garages and what-not making up the west side of Davie Street, there was in those days simply the State of North Carolina. In that wide expanse the horseshoe pitching championships were commonly decided, and Dr. Beall recalls with glee an occasion on which he went out back of Porter's store with a rifleman for a shooting match, and beat him with Porter's pistol.

The presiding genius of this establishment was William Clarkson Porter, whose mother was a Worth, of the well-known Quaker family of that name, and whose father was Sydney Porter—a name destined, with the addition of Clark Porter's first name, to become more illustrious in the literary world than any member of the family at that time had ever dreamed. New Garden School, the ancient name of Guilford College, equipped young Porter mentally, and he went into business on East Market Street in the sixties, transferring to Court Square, just west of the site now occupied by the Jefferson Standard Life Insurance Company's building, after the Civil War. There is some recollection of a stand on the southwest corner of Elm and Sycamore Streets before he finally set up the establishment under the sycamore tree.

All the testimony goes to show that Clark Porter was a quiet man who attended to his own business, and was as little given to spectacular words or acts as any man in the town; and yet there is the best possible proof that under his quiet exterior he concealed a capacity for action, when the occasion warranted, of the most energetic and determined kind.   He was married March 31, 1873, and after the lapse of 50 years the story of that wedding still lingered in the memories of the older citizens, and was told by them with appreciative delight.   Furthermore, the story is not legend. It is authenticated by the Greensboro Patriot in its issue of April 2, 1873.

According to that account, the Rev. Dr. J. Henry Smith announced to his congregation at the First Presbyterian Church one Sunday that a wedding would occur there the next day, but omitted to name the contracting parties.   Nor could all the persuasions of his intensely curious parishioners induce him to let the names pass his lips.   Nevertheless, it presently became known in the village that the bride-elect was one of the prettiest and most popular girls in town, Miss Berta Sloan, daughter of Mayor Robert M. Sloan, one of the dignitaries of the town.   But that served only to increase the tension, for Berta Sloan had innumerable admirers, and after the process of elimination had been carried to its farthest limit there remained two, between whom no one could choose with certainty.   One was a man from Baltimore, the other a Greensboro boy, and while the town naturally whooped for the local favorite, it was impossible to say with certainty that he was in the lead.   Discussion swiftly developed into argument, and excitement mounted to such a pitch that presently certain ribald fellows began to lay wagers, which was like touching flame to tow.   By the time the wedding morning dawned all the sports in town, and not a few grave and dignified citizens, had bets placed on the outcome.   Of course the church was packed at the hour set for the ceremony; but the identity of the bridegroom had not been revealed when the organ began to play the wedding march and the first of the attendants started down the aisle—was not revealed, indeed, until Clark Porter stepped through the church door to meet his bride.

And in church, under the stern and quelling eye of Dr. Smith, not even the winning betters dared to cheer!

So the quiet, unostentatious druggist had the honor of having carried the colors of his city to triumph at least once in his career. The good will of his city he carried all his life long, for the city had his good will. Indeed, his failing was too much tenderness of heart, if that can by rights be called a failing. When business troubles came upon him late in life the final estimate showed that they were attributable to that kindliness that could not refuse aid to any who applied for it. He had granted credit to men who were utterly unworthy of his trust. His career in the end proved a bitter commentary on human nature that makes "the larger heart, the kindlier hand" perilous to their possessor; but rare indeed are the spirits whose very generosity proves their undoing, so rare that, as in the case of Clark Porter, their memory lingers long after they are dust, lingers delicately and beautifully in the minds of those who knew them, like faint perfume clinging to old lace.

But in the early eighties the last act in the quiet drama of the drug store was yet to come. In the eighties, when young Dr. Beall found Greensboro not even an adolescent city, but more like an overgrown country boy, with all the triumphs and the disappointments of his life yet before him, Porter's drug store flourished as the heart of the village. In the brave eighties youth, with great expectations, ruled the place, untouched as yet by fame and tragedy.

Such a statement would have surprised Clark Porter, then in middle age. It would not only have surprised, it would probably have incensed old Dr. Hall, dean of the profession in the town, and by virtue of seniority, a bit of a lord in the drug store. It would doubtless have much amused his six professional brethren, Doctors Cheek, Glenn (the elder), Alford, Marley, Logan and Lindsay, all of them men of mature years. Nevertheless, in so far as we of a later generation are concerned, the statement holds good, for we can see the place at all only through the eyes of the junior physician and an adolescent drug clerk, one of whom sketched it with swift pencil strokes on odd bits of paper, while the other took an afternoon off in 1923 and sat down to reconstruct it in imagination. The junior physician was Dr. Beall. The drug clerk was he whom the world knows as O. Henry.

This mild-mannered, unobtrusive clerk was but little regarded by the hardier spirits that frequented the store, but he, on his part, missed never a word nor a gesture of theirs. Years later those words and gestures were destined to start out suddenly from the pages of one of the supremely great masters of the short story, worked into strange surroundings, but instantly recognizable by those who had been there when they were spoken or made, spectators who had perhaps never noticed that Will Porter was standing by, and who never dreamed that the quiet clerk was marking everything that passed, and noting it down in one of the most wonderful brains of the century.

These sketches of a young artist and memories of a young doctor reveal the Porter establishment as a typical village drug store, prototype of the hill named for Mars in the most illustrious of cities, where active-minded citizens congregated daily, seeking to learn some new thing. Here all the life of the village was passed in review and commented on, usually jocosely, sometimes mordantly. Here were heard the local echoes of the battles of ideas that roared through the great world. Here was presented for the study of a man who later was to comment wittily and wisely upon it, a fairly representative cross-section of American life. The conservative was there and the wastrel, the pietist and the drunkard, the wit and the hopeless fool. The left wing also had its representative, at the time a snorting Greenbacker, which was for that day about the extreme of radicalism. No doubt in village drug stores of forty years later the same type of man is proclaiming his leaning toward communism.

But the mind of youth was struck, as it is always struck, by the merriment that pervaded the back room that inclosed the fat-bellied stove, or the group of decrepit chairs around the bole of the sycamore tree. Grave discussions there were, without doubt, but a merciful provision of nature assures that gravity and care slip lightly from youthful minds, while the impressions of gaiety remain forever. So it is that from those days in Porter's drug store the impression that comes down to us is no prosy sketch of prosaic happenings, but a merry collection of jests, oddities and whimsicalities that youth seized upon avidly and preserved forever. Will Porter gazing soulfully into the far distance, while under cover of the showcase his clever fingers mercilessly caricatured some pompous citizen standing across the store, stands out clearly, while the commercial transactions of the day have been deservedly forgotten. The eccentricities of various inhabitants of the village are preserved, while their ordinary doings and their far from remarkable opinions have faded into oblivion.

Yet in this quiet corner of the world, where the village idlers loafed and laughed, history was being made, not the commonplace political history of conquests and battles and sieges, but history of the enchanted realm of art. A new Ulysses was being given the sprig of moly that should one day preserve him against the horrible spell that turns men into worse than swine. William Sydney Porter was learning the science of pharmacy under the tutelage of his uncle. Years later, in the hour of his bitterest need, that skill in pharmacy was to serve him well. It was to deliver him from the more extreme ferocities of our frightful penal system, and to purchase for him, within prison walls, the privileges of a quasi-privacy and a certain amount of leisure, in which to begin the practice of his own white magic which was soon to astonish and delight the world. Therefore, by a curious irony of fate, the future city of Greensboro was to owe to Porter's drug store the salvation of that genius that has brought the city its greatest fame.

Yet not for that alone are Clark Porter and his drug store worthy of remembrance. Sycamore trees will never grow in Elm Street again. Business and professional men no longer spend their rare moments of leisure idling around a drug store, presided over by some such genial personality as Clark Porter. Nevertheless, these things are in the background of the modern city, an ineradicable part of its history. Surely, it is no bad thing for the city, with its accelerating speed, its tendency to raise the boiler-pressure of its life ever higher and higher, to look back occasionally on that time, to remember that the men who built the foundations of the city and made them sound and strong, were wise enough never to drive ahead too furiously, never to take themselves too seriously.

Leisureliness and quiet, trees and the sound of laughter in the streets—"somnolent" it doubtless was, but the old southern town had charm.

GERALD W. JOHNSON.

JOHN WILLIAM SCOTT

JOHN WILLIAM SCOTT
1843 - 1918

John William Scott was born October 14, 1843, in Guilford County, North Carolina, near Buffalo Presbyterian Church, the son of Dr. William B. Scott and Margaret Rankin Scott, and died in Greensboro, North Carolina, March 30, 1918. He had two brothers and one sister, all of whom he long outlived. Educated in the schools of Guilford County, he was preparing to enter the University when war between the states was declared. Sacrificing his educational ambitions, he volunteered at the age of eighteen, and became a member of the 53rd North Carolina Confederate Regiment, commanded by Col. James T. Morehead, of Greensboro, North Carolina. Though a boy in years, he early proved his manhood. By rapid promotion he became chief of the sharp shooters of the regiment and first lieutenant of Company A. His courage and ability were conspicuous. Col. Morehead said of him that he had no better soldier. A higher rank was planned for him and would have been his in a few days, when he was captured at Winchester, Virginia, in 1864, and kept a prisoner at Fort Delaware till the close of the war.

Though not given to speaking of the war or his part in it, yet I have often heard him say how decisively the war tested men's character. On the frequent occasions when I would ask him confidentially about this or that Guilford County man—since he had an amazing range of acquaintance—I recall how invariably, if the person inquired of had been a soldier, Mr. Scott would tell me his war record. If the man had been a good soldier, he was usually all right.

Returning to Greensboro at the close of the war, he was employed by Bogart & Murray, and later by Newton Caldwell, local merchants, from whom he learned much of the business he was later to operate for himself. In January, 1871, he established "J. W. Scott & Company", with Thomas D Sherwood, who many years later became the husband of Mr. Scott's beloved niece, Miss Bessie McMasters, as his associate, and also W. C. McLean, his brother-in-law. Until his death he was president of this corporation. The company did a retail grocery business at first. In 1878 a dry goods line was added, which developed so successfully that in 1908 the grocery business was discontinued, the company becoming a highly prosperous wholesale dry goods firm.

Although this was Mr. Scott's chief business interest, yet his business abilty was so marked, his personal popularity so great, and his reputation for integrity so outstanding, that his name and counsel were much sought after. He was vice-president of the American Exchange National Bank, director of the Greensboro Loan and Trust Company, director in several of the insurance companies of the Southern Loan and Trust group, being a charter member of the first of these formed, and one of the organizers of the old Security Life and Annuity Company, merged later into the Jefferson Standard Life Insurance Company. He was one of the five men who organized the Guilford Battleground Company and redeemed from oblivion the ground which has now become a national park. He was made treasurer of the company when the five men first met to organize, and held the office until his death. The other four were Judge David Schenck, Julius A. Gray, Dr. D. W. C. Benbow, and Thomas B. Keogh.

For forty years before his death Mr. Scott was one of the leading business men of Greensboro and of the state, and his name the synonym of ''whatsoever things are honest, whatsoever things are of good report.''

On January 13, 1870, he married Katherine McLean, daughter of John C. McLean and Rebecca Rankin McLean. Mrs. Scott died August 30, 1879, leaving a daughter, Lizzie, who died a few years later in her beautiful young womanhood, leaving her father bereaved indeed. Another daughter, Minnie, had died years before at the age of seven years. After Lizzie's death Mr. Scott made his permanent home with his sister-in-law, Miss Lou McLean.

In 1882 Mr. Scott was elected a deacon of the First Presbyterian Church of Greensboro, at the same time with William E. Bevill and Dr. Robert F. Robertson. In that office he was eminently faithful and useful. In 1892 he was elected ruling elder at the same time with James T. Carson and Lunsford Richardson. As an elder he ruled well, leaning ever to the side of mercy, like his Master, hating sin but loving the sinner.

There has never lived in Greensboro a man more widely loved and trusted than J. W. Scott. It was my privilege to spend over forty years of my life in the same town and I do not recall that I ever heard a word from anyone in depreciation of him. His personal friendship, since the time I was old enough to know him, has been one of the blessings of my life, as my father's friendship was one of the blessings of Mr. Scott's life. As a young minister in another section of the town, and later as his pastor for twelve years, I continually sought his counsel and learned to rely, with an ever-deepening confidence, on the shrewd yet kindly wisdom that so eminently characterized him. It is rare that so keen an insight into human nature is accompanied with so loving a spirit. Firm when necessary, he was ever gentle and affable, with a quiet but delightful humor habitually brightening his face and speech and manner.

His generous sympathies and the affectionate esteem in which he was held knew no limits of race or creed. When the effort was made to establish The Agricultural and Mechanical College for colored people in Greensboro, Mr. Scott was the first citizen to whom the colored committee applied for funds, because they knew his heart. During an unusually severe winter when there was much suffering among the poorer classes in the city, a committee composed of members of both races was appointed to search out the needy. Mr. Scott, who was then at the head of his large grocery business, went at once to the colored representative on that committee and said: "Whenever you find any of your people in need of groceries or fuel, make out a list of their needs and send them to me here at the store, and I'll honor your orders." That act, known only to a few people, was characteristic.

Though with abundant means, his manner of living was always simple, modest, inexpensive. What God gave him he used for others.

After his death a well known newspaper editor published a letter, which two years before, while on a health sojourn in Arizona, he had written to Mr. Scott, in which, among other things, he said:

"I told Dr. Clark that I thought you were the most exemplary man in Greensboro, so calm, so cheerful, so thoroughly in earnest, and so honest, that to live to be a grand old man like you was well worth while; that you were my ideal of what Joe Caldwell called 'a good citizen'. I hand this to you across the deserts and the dreary miles which separate us, because I want you to know that I said this, and it might be that I could never tell you."

Another editor wrote of him:

"It has been almost universally agreed that John William Scott was 'the best man in Guilford County'. Gentle as a May day, thoughtful, courteous, always considerate of his fellow brother, caring nothing for wealth except the real good he could do with it by helping others, he lived and died without an enemy, the friend of all who knew him."

Another wrote of him:

"He had no enemies because he would never press an advantage of any kind against his fellow human. He always refrained from expressing a bad opinion of another. No one could be found, perhaps, who could recall an adverse criticism from him in the manner the average man criticises. He declined, too, to prosecute anyone in the courts for misdemeanor or wrong done him. Several times in his business life thefts from his company were revealed, as they are revealed in nearly all large concerns, but the head of it invariably avoided carrying the matter into the courts. This love of humanity, displayed thus and in all the other ways of the man, was the big thing which set him apart, and made him loved of black and white, rich and poor, old and young".

We know what true religion is and how it shows itself in a human life. "Pure religion and undefiled before God and the Father", says the Scripture, "is this, to visit the fatherless and widow in their affliction, and to keep himself unspotted from the world." Active benevolence and personal purity, these, the twin fruits of true religion, were the twin features of Mr. Scott's character.

As I think of him, two familiar quotations come to mind:
"Do good by stealth and blush to find it fame".
"So didst thou travel on life's common way,
    In cheerful godliness."

The simple tastes, the sound religious principles, the church-going habits, characteristic of the godly country home in which he was reared and which has been our nation's chief nursery of noble characters, were his to the end. Though a much afflicted man, bereaved successively of his wife and his two children, yet his faith in God never wavered. The cheerful courage with which he faced life and its duties was never dimmed. From the Unfailing Source he drew strength for every need.

The value of such a man to a community it is impossible to estimate. Of far greater benefit than his generous encouragement of all that made for the commercial and educational upbuilding of the city was the shining proof afforded by his life that business success is not inconsistent with integrity and unselfishness. The strength of cities, of states, of nations, their value to the world, their power to lift humanity to ever higher levels of character and happiness, are measured by, and only by, the proportion of such men among their citizenship.

EGBERT W. SMITH.

JOSEPH MARTIN REECE

JOSEPH MARTIN REECE
1848 - 1915

"As a builder of Greensboro" one must measure Joseph Martin Reece from the standpoint of an editor and publisher of a daily paper, the Greensboro Daily Record, which he, in conjunction with Harper J. Elam, established in 1890, and in which work he continued until his death.

He was a practical printer and learned his trade in the office of the Greensboro Patriot, of which his brother-in-law, Robert Albright, was one of the proprietors. He later became connected, as business manager, with the New North State, of which Capt. W. S. Ball was editor. He loved to recount the many events which transpired during these years and to revel in the memory of the rare actors who came upon the stage during that period.

He was working in the office of the New North State, which was Republican in politics, during the Tilden and Hayes campaign in 1876, and a very amusing incident for the Democrats, but a very serious one for the Republicans, occurred during the last week of the campaign. The last shot had been prepared for the Democrats, the "forms" were locked up and brought near the stove to dry while the Washington hand press was being put in order to run off the last two pages, which contained the editorial and local matter. It was the custom of a certain negro man in the Center neighborhood to come and get his paper on the day of publication. The negro was standing by the stove seemingly much interested, as usual, in the modus operandi of printing a paper, when suddenly he fell on the floor in a terrible fit, kicking and writhing in a terrific manner. His feet came in contact with the forms through which he kicked holes and both pages of the paper were "pied". The office did not have sufficient additional type to set up the two pages. The times were too hot to borrow type from the Greensboro Patriot, a Democratic paper, so the proprietors called on Rev. J. L. Michaux, editor of the Central Protestant, who loaned them the necessary type.

Mr. Reece was a good musician and did much in organizing, instructing and keeping alive a good brass band in this town, but he always insisted that a good brass band could not be kept alive in a live town! For many years he was the sustaining influence and one of the most faithful instructors and performers in the Greensboro Cornet Band. He enjoyed music and contributed much to the pleasure of the community by his efforts in behalf of the band. In those days it was with difficulty that instruments could be procured and the boys were compelled to use the slow process of lawn parties and private subscriptions to that end. The band had more than a local reputation and it was employed to play during political campaigns, at college commencements and other public gatherings. In the early seventies Maj. William A. Smith was elected president of the North Carolina Railroad Company. The president's office was at Company Shops, N. C. (now Burlington). On a certain occasion the Greensboro Cornet Band was employed to go to Company Shops to serenade Maj. Smith. It transpired that the band had just before this engagement, at great expense and deprivation, purchased a large bass horn, or tuba. It was the largest instrument in the band, save the drum. It was the pride of the band and shone resplendent in the sun. After playing several selections to the delight of Maj. Smith and his guests, the much-prized horn was hung on the outside of the building about eighteen inches from the ground. The members of the band sauntered around, but ever and anon casting a loving eye towards the tuba. Presently a large bull, the property of Maj. Smith, came in position to catch the glint of the sun upon the precious horn. Immediately, with distended nostrils, glaring eyes, tail lifted on high and with a bellow that jarred the earth, the bull made a charge upon the pride of the band; the terrific impact mashed it flat. Old man (Paddy) O'Sullivan, a member of the band and a tinner by trade, took the remains in hand and succeeded in hammering the horn again into shape, but it never looked the same.

For some time after his connection with the New North State, Mr. Reece had charge of the job office of that paper. Later he formed a co-partnership with Messrs. Frank and John Thomas in the job printing business.

The Daily Record was established in 1890 by Mr. Reece and Harper J. Elam, Mr. Elam selling his interest to Mr.

Reece in 1901. The paper was printed on South Elm Street, under the Benbow Hall building, for a number of years. Later the old wooden building, occupying the corner where the present building stands, was torn down and the present one erected. The Record started the year before the extension of the corporate limits of the city, which took in South Greensboro and some additional territory. On July 28, 1891, the people of Greensboro voted $30,000.00 in bonds to secure the location of the State Normal and Industrial School in this city. There were 975 names upon the registration book and 771 voted in favor of the bonds and none against. The financial statement for the year ending May 1, 1891, showed the total income of the city for all purposes was $28,312.75.

This year was the beginning of the development which put Greensboro upon the road to larger and greater things. Mr. Reece through the Record and personally, favored the movements that culminated in the years that have passed in putting Greensboro in the splendid position which it now occupies. Soon after the extension of the corporate limits the Messrs. Cone established the Finishing Mills in the then northern suburbs of the city, and in 1896 made plans for the opening of Summit Avenue and the building of the cotton mills, commencing with Proximity, then following with Revolution and White Oak.

Following the growth of the city it became necessary to have a better water supply and to put in sewer lines and to improve the streets. A proposition was placed before the people by the board of aldermen for the issuing of $300,-000.00 in bonds, which then seemed a huge amount, for the following purposes: streets, sewer, water and lights. Mr. Reece and the Record came out for the proposition, and in addition tendered one page of his paper for reading matter stressing the importance of the bond issue. This page was used effectively by a committee of citizens, at the head of which was Dr. J. Y. Joyner, in presenting the needs and the wisdom thereof.

In the progress of the city during the years from the year 1890 to within a short time before his death, August 24th, 1915, Mr. Reece took a leading part through his paper in all activities. A native of Guilford County, the son of William H. and Susan Greene Reece, and moving to this place from

Jamestown in 1865 with his father's family, he took a special pride and interest in Greensboro and Guilford County,

An an editor, Mr. Reece was unique. The Raleigh News and Observer said of him upon his death: " 'Joe' Reece, for so those who knew him well loved to call him—and there are few in Greensboro and Guilford County who did not love that true and sturdy North Carolinian—was of the 'personal' type of the North Carolina editor. His brethren of the press would talk of what 'Joe' Reece had to say more frequently than they would speak of things in the Greensboro Record. 'Joe' Reece was the Greensboro Record. The Greensboro Record was 'Joe' Reece. In that paper his utterances rang clear and true for the highest ideals. He was an editor unafraid, a man loyal and true."

Said the Charlotte Observer: " * * * Mr. Reece had naturally dropped into journalism and early developed a talent for saying the truth in a picturesque way. He was not what might be called a polished writer, yet he was versatile. He was of the character of writers described in Goldsmith's epitaph, "who scarely left any class of authorship untouched, and who touched none he did not adorn."

Said the Winston-Salem Journal: " * * * Mr. Reece came nearer being what is known in journalistic tradition as an old-time editor than any other now in the state. By that is meant, editor who is not a cog in a machine, but who is largely the paper itself. Mr. Reece was a born optimist and he preached a gentle doctrine of love and cheer in his editorial column daily that has come to be one of the priceless possessions of the city in which he spent his life. Only those who knew the haunts and the gentlemen of whom he wrote daily could appreciate his ready wit and his love for his fellow beings. The old guard that for years sat in the shade of the court house trees in Greensboro were his best friends, and slowly they are passing away one by one."

. Mr. Reece was extremely fortunate in the choice of a partner for life, as his wife was truly a helpmeet and a faithful and loving partner in all that the term implies. He was married to Miss Alice McMurray, daughter of Mr. and Mrs. John W. McMurray, who lived about two miles south of town on the Asheboro road, September 26, 1873, and who still survives him. No children were born to this union, but their parental love and care were lavished upon the three children of Mrs. Reece's deceased sister, Mrs. Samuel C. Robertson. These children were Mrs. Frank P. Morton, Charles C. Robertson, of Peoria, Illinois, and Mrs. John A. Williams, and all are living except Mrs. John A. Williams, who died about two years ago.

The family of Mr. Reece were Methodists, but he joined the First Presbyterian Church, of this city, of which his wife was a member, and ever remained a loyal and devoted member of that congregation. His funeral took place from that church and his body was interred in Greene Hill Cemetery.

JOHN S. MICHAUX.

ROBERT MARTIN DOUGLAS

ROBERT MARTIN DOUGLAS

1849 - 1917

Robert Martin Douglas was born at Douglas, Rockingham County, North Carolina, on the 28th day of January, 1849, and died in Greensboro on the 8th day of February, 1917.

His father was Stephen A. Douglas, United States Senator from Illinois, and candidate of the Democratic Party for President in opposition to Abraham Lincoln. His mother was Martha Martin, daughter of Col. Robert Martin and grand neice of Alexander Martin, first Governor of North Carolina under the Constitution.

He was educated at Georgetown University from which institution he received the degrees of A. B., A. M., LL. D.

At the age of eighteen he was appointed private secretary to the Governor of North Carolina (Holden) and made colonel of the militia. After about one year, and while yet under twenty-one years of age, he was appointed private secretary to the President of the United States (Grant), which position he held for four years. Then in 1873 he was appointed by President Grant United States Marshal for the State of North Carolina, which position he held until the state was divided into two districts, when he was appointed Marshal for the Western District of North Carolina.

Upon the expiration of his term of office, he studied law and was admitted to the bar in 1885, and began the practice in Greensboro. In 1886, one year later, he was appointed Standing Master in Chancery of the United States Circuit Court, an office now abolished, which he held until 1896. In 1896 he was elected Associate Justice of the Supreme Court of North Carolina. Upon the expiration of his term of office, he resumed the practice of his profession in Greensboro and devoted a great portion of his time to literary work. He wrote extensively for magazines and encyclopedias upon historical, economic and political subjects, probably his most widely known articles being his reminiscences of General Grant, published in the Youth's Companion.

He married, June, 1874, Miss Jessie Madeleine Dick, daughter of Judge Robert P. Dick (q. v.). His children were, Robert Dick Douglas, Stephen A. Douglas, who died in 1907, Martin F. Douglas, and Madeleine, wife of Colonel Edward Warren Myers.

Perhaps the most conspicuous and able public service of Judge Douglas was rendered while he was Private Secretary to the President and his personal friend General Grant. The complicated questions of states rights and slavery were forever settled by the arbitrament of the sword. But the status of the seceding states and their populations in relation to the Union became increasingly involved and disturbed until the term of General Grant as President. And it was as the only representative of the South in Grant's official family that Judge Douglas was in a position to render invaluable aid to the South and particularly to his native state, North Carolina.

One instance will serve to illustrate the nature and extent of his service. It is taken from the reminiscences of Judge Douglas as published in the Youth's Companion. It is told in his own modest way, but many eminent Virginians have testified their lasting gratitude to Judge Douglas' great influence with President Grant. The excerpt is as follows: "The Constitutional Convention of Virginia, convened under the reconstruction acts of Congress, and especially the act of 2 March, 1867, framed a constitution that practically disfranchised all who had taken any part in the rebellion, or had done anything to aid the South or its soldiers in the slightest degree. Clause 4, Section 1, Article 3, disqualified from holding any office in the state from governor down to constable 'every person who . . . held any office, civil or military, under the United States or under any state, who, having previously taken an oath as a member of Congress, or as an officer of the United States, or as a member of any state legislature, or as an executive or judicial officer of any state, shall have engaged in insurrection or rebellion against the same or given aid or comfort to the enemies thereof'. Section 7, of Article 3, required all prominent state and municipal officers to take the so-called 'test oath' before entering upon the duties of their respective offices.

"This elimination of the dominant element of Virginia from all active participation in public affairs was extremely distasteful to its people, and was strongly opposed by many prominent Republicans, who did not regard the restoration of the Union as depending upon conquest alone, but looked forward to a complete reconciliation of the sections as the only true basis of national peace and prosperity. The situation was further intensified by the fact that the negroes were allowed to vote upon these constitutional questions while the disfranchised classes were not. · Accordingly, Congress passed an act in April, 1869, empowering the President in his discretion to submit the proposed Constitution to a vote of the people without the disfranchising clauses, and at the same time to submit the latter to a separate vote.

"General Grant was a true friend to the South, and opposed to the test oath or any form of disfranchisement, but in this case very strong personal and political influences had been brought to bear upon him, which were met by many of the Democratic leaders with idle threats and useless denunciation. One day Col. L. G. Washington, a prominent newspaper correspondent of Washington, asked me if I would arrange an interview with the President for a committee composed principally of old Union men, if they should come to Washington. I told him that I would gladly do so, as I never lost an opportunity of bringing the old Union element of the South into personal contact with the President. Soon after I received a note from Col. Washington, dated Friday, 14 May, 1869, saying, 'I am happy to be able to say that the committee representing the conservative organization of Virginia arrived here this morning and are exceedingly anxious to have an interview with the President this morning, as they are compelled to return this evening. It is also understood that the order which is to direct the submission of the Constitution is to be issued on Saturday. The committee consists of Hon. John R. Edmunds, Chairman, Col. Frank G. Ruffin, James A. Cowardin and Franklin Stearns.'

"To my intense surprise the President declined to see them. I felt deeply hurt, not only on account of these gentlemen, but for the great and lasting injury which I feared would result to Virginia and the entire South. The only course open to me was an earnest personal appeal to the President. I told him that these men came on my promise to get them an interview, a promise I had given, knowing his high appreciation of the Union element of the South; that they came to present their side of a matter pregnant with vital consequences to their state and perhaps to the nation; and I asked him as a personal favor to see them and hear them. 'Bring them in,' was his simple answer.

The interview was eminently satisfactory. The Virginians were firm but conservative, and with high personal respect for General Grant, they presented their case respectfully, but with clearness and decision. The President granted their request, and eliminating the objectionable clauses from the Constitution, submitted them and the remainder of the Constitution to be voted on separately by the people. This action of the President was construed as indicating his personal objection to the disfranchising clauses; and thus the weight of his great name was once again in favor of peace and reconciliation. The vote was taken on 6 July, 1869, when the Constitution was adopted by over two hundred thousand majority, while the disfranchising clauses were rejected by a decisive vote''.

This is but one instance taken from the daily routine of his life as private secretary to President Grant. The dominating idea of his life was to reconcile the northern and southern sections of his country, the homes of his father and mother respectively.

The National Cyclopedia of American Biography states that Judge Douglas was largely responsible for the size of the Republican Party in North Carolina. And it is a fact that in the Presidential elections Guilford County alone, the home of Judge Douglas, casts more Republican votes than the entire State of South Carolina. It is said that Stephen A. Douglas inaugurated the Democratic Party in power in North Carolina by urging David S. Reid, the first Democratic Governor and first cousin to Mrs. Douglas, to run upon the platform of ''manhood suffrage''. It seems strange that Robert M. Douglas, his son, should have been such an influential factor in establishing the Republican Party in the same state.

Aside from his political career, much could be written about the judicial career of Judge Douglas and his influence upon the corpus juris. His fame as a student of the law and writer of lucid opinions passed beyond the boundaries of his native state. Two illustrations might not be inappropriate.

In volume 69, page 131, of the Central Law Journal, in an article on "Government by Injunction", the author says: "The case of the State v. Van Pelt, decided by the Supreme Court of North Carolina in 1906, is the best reasoned, the profoundest and most analytical of all decisions rendered by judicial tribunals in the United States in these so-called boycott cases. I commend to the attention of judges everywhere the concurring opinion of Judge Douglas in that case." The Hon. Thos. W. Shelton, in an article on the law of the "Last Clear Chance", appearing in the Virginia Law Register of August, 1904, begins by saying: "Probably the best exposition of the doctrine of the last clear chance is set out in the case of Bogan v. Ry. Co., reported in 129 N. C., 154, and it is prominently referred to on account of the facts involved, as conveying an object lesson, as well as the able opinion of Judge Douglas". There are numerous other illustrations that might be used, but the limits of this article will not permit. Long after Judge Douglas' memory shall have passed from the mind of the common man, his salutary exposition of the law shall continue to control and safeguard the property, happiness and destiny of the future generations of men.

As a writer of pure, lucid, concise and eloquent English Judge Douglas will take a high rank. His articles in magazines and encyclopedias, as well as his judicial opinions and pamphlets on historical, economic and industrial subjects, all bear testimony to this fact. The limits of this article will not permit of any adequate examples of his literary style. However, we will insert a brief extemporaneous address delivered by him before the Universal Congress of Lawyers and Jurists in St. Louis in opposition to alimony, which was taken down by the stenographer and published in the proceedings of that body, under the chapter on divorce, which was under consideration at that time:

"Mr. President: This is neither the place nor the occasion for unprepared addresses, but sometimes free expression in simple words of the convictions of a lifetime have greater effect than any power of studied words.

"Coming directly to the point, while recognizing the fact that divorces granted in one state must of necessity be universally recognized, as they in fact break up the marriage tie, I do not think that a decree allowing alimony should have any extra territorial effect.

"Divorce may at times become a necessary evil, but it is still an evil that should receive neither moral encouragement nor pecuniary reward. Many states, including our own, deem it contrary to public policy to allow any alimony whatever in a divorce, and hence are loth to enforce any such decree, which they regard as directly opposed to the letter and spirit of their laws and the welfare of their people. Petitioners obtain divorces purely on the sworn allegation of bona fide residence in the state whose jurisdiction is invoked; therefore they should be content to abide there and enjoy such pecuniary advantages only as its laws may give and its courts can enforce.

"I am personally opposed to absolute divorces, that is, divorces permitting remarriage. Aside from its religious phase, it strikes at the very root of society by destroying its chief constituent of unity, the family home. If the parties alone were affected, I would care but little; but it directly affects the helpless child as well as society itself. Especially repugnant are those carpet-bag divorces which are so freely granted in certain states to merely nominal residents, in proceedings which are, in their essential nature and purposes, purely ex parte, although dignified by the title of actions at law.

"Remarriage after divorce has well been called successive polygamy, and it seems to me that it is but little removed from the contemporanous polygamy which we so freely denounce in our Mormon citizens. Should not we avoid even the semblance of that sin which we denounce so strenuously in others?

"I am aware that our own state has always permitted divorces for certain causes, and has recently further relaxed its ancient rule apparently to meet the unusual hardships of special cases, but I am sure that the trend of public thought is strongly in favor of its restriction. North Carolina feels a just pride in her material development, but she is prouder still of the manhood of her sons and the womanhood of her daughters. Around the family hearthstone clings her fondest affections, and from it emanate her noblest aspirations. I know she is called the 'Rip Van Winkle' of the Union, and we have frequently heard that she will awake from her slumbers and follow what is called the Progressive Thought of the Age; but it were better to let her sleep forever than to awake to infamy and shame.''

Judge Douglas moved to Greensboro in 1873 and made that city his home during the remainder of his life. He was an active and influential factor in every phase of community upbuilding. He helped organize and was an officer of the first Chamber of Commerce, was president of the first street car company, was a director in several banks and various corporations, and donated to the city the public park which bears his name.

He lived in a turbulent political age, and his life was filled with many exciting, and at times, acrimonious incidents; but this is neither the time nor place for an exhaustive analysis of his contributions to statesmanship, literature and law. Suffice it to say that upon the scroll of North Carolina's history Judge Douglas will be inscribed as an author of unusual literary ability, a statesman and valuable friend to the South in a troublous political era, a just, able and humane judge.   WALTER F. COLE.

CEASAR CONE

CEASAR CONE
1859 - 1917

There are men born, from time to time, as the world rolls on, who are cast in heroic mold—men mentally able to look into the future and see far ahead of the other fellow—men who take time by the forelock—men devoid of fear and of abounding faith and truly possessed of a tremendous strength of both will and body. Such men become empire builders and add to the wealth of the world by making two blades of grass grow where only one grew before. Such a man was Ceasar Cone.

Mr. Cone inherited the steady traits of his father, Herman, who came from Bavaria, Germany, to this country in 1845, at the age of seventeen, and started with a capital of fifty cents. His son, Ceasar, was born in 1859, at Jonesboro, Tennessee, and lived there until 1870, when his father removed to Baltimore and established a wholesale grocery business. Ceasar remained in the public schools of that city until he reached the age of fourteen years. This completed his education. His inheritance from his mother was potent for good. Her name was Helen Guggenheimer, and she also came from Bavaria, Germany. At fourteen years of age the boy started in the stationery business in a Baltimore firm. He never departed from the methods and precepts inculcated during his tender years. The paternal lesson was rigid honesty, rigid economy and rigid observance of every obligation. The life of Ceasar Cone was a living exemplification of these principles.

In 1894 he married Miss Jeanette Siegel, who, with three sons, Herman, Benjamin and Ceasar, survives him.

In the development of the Piedmont section the Cones were among the most powerful factors. Moses H. Cone, in the early nineties, brought to life the Cone Export and Commission Company, and through its co-operative agencies saved from bankruptcy many of the older cotton mills of this state. In the projection, organization and successful operation of this company, his brother, Ceasar Cone, with clear head and steady hand, stood by his side at every step.

In 1890 the old and successful firm of H. Cone & Sons was dissolved. The two brothers had been members of this firm and through its connection had obtained an accurate knowledge of the conditions and resources of the South. With prophetic eye they saw the development of its vast resources. The Cone Export and Commission Company was their first venture in the handling of cotton goods. This put them in close touch with the cotton mills and led them into the unexplored territory of southern industrial life and possibilities.

In his survey of the field, Ceasar Cone was attracted by the advantages of Greensboro, N. C. In conjunction with his brother, Moses H. Cone, who was associated with him in all his enterprises and extensive investments, he acquired several hundred acres of land lying inside, outside and adjoining the then corporate limits of the Gate City, on which was erected, in 1895, the large cotton mill of the Proximity Manufacturing Company, of which he was the acting and active president. Starting with 240 looms, this company has increased its number to 4600 looms, including another mammoth plant known as the White Oak Mill, which is one of the largest cotton mills in the South and the largest denim manufacturing plant in the world. These mills require the employment of more than 2500 people. The annual consumption is more than thirty-five million pounds of cotton, which will turn out more than seventy-five million yards of cloth every year. Nor were these all. He was primarily responsible for the erection, and later the enlargement of the Revolution Cotton Mill, in which he was a large stockholder and director.

His master mind, indomitable will and restless energy were concentrated in the successful operation of these mammoth plants. Due to his directing genius, the towns or villages surrounding these plants have become models of cleanliness and beauty. In his broad, humane and generous provision for the comforts of the operatives, he led the manufacturers of the South. He established a system of offering prizes or rewards to those who excelled in the neatness and adornment of their homes and encouraged the planting of shrubbery and flowers in their yards. Nor was he content to stop there. He took another advanced step in providing, at the expense of his company, the very best school facilities, including kindergarten work, in modern and comfortable school buildings for all the children of school age. He was a pioneer in welfare work and one of the first manufacturers in the state to employ district nurses in his mill villages. He also saw to it that ample boarding houses, hotels and churches were built and maintained and that every accommodation necessary for the well-being and welfare of his people was secured. His broad-minded policy went beyond the mere exchange of money for labor and sought the promotion of his own interest in the comfort, contentment and happiness of his employees.

Mr. Cone possessed to a marked degree a keen and quick sense of values both in men and goods. A man who would "make good" with him must ring true, must have common sense and be efficient. He always knew how to do things and make other people do things and do them right. Notwithstanding his fame and fortune—his unusual success—he was simple and democratic, he was easily approached, was magnetic and a popular man with all classes. His employees swore by him.

He was a great man in heart, mind and intellect. He was clean, sincere, upright, honorable, truthful and industrious. No day was too long, no work too hard for him to do. He was simple. He had no peculiar notions as to his own superiority. He was a common, everyday citizen of this great state. There was no subject too great for him to approach and no question too small to engage his attention.

Mr. Cone died at his home in Greensboro, North Carolina, on March 1st, 1917, from an intestinal hemorrhage, after about a week's illness.

In a spot selected by himself as his last resting place, overlooking the mills which were the objects of his pride and his care, and the homes of the people whom he loved so well, this builder and benefactor was laid to rest in the presence of thousands of sorrowing friends who had gathered from every section of the state, and from every walk of life, to pay their last homage to his memory. Such a life and character must have been the inspiration of the poet when he wrote:

"So live, that when thy summons comes to join
The innumerable caravan, which moves
To that mysterious realm, where each shall take
His chamber in the silent halls of death,
Thou go not, like the quarry slave at night,
Scourged to his dungeon, but, sustained and soothed
By an unfaltering trust, approach thy grave
Like one who wraps the drapery of his couch
About him, and lies down to pleasant dreams."

SIDNEY J. STERN.

CHARLES DUNCAN McIVER

CHARLES DUNCAN McIVER
1860 - 1906

It is eminently fitting that in a sketch of some of the more noted men of Greensboro and Guilford County, Dr. Charles D. McIver's name should be included. Certainly among those who did much for education and emancipation from ignorance he stands out most prominently.

Guilford County and Greensboro claim him by adoption. He was born on a farm near Sanford, North Carolina, in Moore County, on September 27, 1860.

His parents, Matthew Henry McIver and Sarah J. Harrington McIver, were Presbyterians of Scotch ancestry. Thus there was early brought into his life influences which we have come to accept without question as belonging to the sturdy Scotch Presbyterians.

With them there was no compromise with truth. They believed and incorporated into their lives the teachings of the Sermon on the Mount, and they recognized individual righteousness as the chief factor in the nation's strength and growth.

In such a home with such parents the early training was all that could be desired and there was early implanted in Charles D. McIver a reverence for and love of the truth, integrity of purpose, hatred of sham and deceit.

When started to school he was most fortunate in that he came under the influence of one of those old masters who believed that a thorough knowledge of the classics and mathematics was an essential for a broad and liberal education. Here he learned well a few things which in those days were considered essentials and was well prepared for the four years' course which he took at the University of North Carolina.

Dr. Edwin A. Alderman, his college mate and lifelong friend, says of this part of his life: "After four years of steady growth in scholarship and character McIver passed from the University to the school room in 1881. He did his duty as an undergraduate, respecting his body and his spirit.

He even won Greek medals, but his thought was on men and student issues and college policies.''

From this time on whatever his work, his real purpose was to use his every effort to bring more light to the manhood and womanhood of the state, and with his clear vision he saw that the best way to do this was to bring to all equal educational opportunity. ''Without vision the people perish'', and vision comes through education. This was his gospel.

From 1881 to 1886 Dr. McIver was engaged in public school work, not simply in teaching so many hours a day in the schools of Durham and Winston-Salem, but in giving the whole of his effort and energy to the cause of education.

In 1885 he was married to Lula V. Martin, of Winston-Salem, a woman of rare power and beauty of character, who was interested in his work and ready and eager to help in its accomplishment. Together they were able to plan and accomplish great tasks, which would not have been possible for him alone. Together they held institutes, conducted normal schools, gave lectures and readings all over North Carolina.

It was during these years that Dr. McIver was patiently and persistently working out the problem the solving of which was to constitute his chief work, the establishment of a college which should offer to the women of North Carolina educational opportunities equal to those offered the men at the University. This was his task and toward its accomplishment he set his face with undaunted courage.

It was seldom that there was an educational gathering, local, state or national, which did not find Dr. McIver present, and wherever he was, whether on the train, on the street, in hotels or in public meetings, he made friends both for himself and the cause which was always uppermost in his mind.

He was interested in all civic improvements and in all movements, whether local or national, which would help to raise our standards of living.

He was much interested in and worked for the education of the negro and was always considerate of his rights. His first vote was cast for the bill to establish the Durham Graded School, although its passage meant the closing of his own private school and financial loss. He was chosen a member of the first faculty of the Durham Graded School and remained there until he was called to Winston to help organize the Winston Graded School, and to become the first principal of the high school. He next accepted a position at Peace Institute, a Presbyterian school for girls at Raleigh, where he learned to solve some of the problems which come in connection with the management of such an institution as he had in mind, and where at the same time he was so situated as to keep in touch with public movements and their leaders.

The history of the establishment of this institution is open to those who care to look it up.

There were years of untiring effort given to the cause. There was much of prejudice and hostility to be overcome, and it took patient, persistent effort to accomplish the task. Dr. McIver and his co-laborers were too much in earnest to be discouraged, though their bills for the establishment of the school failed to pass in the legislatures of 1887 and 1889. They worked on for five years with undaunted courage and, finally, in 1891, the legislature of North Carolina passed the bill establishing the "North Carolina State Normal and Industrial School", which has now grown into the North Carolina College for Women.

The school was opened with Dr. McIver as president October 5th, 1892. To the great task he brought his youth, enthusiasm, love of truth, honesty of purpose, determination to succeed, and to the little group of faculty, eight in all, he imparted much of his enthusiasm and earnestness.

Dr. McIver had the peculiar ability to get the best from those with whom and for whom he worked.

To all of us in those early days he was not only our college president, but a close personal friend.

He is well characterized in the following words from the tribute paid him by the college faculty at the time of his death:

"Dr. McIver's was a soul too generous to entertain jealousy, too noble for pride. Neither wealth nor public honors could tempt him from his unselfish devotion to what he regarded as the state's greatest need. His was the truly great character that stands the crucial test of service to humanity. For him no undertaking was too difficult, if its accomplishment meant a larger life for his people.

"We delight in bearing tribute to the fact that his life was a beautiful illustration of that sublime truth which he so often read in our presence: 'Now abideth faith, hope, charity, these three; but the greatest of these is charity'."

The place given him by the students was not only that of president of the college, with all that this should mean, but he was for each student, guide, counsellor and friend. He knew the parents and home conditions of a large majority of the girls, and if he did not know them at first he was not long in ignorance. He believed in and trusted the students, and appeals made by him to their honor and loyalty never failed to call out the best from them. It was his constant endeavor to do all in his power to keep the girls from being what might be called provincial, and to this end he was continually alert and active in bringing to the college men and women of prominence and power. Few people of note were allowed to pass through Greensboro in those days without being taken from the train and brought out to meet the girls and speak to them if there was any opportunity.

The following is a fair and just estimate, taken from the Memorial Volume, of the feeling the students had for him during those early days:

"On entering college his strong personality was felt by every individual student and in a short time she felt herself the possessor of a true friend. Narrow opinions were changed to broader views and the horizon of girl-life soon enlarged. As the years passed his influence was more keenly felt as he impressed upon each class the fact that graduation meant the beginning of work as a citizen. His influence upon all students illustrates the force of Owen Meredith's lines:

'No life can be pure in its purpose and strong in its strife
And all life not be purer and stronger thereby!'

"His life was pure, his purpose strong and therefore our lives are purer and stronger for his spirit among us."

Certainly a large majority of the students who left the college walls went out with a feeling of responsibility to the state and a determination to strive earnestly to do their part toward removing the burden of illiteracy, which so oppressed and held us down.

The Southern Education Board was organized in 1901 for the purpose of investigating the educational conditions and needs of some of the southern states. Its fundamental purpose was to uplift and advance the rural public school, and to furnish accurate information respecting conditions and needs to newspapers, preachers and teachers and to any others who were interested in the question of public education.

Dr. McIver was a member of this board, and his ability as an organizer was recognized when he was chosen as chairman of the committee for directing a campaign for popular education in the southern states. In reports of work done by this campaign committee no state made a better showing in work done along the lines of educational conferences, campaigns for local tax, organization of "Women's Associations for Betterment of Public School Houses", than did North Carolina, and there is no question but that the success of the work in North Carolina was in a very large measure due to the continuous devotion of Dr. McIver to the cause to which he had wholly committed his powers.

Dr. McIver's death, which came suddenly on the train between Durham and Greensboro while he was making a tour with his friend William J. Bryan, was a terrible shock, not only to his wife and children, but to the entire state, and to the nation as well if one is to judge by the accounts in the press outside the state. The tributes to his memory are many and beautiful. They were spontaneous outbursts from friends everywhere who felt themselves, the institution which he had builded and cherished, the state he loved, the cause of education, stricken almost beyond recovery. One has only to look over the files of North and South Carolina, Richmond, Baltimore and New York papers near the date to see how he was regarded and the great esteem in which he was held and with what sincere affection his friends and admirers gave voice to their appreciation and grief.

Dr. Albert Shaw, in the Review of Reviews for October, 1906, pays the following beautiful tribute to Dr. McIver:

"He was a man of remarkable eloquence and of great readiness and power on all occasions in public speech. He was famous for his wit and for his unlimited store of amusing incidents and anecdotes.

"His efficiency and his gifts of leadership would have made him a marked man and a rare success in any profession or calling. But he gloried in the work he had chosen, and believed that the right training of women, for the sake of the home and the common school, was the most fundamentally important thing with which he could possibly concern himself, and so it was that he gave his strength and life to that work. He can be ill spared, but he had builded so broadly and staunchly that what he had done will remain. . . . His memory will long be honored in North Carolina."

"He was made not after the law of a carnal commandment, but after the power of an endless life."

GERTRUDE W. MENDENHALL.

INDEX

INDEX

www.ingramcontent.com/pod-product-compliance
Lightning Source LLC
Chambersburg PA
CBHW021848020426
42334CB00013B/231